WINNING IN REVERSE

DEFYING THE ODDS AND ACHIEVING DREAMS: THE BILL LESTER STORY

BILL LESTER

WITH JONATHAN INGRAM

T03069I7

PEGASUS BOOKS
NEW YORK LONDON

WINNING IN REVERSE

Pegasus Books, Ltd.
148 West 37th Street, 13th Floor
New York, NY 10018

First Pegasus Books paperback edition February 2022
First Pegasus Books cloth edition February 2021

Interior design by Maria Torres

ISBN: 978-1-64313-945-6

10 9 8 7 6 5 4 3 2 1

Printed in the United States of America
Distributed by Simon & Schuster
www.pegasusbooks.com

Praise for
Winning in Reverse

"I remember racing with Bill Lester for the first time in 1998. Being unfamiliar with the name, I assumed he was a long-time journeyman road racer who was looking for a new challenge in stock cars. Turns out his journey was anything but typical. Deciding to become a professional stock car driver in your 40s is next to impossible. In the pages of this book you'll learn Bill is a determined enthusiastic individual whose passion to succeed made the impossible a reality."—Dale Earnhardt Jr.

"Motorsports—an industry where you won't find much color. Being Black in NASCAR, you have to have the talent. You also have to have thick skin. You are already looked at with many more eyes expecting immediate success no matter the equipment or circumstances you're in. As soon as you don't perform, your opportunity is immediately labeled as a handout, based solely off the color of your skin. When your time comes, you have to be twice as ready to seize and capitalize on the task in front of you. Bill Lester embodies this and reveals his struggle and triumph in this book."

—Bubba Wallace

"Bill Lester's story is instructive for any person at any age to understand that when we have a deeply embedded passion, it is never too late to make it come to fruition. I strongly believe there are many people in this world who have been waiting for this book at this moment in their lives!"

— Roland S. Martin, host/managing editor,
#RolandMartinUnfiltered Daily Digital Show

"Bill Lester is a trailblazer. Like many who brave the front lines, he had to take risks. He lived his childhood dream, but he had to persevere to succeed in a sport that had few people of color and a reputation for being unwelcoming to African Americans. *Winning in Reverse* is his story of his achievement. In spite of adversity and tremendous odds stacked against him, Lester's hard work and tenacity served him well. Readers facing similar hurdles will gain motivation from the pages of his book too. *Winning in Reverse* is an invaluable tool for those looking for a guide to the winner's circle."

—Ed Gordon, broadcast journalist and
author of *Conversations in Black*

"An affecting memoir. Lester's inspirational story of resilience in the face of daunting obstacles wins big."—*Publishers Weekly*

"Since his retirement, the iconic racer has used his large platform to represent auto racing, businesses, and the black community in engaging in and helping bring an end to racial injustice. A recommended read for many, this book will make you believe that your dreams are so much more than 'what-if' scenarios."—*Racing Refresh*

To the three women who have always believed in me:

my mother, my sister, and my wife;

and the man who set the bar high for me, my father.

I am eternally grateful for your love and support.

To my sons, Alex and Austin,

I hope my story further encourages you

to reach your potential and live your dreams.

CONTENTS

A GLOSSARY OF RACING TERMS

RACE ORGANIZATION

AMATEUR RACING: Drivers race for a checkered flag and a trophy.

PROFESSIONAL RACING: Drivers race for a checkered flag, a trophy, and prize money from a posted event purse.

SANCTIONING BODY: An organization that hosts racing events, establishes the rules, and enforces them. Drivers and teams officially enter racing events through this group.

SCCA: The Sports Car Club of America sanctions events on US road racing courses, hosting primarily amateur and some professional races. The SCCA has twenty-eight car classes, including sedans, sports cars, formula cars, and Prototype cars.

IMSA: The International Motor Sports Association sanctions professional road racing events in North America. Its top classes compete simultaneously under an endurance racing format with co-drivers sharing either Prototype or GT-class cars.

NASCAR: The National Association for Stock Car Automobile Racing was launched in 1949 by Bill France Sr., who first began organizing stock car races on the Daytona Beach and Road Course in 1938. NASCAR is America's largest and most successful sanctioning body.

NASCAR TRAVELING SERIES: Three major professional series of NASCAR compete across the United States. The races are predominantly run on ovals and often at the same track over the course of a weekend.

- **NASCAR CUP SERIES:** The fastest and most competitive echelon for stock cars, demanding the largest budget for a thirty-six-race season. The Cup Series draws the most viewership and fans of any American racing series.

- **NASCAR XFINITY SERIES:** The understudy, or minor league, series where drivers gain experience in hopes of moving up to the Cup Series. It can be a training ground for teams as well.

- **NASCAR TRUCK SERIES:** Considered the entry level of NASCAR's national professional ranks, vehicles in the Truck Series compete with a stock car chassis under a pickup truck body instead of a car body. Trucks race the fewest and shortest events in order to keep operational budgets lower.

ARCA: The Auto Racing Club of America sanctions stock car races on a variety of courses including dirt tracks, road courses, and super-speedways. ARCA sometimes runs preliminary events prior to NASCAR races.

CART: Championship Auto Racing Teams was a sanctioning body that hosted races for Indy cars and development series like Indy Lights, among others. Launched in 1979, it went out of business in 2003.

FLAGS: The primary means of communication by race officials with drivers during a race. Flags are deployed at the starter's stand at the start/finish line for oval races and at corner worker stands for road races.

- **GREEN:** Signals the start of the race, or a restart after a caution period.

- **CHECKERED:** Designates the end of the race.

- **YELLOW:** Signals a potentially hazardous condition, and that drivers must slow down. Also known as a caution flag.

- **RED:** Cars must temporarily stop due to an extremely hazardous condition or a problem on the track.

PACE CAR: A control vehicle used to bring a field of cars to the green flag for a rolling start at the beginning of a race or for a restart after cautions. The pace car is dispatched during caution periods to gather the field at a slower speed, enabling safety personnel and track workers to attend to an incident under safe conditions.

PACE LAP: A lap where the speed is controlled by a pace car at the head of the field prior to the start.

POLE POSITION: The number one starting position awarded to the driver who posts the fastest time in qualifying.

QUALIFYING: Drivers must set a time on a solo lap or during a session with other cars on the track to determine the starting order. Qualifying can also determine who will start the race and who doesn't if there are more entries than positions available in the starting field.

RACE CARS

STOCK CAR: A purpose-built racing vehicle with a tube frame chassis, a racing engine, and a body that approximates the look of a street car. Stock cars are not street-legal and compete on racing tires.

PROTOTYPE: Full-bodied race cars built from the ground up for racing and designed to maximize aerodynamics. They are created and built by specialty manufacturers for road racing.

GT: Grand Touring is a road racing class. The category features modified versions of production street cars like those purchased at dealerships and have a similar appearance to street cars.

INDY CAR: An open cockpit car with exposed wheels that races in the Indy 500 annual event and on other ovals and road courses. They are distinguished by powerful engines and can attain speeds well over 200 mph on large oval tracks.

OPEN WHEEL: A term for American race cars with a single-seat cockpit and exposed wheels. In addition to Indy cars and Indy Lights, the term includes two popular categories known as midgets and sprint cars that race on short oval tracks.

FORMULA CAR: A vehicle made for road racing with exposed wheels and a single driver's seat in an open cockpit. Formula 1 racing is the pinnacle of motorsports outside of the United States.

STREET CAR: Production car purchased through a dealership. Typically it can be enhanced with performance modifications and converted to use on road courses for actual competition.

GO-KART: A small, tube-frame vehicle that younger people can race. Karting has numerous sanctioning bodies around the world and often is a stepping-stone to professional racing.

DRIVING

DRAFT: A draft occurs when two or more vehicles travel together in a straight line at high speed. The lead vehicle punches a hole in the air and any following vehicle can ride in its wake while experiencing less wind resistance. Trailing vehicles can then gain speed to attempt a pass or stay in line to save fuel by using less horsepower. Speeds in a draft can exceed 200 mph.

THROTTLE MODULATION: When a driver adjusts foot pressure on the gas pedal to maintain maximum speed without losing control.

RUBBING: Light contact between race cars. It's often said, "Rubbing is racing."

RACING LINE: The optimum line around the track for speed.

INSIDE LINE: By choosing a racing line closest to the inside of a corner when passing, a driver is taking the "inside line." On ovals, it's also known as the lower groove.

OUTSIDE LINE: By choosing a racing line with greater circumference in a corner when passing, a driver is taking the "outside line." Also known as the high groove on ovals.

PUSH: Term given to describe a lack of front traction while turning a vehicle. The driver turns the wheel and the vehicle tends to continue going straight.

LOOSE: Term given to describe a lack of rear traction when turning a vehicle. The driver turns the wheel and the rear slides sideways.

PITCH AND ROLL: Term used to describe the way a vehicle's front end lifts up under acceleration, dives under braking, and leans over when cornering due to lateral force.

DRIVING IN TOO DEEP: Driving too far into a corner after braking late. It is not the typical line around the track and usually produces a slower a lap time.

COLD TIRES: Race tires on a car that have not yet generated the heat required for optimal traction and grip.

RAIN TIRES: Treaded, purpose-built race tires with grooves that more efficiently expel water on the track during competition in the rain.

SLICK TIRES: For racing under dry conditions, these tires have a flat, uninterrupted tread to increase traction and reduce heat buildup. Absent treads, they are "slicks."

STINT: Term often used to designate a driver's turn behind the wheel when there are co-drivers.

THRESHOLD BRAKING: Braking hard for as little time as possible before immediately going back to the gas.

SPINOUT: When a driver's car loses traction, slides sideways, and spins out of control.

RIM RIDING: Driving around the top edge of an oval track along the outside wall.

FLAT-SPOTTING A TIRE: When a wheel and tire are locked up under braking, the tire slides on the track, which can create a small area that is ground flat, often ending a tire's useful life.

WEAVING: Continually changing lanes in order to pass cars.

GOT UNDER: When a car overtakes another going into a turn and passes it on the inside.

THREE-WIDE: Three cars riding side by side.

RACE CAR PERFORMANCE

CHASSIS: The frame of the car.

SOFT CHASSIS: A suspension more compliant in slippery conditions and less likely to suddenly let the tires break loose.

STIFF CHASSIS: A suspension that typically optimizes performance and handling in dry conditions.

AERODYNAMICS: The effective use of air to maximize vehicle speed by creating downforce with the bodywork while reducing the amount of air the vehicle pushes against, by minimizing drag.

DOWNFORCE: The downward air pressure generated at speed by the vehicle bodywork. The goal is to improve traction and handling by pushing the car down on the track.

BODY KIT: A set of uniquely designed body components (fender, hood, trunk, bumpers, etc.) that are different than the originals and made by a specialty manufacturer.

PERFORMANCE MODIFICATIONS: Equipment added to a street car to enhance performance and appearance. It can be purchased from a manufacturer or a specialty company in what's known as the aftermarket.

AFTERMARKET: Designates car parts not produced by the original manufacturer but by a specialty manufacturer.

TRACKS

SHORT TRACK: An oval track that is one mile or less in length.

INTERMEDIATE TRACK: An oval track that is between one mile and two miles in length.

SUPER-SPEEDWAY: An oval track that is two miles or greater in length.

OVALS:

- **BANKING:** An oval track is often banked to enable cars to carry more speed in the corners. The degree of banking varies from track to track.
- **THE APRON:** The flat part of the track around the bottom edge of an oval. It is typically not associated with the racing line but can be used when necessary.

- **FRONT STRAIGHT:** The straight on the same side where the pit road and start/finish line are located.
- **BACK STRAIGHT:** The straight on the opposite side from the start/finish line.

GREEN TRACK: A green track means that rain has washed away the tire rubber that has been ground into the track during the course of a race weekend. A green track has less grip for tires.

ROAD COURSE: A paved racing circuit where the layout resembles a road with left and right turns and typically includes elevation changes.

CIRCUIT: Another word for race track, usually applied to a road course.

THE ESSES: A squiggly series of turns on a road racing course that are shaped like an *S*.

PIT ROAD: The non-racing portion of the track where drivers enter and exit the pits.

PIT BOX: Designated area on the pit road where a driver's crew services the car during the race.

PADDOCK: The area used at a road racing circuit where teams set up to prepare their cars for competition. At ovals, this area is called the garage.

VICTORY LANE: The designated section of the track where the winners of a race go to receive trophies and celebrate.

GOING RACING

DAYTONA 500: NASCAR's biggest race at the Daytona International Speedway; it opens the Cup Series season each February.

ROLEX 24: A 24-hour endurance race held annually at the Daytona International Speedway for IMSA classes representing Prototype and GT cars, each typically shared by four drivers.

24 HOURS OF LE MANS: A 24-hour race that has been held in Le Mans, France, since 1923, and is one of the world's biggest sporting events. Each Prototype and GT car is shared by three drivers.

SPONSOR/SPONSORSHIP: A person or company providing financial or other support to a driver or team, usually in return for publicity.

FACTORY CAR/TEAM: A racing program that has the financial backing and technical support of a manufacturer.

NON-FACTORY CAR/TEAM: A racing program that does not enjoy the financial backing or technical support of a manufacturer.

PIT CREW: The team that services a car during a race, usually limited in number by the rules.

PIT STOP: Stopping in the pit box during a race to get additional fuel, fresh tires, and other service. In endurance racing, driver exchanges take place during pit stops.

FIELD: The sum total of cars on a track, as in, "The starting field is ready to race."

TO FIELD: When a team enters a car, it is said to be "fielding" a car for the race.

SECOND-TIER CREW: A group of mechanics or crew members who are not as proficient or experienced as the primary group.

SPOTTER: A designated observer who has radio contact with the driver and relays real-time information regarding the location of competitors and conditions on the track.

STAYING OUT: During a caution lap, when a car remains on the race track instead of pitting for service, this is "staying out."

TESTING: Practicing with a vehicle on the track in pursuit of optimal performance.

HAULER: The trailer used to transport a team's cars and equipment.

THE DRIVER CHAMPIONSHIP: Awarded to the driver with the most points for the season. Points are earned in each race according to the order of finish and sometimes as a performance bonus such as a fastest lap.

THE TEAM CHAMPIONSHIP: Awarded to the team whose car has earned the most points, regardless of drivers.

THE MANUFACTURER CHAMPIONSHIP: Awarded to the car manufacturer whose brand collects the most points over the season.

ADDITIONAL TERMS

STREET RACING: Illegal, oftentimes dangerous, racing on public streets by a solo driver or drivers competing against one another. Not sanctioned by an organization and typically done late at night when roads are vacant and police scarce.

DRAG RACING: A short, two-car race in a straight line, usually over a quarter mile. Drag racing is a popular form of sanctioned racing for weekend warriors at local drag strips. It is also a common form of illegal street racing.

D4D/DRIVE FOR DIVERSITY: A program devised by NASCAR in 2004 to create opportunities for underrepresented drivers, crew members, and front office workers in NASCAR.

DIVERSITY COUNCIL: Before D4D was introduced, a Diversity Council was created by NASCAR in an initial effort to diversify participation. It no longer exists.

GONG SHOW: Slang for an audition held by a racing team or manufacturer to evaluate potential drivers; derived from the 1970s TV talent show where contestants were "gonged" off the stage for a bad performance.

LADDER BARS: A device resembling a metal ladder used on muscle cars on each side of the rear suspension. During hard acceleration, they help secure the back of the car, increasing rear wheel traction.

ROLL BAR: A bar, or set of bars known as a cage, that strengthens the car's frame, protecting the driver during impacts, and preventing the roof from being crushed in a rollover.

ENDURANCE RACING: A form of racing where teams use more than one driver per car and compete on a track for a specified time period or for a long distance.

SLOT CARS: Scale-model race cars with electric motors designed for tracks with electrified grooves that the cars follow. Performance is controlled by a hand-held pistol grip device.

SPRINT RACE: A short race on a circuit that typically has only one driver. The duration varies depending on the sanctioning body.

SPORTS CAR RACING: Historically, this type of racing featured two-seat production vehicles known as sports cars. Currently, several classes at the SCCA feature two-seat sports cars.

TRACTION: Another term for grip.

INTRODUCTION

How I Defied the Motor Racing Odds

HOW DOES A PROJECT MANAGER on the fast track in the high-tech industry become a full-time professional athlete in his forties? Why does an amateur sports car driver with no experience on high-speed ovals switch to racing stock cars at 200 mph? How does a black man from Northern California seemingly materialize out of thin air in the Deep South to make history by competing in NASCAR's premier Cup Series? It took passion, determination, enthusiasm, gratitude, hard work, raw talent . . . and a little bit of luck!

The things I accomplished are not supposed to happen in sports—unless it's in a movie or a novel, and certainly not in major league racing. At forty-five years of age, I made history by being the first black driver in twenty years to race in NASCAR's elite series. That weekend in Atlanta, I was one of only forty-three drivers to race in the top level of NASCAR, the Cup Series, the most popular and competitive form of professional motor sports in the United States.

Defying the odds, overcoming the challenges and adversity, and prevailing over cynicism and racism, I lived my dream as a professional race car driver. I competed for over thirty thousand laps and eventually stood on the top step of the podium. I had made it and, for me, that was the true win. Any trophies I might win along the way would merely be icing on the cake.

My road to success was in stark contrast to the career of the typical, professional race car driver. Most drivers usually start by the age of ten, with some as young as five. They begin racing go-karts or quarter midgets, which are miniature open-wheel race cars designed for kids, and, if successful, they climb a racing ladder composed of larger, faster, higher-horsepower cars. By their early teenage years, those who have won prestigious championships during their ascension begin to catch the eye of race team owners at the professional level. By the time they have reached their late teens or early twenties and demonstrated consistent success, they have the opportunity to begin their career as a professional driver.

My career did not follow this path. Not even close. I did not race go-karts as a kid, nor did I compete in any officially sanctioned wheel-to-wheel competition as a teen. Unlike my future competitors, when I was in my twenties, I worked as a computer scientist in Silicon Valley at Hewlett-Packard in order to fund my desire to race. I did not become a professional race car driver until my fourth decade and, ironically, my last competitive racing came in karting in my fifties. My racing career unfolded in almost the exact opposite way of a usual one—in reverse!

There were many lessons to be learned during my difficult journey. Risks were taken and opportunities were created in order to live out my dream. Acquiring the right set of values and attributes became fundamental to my success. At the very beginning, long before I started racing, I recognized that I had a passion for the sport. But if I was going to make my dreams a reality, I was going to have to think outside the box and be willing to get out of my comfort zone. Sacrifice and self-discipline were a potent combination that I learned to harness. I taught myself how to network with people and how to present myself with integrity, confidence, and professionalism. But the most effective calling card in my arsenal was my unrelenting enthusiasm for racing. As time went on, some other drivers and industry professionals began to believe in me and offered to help me. Armed with my resolve and solid support from my family, I was poised to reach my goals.

All of my experiences have helped me develop character and cultivate what I refer to as my "Winning Circle." Specifically, there are eight key attributes that I have identified and applied to every step of my path to success: Getting out of your comfort zone, passion, sacrifice, persistence, discipline, enthusiasm, networking, and gratitude. Each of these key attributes helped me grow as a person and propel my career forward. Because I embraced and implemented these qualities from an early age, I was able to achieve a level of happiness, both personally and professionally, that I never could've dreamed possible.

At the end of each chapter, I have reflected on specific values from this Winning Circle that helped me along the way. I call these reflections "Racing to the Front."

I hope my story will resonate with you and inspire you to live out your dreams.

1

Qualifying for My Big League Debut

The sun had set below the rim of the steep banks of the Atlanta Motor Speedway, leaving one-and-a-half miles of asphalt surrounded by whitewashed walls bathed in the radiant brilliance of the track's lights. My time to step up to the big leagues of racing had arrived, and with a deep sense of satisfaction that helped settle my nerves, I surveyed the scene of cars in bright sponsor colors lined up on pit road. After years of preparation, sacrifice, and more than a few setbacks, I was about to get my shot at qualifying for the Golden Corral 500. If successful, I would earn a starting spot in my first NASCAR Cup Series race. It had been twenty years since someone who looked like me had raced in NASCAR's top series.

Historical significance aside, I stood beside my Dodge Intrepid on pit road, mentally focused on driving the two fastest laps I could without crashing the car. Eleventh in the qualifying line, my car looked fabulous with my Waste Management sponsor's unmistakably large *W* and *M* in green and gold dominating the real estate on a brilliant cream-white hood. A big green *23* marked the side, and a billboard-sized *23* filled the roof, where my name in the form of my autograph ran across the top of the door. Gold highlights made the paint scheme pop.

Ahead and behind stood a line of Chevys, Fords, and Dodges glinting under the track's lighting. Trumpeting a kaleidoscope of logos and colors, each paint scheme represented annual sponsor investments of at least $20 million. Sitting like silent sentries with their aggressive built-for-racing stance and aerodynamic bodywork, the cars were attended by proud crew members slowly pushing them up the line. The crews waited impatiently to peel off and head back to the pit area once the driver had climbed in and fired the engine for the launch onto the track and two solo qualifying laps.

An ESPN crew floated nearby with a shoulder-mounted camera ready to capture the thunderous takeoff of each car. Across the way, relatively mild March weather had brought out a decent-sized crowd to the gigantic grandstand, with most of the fans clustered in the seats closest to the track along the front straight.

Was I nervous? Yes and no. I had not practiced well earlier in the day. That didn't give me the confidence I'd wanted for the qualifying race, but I forced myself to focus on the positives. I reworked the mental imagery. I had already driven the two upcoming qualifying laps in my head. I knew what I needed to do. Now I just had to do it.

It wouldn't be easy with fifty-two cars trying to qualify in a forty-three-car starting field. Nine drivers would miss the race. Many of the drivers had the security of a guaranteed starting position owing to their cars ranking among the Top 25 in point standings. They were "locked in" to start the race. I did not have that luxury since my car had not raced regularly in the series. I was one of the "go or go home" entries, meaning that if I did not drive fast enough in qualifying, I would not be racing on Sunday.

I was on a mission. I had to prove to myself and everyone else that I was one of the forty-three fastest stock car drivers in the world. I was someone with no prior Cup Series-level experience on one of the fastest tracks on the NASCAR circuit, a super-speedway with 24° banking in turns enclosed by concrete walls. I would be entering the corners at over 200 mph hoping—no, praying—that the car would maintain the grip needed to come out on the other side.

There's a reason why stock cars have a surplus of dashboard gauges but no speedometer. Drivers don't focus on speed; we focus on beating each other. Although qualifying is all about speed, we don't have time to look down at our dash to see how fast we're going—that would take away from focusing on every input we can make behind the wheel to maximize our performance. Complete attention is needed to choose the line driven around the track or to adjust inputs to the brake and gas pedals. When you're dancing on the edge at 200 mph, and a 3,400-pound car is your partner, the slightest error means you can lose control and suffer very painful consequences in front of your team, industry professionals, the fans in the stands, and upward of several hundred thousand people watching on live TV.

While slowly walking toward the front of the qualifying line alongside my car, I occasionally bantered with my crew to help calm my anxiety. I was trying to keep the gravity of the situation in perspective and my nerves in check. When my car came to fifth in line, I climbed in.

Once I was sitting comfortably in my "office," one of my crewmen locked the window net into place. The custom-built, contoured racing seat fit tightly and held my body in attack position. It would firmly support me against any g-forces or impacts I might sustain. The steering wheel that locked onto the column stood at the perfect distance and angle to maximize turning leverage while minimizing fatigue over a race distance. All of my gauges were in full view on the dash. My helmet and gloves were on. If my six-point safety harness had been pulled any tighter, I might not have been able to breathe.

I had only a moment to close my eyes and offer a brief prayer to the power above. I asked Him to watch over me and allow me to do my best. Then I stared down the track into Turn 1 as my crew finally pushed my car into position at the front of the qualifying line.

With all the pre-event promotion surrounding my presence, a sense of expectation thickened the air, but nobody's expectations were higher than my own. I blocked out all distractions and immersed myself in my laser-focused zone, having already forgotten about the well-wishes from my wife, my parents, my crew, friends, and other supporters along pit road. Given the indication by the NASCAR official to go, I took a deep breath, fired the thunderous V-8 engine, pushed the clutch to the floor, and slid the shifter into gear. After letting out the clutch, I accelerated as hard as I could through the gears as I headed up the banking of Turn 1.

During the warmup lap, I reached fourth gear coming off of Turn 2 and started to weave the car back and forth on the back straight to generate enough tire temperature for maximum grip. I needed to quickly heat up the new set of tires that had been bolted onto the car after the last practice session. If I didn't bring them up to temperature quickly, I wouldn't make it through the sea of high-banked asphalt waiting in Turn 3.

In order to hit the start of my first official qualifying lap at top speed, I had to get through Turns 3 and 4 as fast as possible. Earlier in the day when I was practicing on worn tires, it had felt as though the car was sliding on ice, but now—thanks to the new tires—the car stuck hard through the corner like a roller coaster tightly clenching the rails. When I came across the start/finish line to take the green flag for the first of two qualifying laps, I was hauling!

My right foot had the gas pedal nailed flat to the floor as I approached Turn 1. I lifted slightly off the throttle to scrub off some speed, then turned in and quickly mashed the throttle again. I could feel the tires bite into the track surface as they gave me maximum grip, and the car shot me off of Turn 2. I barely had time to process my thoughts before entering Turn 3 at maximum pace. Again, my car did not disappoint as I made it through the exit of the corner of Turn 4, completing my first lap at an average speed of 190.5 mph.

I don't remember even taking a breath before diving into Turn 1 for my second lap. The feeling of grip surprised me. Racing tire performance degrades from the time they hit the track, with the only variance being how quickly the grip falls off. I was amazed that my tires had kept their edge. I drove that second lap like the first and came across the finish line within two one-thousandths of a second of my first lap! The times virtually mirrored each other, which is a rare occurrence over the length of a 1.5-mile track.

When I later looked at the video on a Fox Sports telecast, I saw that I had demonstrated a speed and consistency that impressed former NASCAR Hall of Fame and Cup Series Champion Darrell Waltrip and former Cup Series crew chief Larry McReynolds, the veteran broadcasters who were commenting on each driver's qualifying attempt. They initially expressed concern and skepticism over my driving technique until they saw the impressive lap times I posted. It prompted them to make an immediate about-face from their prior on-air comments. They quickly started singing my praises, crediting my skill, and admitting they had misjudged my performance earlier. While they may have doubted me, I had never doubted myself.

My time had come. I had arrived.

When I returned to pit road after completing my two laps, I really had no idea how fast I had run. My crew chief, Ricky Viers, had purposely kept quiet on the radio during my laps so as to not break my concentration.

Once I parked and unbuckled, he finally let his guard down.

"Congratulations, Bill. I think it's safe to say that you've made it into the show!"

A lifetime of determination, continued persistence, and years of hard work had finally paid off. History was mine for the making.

I would be racing on Sunday!

■ ■ ■

RACING TO THE FRONT

How did I get across the finish line that day in order to get to that coveted starting line the next?

It may be surprising, but *gratitude* was a key factor in qualifying for my first Cup Series race. Recognizing what has been given to you can be a great motivator. The night I qualified, I wanted to make myself proud, but I also wanted to make all of the people and organizations who had helped along the way proud of me.

I had *gratitude* in the sense that being a black man in the predominantly white world of motor racing may have been isolating but also had its advantages. NASCAR and the sport of racing needed more black participation for a wide variety of reasons, and I appreciated the fact that I acquired unique opportunities as a result.

I was also grateful to have the God-given talent, athleticism, stamina, and bravery needed for high-speed competition, and to be able to accomplish something with those skills that others appreciated and gained enjoyment from as fans.

Taking the time to appreciate success and those who help make it happen provides motivation for the next step.

2

An Early Need for Speed

I became hooked on high performance cars that commanded excessive speeds while growing up in San Jose, California. As a kid, I initially fed my car obsession by racing slot cars, reading my father's car magazines, and racing my bike around the neighborhood. The point of no return came when my father took me to my first auto race when I was seven years old. It was a Can-Am event in 1968 at Laguna Seca Raceway in Monterey.

My father knew about my interest in cars because he always saw me thumbing through his car magazines after he was finished with them. I liked *Road & Track* the most because it had regular racing coverage that included photographs of the cars. When one of my father's friends planned to attend a race at Laguna, my dad decided to go and bring me along. He had a strong impression that it would be something that I would enjoy and he was right. Little did he know how much of an impact this experience would have on my life.

Can-Am, officially known as the Canadian-American Challenge, became a groundbreaking series in the mid-1960s that created a lot of fan interest because of its extraordinarily powerful sports cars, which were unlike anything else being raced in the world. The cars featured open-top cockpits for the drivers, big engines, space frames and bodywork made from fiberglass and aluminum. The series generated a lot of excitement with fans due to the combination of lightweight cars, high horsepower, huge tires, and drivers clearly visible in the seat.

Some of the biggest names in professional racing at that time competed in Can-Am: Bruce McLaren, Denny Hulme, Jim Hall, and Peter Revson, among others. Too young to know all the specifics about the cars or the drivers, I just liked what I saw on the track and brought home an official program, which I still have.

The lax rules about safety back then enabled the fans to stand very close to the track. We watched the action while standing at the bordering fence on the side of the hill that was just beyond the uphill start/finish line, where the cars crested the rise at the top and raced past us into Turn 1.

From the very beginning of the race, I was on sensory overload. Never had I seen cars go so fast, sound so loud, and smell so sweet! I had a hard time keeping a clear focus on the cars as they whizzed past me. The sound of the engines roaring, the gearboxes whining, the tires squealing, and the wind rushing past, combined with the aroma of spent fuel and hot tire rubber, was intoxicating. The whole scene grabbed hold of me and left me spellbound. Being there was euphoric, and I knew at that point that being around racing gave me more enjoyment than anything else I had ever experienced or could possibly imagine. The impression it made sparked the passion that would eventually guide my life.

This incredibly fast course meant drivers turned left at high speed into Turn 1 and then accelerated out, snaking their way along the ribbon of track up a long hill. Standing there, pressed up against the fence and witnessing this artistry of speed, I watched the cars come through each lap until they went over the top of the hill and out of sight. When the cars shot by me, they were probably going 150–160 mph. At that close range, they were not singular moving entities: they were a fluid blur of colors that fused into one flowing stream. Mesmerized and intoxicated, I could feel the breeze as these cars thundered past. By the end of the day, my neck was sore from whipping my head back and forth as I tried to keep focus on all the action.

I think my father was more blown away by the impression the race left on me than by the race itself. He could not have done anything more substantial than introduce me to the sport that would define the course of my life. It set the hook. I knew then and there that I wanted to be a race car driver. But I had no idea if I could actually be one. Almost nobody at the track looked like my father, his friend, or myself. Unbeknownst to me, this was a theme that would follow me all through the course of my life, from childhood to school to corporate America to NASCAR.

Although I grew up middle-class in Northern California, my life began in Washington, DC, in 1961 when I was born to William Alexander Lester Jr. and Rochelle Diane Reed Lester. I came along unexpectedly while my father was working on his PhD in Theoretical Chemistry at the Catholic University of America. My sister Allison came along a year and a half later, and was also born in DC.

After earning his degree, my father moved the family to Madison, Wisconsin, for a couple of years. He performed postdoctoral work at the University of Wisconsin and later became a lecturer in the Department of Chemistry.

I can't remember anything about Washington, DC, because I was only three years old when we moved, but I do remember living in Madison.

My most vivid memories include its typically cold winters. I remember riding sleds and saucers with Allison down the hills in the snow, and walking to school with her and my mom in the frigid cold. Just as distinctly, I remember my very first slot car racing set and how I played with it constantly until I completely wore it out.

We moved around quite a bit in my early years. When my father accepted a job offer from IBM to become a member of the research staff, we packed our things and settled ourselves in San Jose, California. We lived in a quiet, predominantly white neighborhood. The houses stood fairly close together with small yards and short driveways.

While in grade school, my nearby friends and I devised our very own circuit for racing our Stingray bikes. After finishing our homework on weekends, when we had all the time in the world to indulge ourselves, we would race our bikes like we were on a racetrack. We would start by riding on the sidewalk, turning a hard left on a driveway, crossing the street to another driveway, turning another hard left on that sidewalk, and then back again to complete a lap. We would race four or five of us at a time, as fast as our feet could pedal. Sure, it was dangerous—no one wore helmets in those days, and cars could come down the street or around the corner at any minute—but we didn't care. We were racing and having fun!

More often than not, I would win. Was it just that I was practicing more than the other kids? Was I paying more attention to what I was doing than they were? Was it raw talent or athleticism or an innate sense of racing strategy? I don't know, but *it* was something special, and I had it. Every race was like a conquest that I was learning to master. Every win fanned a fire within me that could not be extinguished. I felt alive—invincible!

I was too young to realize how these afternoon antics were bolstering a dream that would eventually lead to a successful career. Other kids would play baseball and dream of one day being in the major leagues. While racing my bike, I would often envision it was an actual racing car. My primary thought was getting to the finish line first.

Throughout my early school days, as soon as I finished my homework, I would jet outside and find my friends. We'd play all afternoon until the streetlights came on. Then it was time to go home, and the evening became family time. My family routinely ate at the dinner table together. It was a nightly event my mother insisted on and a habit I continue to this day with my own family. We ignored any external distractions like the television, radio, or telephone. It was an opportunity to genuinely enjoy each other's company and talk about our day

My mother graduated from Howard University in Washington, DC, with a degree in English and became a social worker. After having children, she became a devoted housewife and made sure that my sister and I were academically prepared for school each day, fed, and properly clothed. She was the first line of defense when it came to helping with our homework; she also administered the first line of discipline if needed. She was a level-headed, yet tender parental figure.

My father was more authoritative and served as an important influence on how I prioritized school, work, and playtime. Many of his interests and hobbies rubbed off on me. He was a true sports car aficionado. He bought a Marcos, an extremely rare, lightweight English sports car made with fiberglass bodywork. Steel gray in color, it epitomized everything a sports car should be: it was fast, low to the ground with a sleek fastback silhouette, and loud. I fell in love with it.

When I was fourteen years old, we moved once again, this time to White Plains, New York, for a year after Dad accepted a temporary assignment from IBM in nearby Yorktown Heights. When my father took the Marcos to work on rainy days, the car literally flooded. It sat so low that the water from the turnpike would splash up underneath the engine compartment. The distributor would get wet, which then shut down the electronics and the engine. He learned the hard way that the Marcos fared much better on the dry streets of California. Functionality aside, it was because of the Marcos that I favored European sports cars over American muscle cars. I liked cars that handled well and were lighter, sexier, and nimbler than their American counterparts. I had a particular fondness for exotic European sports cars like Lamborghinis, Maseratis, Ferraris, and Porsches.

I became enamored with a beautiful blue Porsche 911 Targa owned by the father of one of my best friends, John Collins, who lived about six houses away from us. It didn't matter where his father would take us, just as long as we got to ride in that Porsche. Unlike my practical and pragmatic father, John's father often took chances and drove like a maniac. He liked showing off his Porsche and the unique sound of its engine. You hear a Porsche before you see it; nothing else has the distinct pitch of its air-cooled engine.

My father's influence went well beyond my taste in cars. He instilled a firm sense of discipline in me that left a lasting impression. He gave me the spanking of my life after I hit a childhood friend in the head with an oversized rock, leaving a large, open gash that gushed with blood. I certainly deserved that one. At the time, I viewed it as two kids innocently playing in the backyard. I didn't understand the gravity of the situation. When you're little, you don't ever think of your own mortality or what's dangerous. You're too busy playing and having fun, consequences be damned! My father made me realize that I had to consider my actions more carefully in the future. This was a lesson I struggled with quite a bit in my formative years before it finally stuck.

My father generally did not rule with an iron fist, but he would swiftly make it clear if my behavior crossed a line. A man of few words, when my father spoke, it usually carried significant impact. Sometimes just his facial expressions were enough to get his point across. He was a loving family man who always did what was needed to keep my mother happy. He was the strong, silent type, and, typical of many men of his generation, kept his emotions close to his vest and didn't readily share his feelings.

I often thought he lacked a sense of humor and was too strict, but there were times when my father gladly let loose and joined me in fun activities. He raced slot cars with me in the basement of our home in Madison. We played basketball in the driveway in front of our home in San Jose, which was challenging for me considering he starred as shooting guard at the University of Chicago, where he's in the school's Athletics Hall of Fame! He never took it easy on me when we played, so I rarely won. But he let me ride shotgun in the Marcos, so that almost made up for my constant losses in basketball—almost.

Although I knew he loved me, my father did not often express it. I could never seem to get as much of his attention as I wanted. He worked too hard for too many hours for my liking. My father spent most of his time at the office and often worked through the weekends. While I knew he was making a better life for our family, he rarely witnessed my youth league football and basketball games while I was growing up.

Despite not getting as much time with him, my father instilled important character traits that governed my behavior throughout my life. He taught me the importance of integrity, hard work, and doing things to the best of my ability. He also influenced my sense of style. Conservative but stylish in apparel and presentation, he always looked dapper. My father was a longtime subscriber to *GQ* magazine, and it showed. He was a great role model for learning how to present myself as a professional. He carried himself with confidence and had a signature stride that people often remarked on.

Though he did very well for himself, success did not come easily for a black theoretical chemist at IBM in the 1960s. My father was very much on an island; African Americans were not exactly the typical IBM employee in those days. He often shared the copious challenges of being one of the few black men in a predominantly white company. It was a lesson I benefited from learning early on and ended up being something I would encounter for the entirety of my career as well. He taught me to be confident and continue on my path of success even when I was the only black person in school, sports, work, or just hanging out in the neighborhood. Because of the way my father held himself with dignity and respect, I was able to learn the importance of self-confidence.

Since my father was not around much, my mother usually had charge of me and my sister. She trusted me implicitly. I didn't give her a lot of reason not to. I earned good grades at school, played sports, stayed away from drugs, and really didn't get into a lot of trouble, so I had a lot of latitude with being able to run the streets. I was not a homebody. I wanted to be everywhere doing everything with everyone. My sister, on the other hand, preferred to stay in the house. I think my natural energy might have made my mom a little crazy at times.

"Billy, why don't you go outside and play?" she would often say.

In other words, "Go do the things that boys do and leave us alone."

That worked just fine for me. There were adventures and adrenaline rushes to be had.

In junior high school, I spent a lot of time hanging around the teenagers in the neighborhood who had flashy cars. Although I was a few years younger than they were, I was grateful that they never seemed to mind me bombarding them with car questions. I truly enjoyed watching them work on their cars, but I was even more excited when they would invite me along for a test drive after they'd finished their latest performance modifications. I remember many smoky burnouts and near triple-digit-mph joyrides on city streets. Looking back, the chances we took seem crazy, but man, it was exhilarating! My mother knew that I spent a lot of time in garages with the older kids, but she had no idea about the shenanigans that ensued. If she had, I likely would not have been able to return for another wild ride.

Jim Quarter was a high school senior who lived around the corner. One day, I was riding my bike and saw that Jim's garage door was open. All I could see were his legs and feet dangling out from under his car while hearing the unmistakable clicking of a ratchet wrench. He had a beautiful Chevy Z/28 with a four-speed transmission and high performance 302 V-8 engine. Blue with white stripes, it was one of the nicest cars around.

Curious, I rode up the driveway, stopping short of the garage, and peered in.

"Hey Jim, what are you working on?" I asked quizzically.

Without moving an inch, he stayed focused on the job at hand.

"I'm putting on some ladder bars," he replied.

I had no idea how to install them, or what they were for, but I wanted to absorb everything Jim was doing, so that when I had my own car, I would be ahead of the curve.

"Can I come in and watch?"

Although we didn't know each other well, Jim had seen me around, racing my bike up and down the streets like a speed demon.

"Sure," he said. "Come on in."

I carefully leaned my bike up against the outside wall of the garage and then stepped inside, anxious to observe and learn something new about cars. It was like being in the inner sanctum. Jim walked me through what he was doing, explaining how the ladder bars stiffened the rear suspension and produced better traction.

I couldn't tell you how long I was in that garage with him that day. I was so enthralled with everything he was doing and even more honored that he was taking the time to actually teach me that time stood still.

Once he finally came out from under the car, he said "Let's see how this thing hooks up. Do you want to come along?"

"Sure!" I exclaimed.

Jim got up off the floor, brushed himself off, and slid into the driver's seat. I excitedly climbed into the other front bucket seat with an ear-to-ear grin locked on my face. Jim cranked the engine, and I felt the sheer power of the Chevy roar to life. The rumbling engine epitomized the thrill of raw power and speed.

We drove several blocks without talking. We just enjoyed listening to the engine purr while it warmed up. Once he felt it was time, we came to a stop sign, and then Jim nailed the gas. The car leaped straight off the line like a frightened cat. We loved the results of the ladder bars putting more power to the ground instead of the car going sideways and fishtailing.

From that day on, I started going back to Jim's more often and frequenting the garages of other guys with nice cars. I wasn't interested in being hands-on with the mechanics. I didn't turn any wrenches; I was purely a spectator observing their craft, and I watched everything they were doing: tuning their carburetors, putting in heavy-duty shock absorbers, and replacing stock exhaust manifolds with headers. I was inquisitive and interested in how things worked. I suppose even as an adolescent I had an engineer's mindset. I liked taking things apart—mechanical gadgets and appliances—to see how they ticked. Guys my age did that sort of thing back then, before technology became focused on wearables and handhelds like it is today.

Although I wasn't the only kid in the neighborhood interested in cars, I probably took it the most seriously and went to the furthest extremes. My desire to immerse myself in the culture of cars was insatiable. If I had any free time, I was in a garage somewhere.

Other kids may have thought, "My older brother is working on his car again, whoop-de-do. I've seen it a million times."

They didn't know how lucky they were. I would've killed to have an in-house role model to show me the ropes. There were plenty of times when I had to pedal my bike all around the neighborhood just to go for a ten-minute cruise in a newly souped-up muscle car. But when I felt the engine rumble and reverberate, I knew it was absolutely worth it.

■ ■ ■

RACING TO THE FRONT

Although we didn't call it *networking*, as kids, we often connected with others by making friends or hanging out in the neighborhood. As I got older, my *passion* for cars and speed led me to start developing *networking* skills that would help me throughout my career.

To gain exposure and familiarity with cars and the chance to participate in automotive performance, I started to create my own opportunities. There weren't many black teenagers where I lived, so it was not always a comfortable proposition to walk up the garage of an older teenager. It required me to get *out of my comfort zone*. But once I followed my *passion*, being around others with similar interests helped me become more engaged in my dream of owning a car and eventually becoming a professional race car driver. By pushing myself to meet people, I learned more than I could have ever dreamed of at that age.

Getting out of one's comfort zone and taking risks are vital elements in achieving one's dreams.

3

A Teenage Life with Cars

Once I got my driver's license at the age of sixteen, my need for speed hit high gear. A driver's license represented freedom to pursue excitement behind the wheel. I started taking advantage of my license as soon as possible. I learned to drive in the family car, a 1969 Buick LeSabre with a white exterior, dark interior, and black vinyl top. It was the first new car my parents had purchased since I was born. It replaced a gray Volvo 122S that we had driven from Wisconsin to San Jose, and frankly, its best years were left back in Madison.

When it was time to replace the Volvo, my father went to Smythe Buick in Santa Clara. I was eight years old and excited to see what our next car would be, so I happily accompanied him to the dealership. We were looking for a practical family car, and this four-door Buick behemoth checked all the boxes, including having an impeccable safety record. *Consumer Reports* was a publication that my parents relied upon heavily to make informed decisions, and they gave this car a glowing safety report.

The Buick was not exactly the flashiest car—it was a land barge. But my parents viewed a car purchase at that time differently than I did. Sexiness, style, and elegance were not the priorities.

My mother primarily drove the Buick, but it was the vehicle I learned to drive in after I got my learner's permit. Washing the Buick became a job my father bestowed unto me. Of course, my father showed me his particular way of scrubbing cars that I was obligated to adhere to. He considered this chore "paying my dues" in order to drive it.

When my mother allowed me to run short errands for her, like buying milk from the grocery store, I jumped at the chance. I never just went there and back. Instead, I took the scenic route. I often drove around exploring local neighborhoods. But sometimes, I'd mix in a little mischief and adventure.

Nothing got my blood pumping quite like doing burnouts after pausing at a stop sign. Though it wasn't a muscle car, the Buick had good torque and, due to its non-locking rear differential, the right rear tire was easily spun upon hard acceleration. On the way home, I always tried to find a puddle of water that I could dip the tire into so that it didn't smell of burned rubber and give my joyride away. How my parents didn't wonder why the right rear tire wore so poorly compared to the left is still a mystery to me.

Autumn was a particularly eventful time of year to be a budding new driver who was on the hunt for the next thrill. All around town, people raked their leaves into neat piles that they left curbside, ready to be picked up by the street sweeper. When I found a pile in a nearby neighborhood, I pulled alongside it with a devious grin. I would back up over it, hold the brake pedal, drop the gear selector into drive, and punch the gas pedal while simultaneously releasing the brake. Through the rearview mirror, I'd watch all the leaves shoot back onto the grass like confetti at a parade. I'm sure homeowners didn't appreciate my foolishness, but I had a blast! To all my neighbors whose lawns I desecrated, please accept my apologies.

I was glad when the Buick was upgraded to a brand-new 1976 BMW 3.0 Si four-door sedan. It was truly my mother's pride and joy. Unlike the Buick my parents had earmarked together, the BMW was my mother's pick. With a maroon exterior and soft, tan leather interior, an injected in-line six-cylinder performance engine, sun roof, Blaupunkt stereo, multi-spoked alloy wheels and four-wheel disc brakes, this car performed even better than it looked.

I soon gained my parents' permission to drive unchaperoned. Once I was alone in the car, each occasion behind the wheel turned into an opportunity to floor the gas pedal, slide the car around corners, or slam on the brakes in order to stop in the shortest distance possible.

About the same time, my friend Mark Mills became one of the biggest influences in my life, especially when it came to cars. A grade ahead of me at Willow Glen High School, Mark lived around the block and was one of the only other black guys in my neighborhood. We quickly bonded and identified with each other through all of our common interests—mainly cars, sports, and girls.

Mark and I had a shared identity as black students at a majority-white high school. There weren't many blacks in the neighborhood our family had moved into, and that was reflected in the school. Our high school had about 2,600 students, and I think the number of black students wavered somewhere between ten and twelve. Having Mark around made me feel less isolated and like less of an anomaly.

I had a lot of friends who were Latino and white, but we didn't share similar backgrounds or cultural experiences. My classmates definitely considered me cool, but I often did not readily identify with the whites or

Latinos. I didn't find common ground with their musical choices—most of the white kids liked rock, and many Latinos liked music with Latin influences and Spanish lyrics, which I couldn't understand. My favorite music was the Motown sound and rhythm and blues.

Willow Glen had a reputation for being strong academically, but there was constant tension between whites and Latinos. Due to desegregation mandates, buses brought Latinos from the east side of town into an essentially all-white, middle-class neighborhood. The culture clash mixed with typical hormonal, adolescent behavior often led to fights. Thankfully, they were not gang-related altercations; they were mostly fistfights with some wrestling. Occasionally, kids had weapons like chains or pocket knives, but that was rare. Standoffs often occurred in the quad area outside the cafeteria. But before things could get really rowdy, teachers usually arrived to break up these showdowns.

I had friends that were Latino and friends that were white, so I was in a tough position. Some of my friends wanted me to choose sides and show support for them, but it was not my fight. I chose to not get involved and let them figure out their issues without my assistance or intervention. In retrospect, I wonder if they were projecting a macho, tough stereotype onto me because I was black. But nothing could be further from the truth. I have always been nonconfrontational by nature and getting into physical brawls was just not my style.

My teenage years were an interesting dichotomy. On the one hand, I sometimes felt isolated among my classmates because of our differences, but on the other, there were plenty of times that I felt a strong kinship with my peers. I was embraced by the student body. I would go so far as to say that I was considered one of the popular kids. Being athletic made it easy to get along with the guys. I didn't have a problem making friends with the girls, either. My sophomore year, I escorted the Homecoming Queen to the big dance. In a graduating class of 2,600 students, it was quite an honor to be nominated to escort her, especially since she was a stunning white girl, and I was one of the only black students in the entire school. There was a sea of white guys who could have been chosen, but I was the winner. She was a beautiful, sweet, girl whom I was fortunate to date briefly, and I was proud of that, too.

In those days, I wore my hair in a gigantic Afro. I would often hear people say, "That guy looks like Michael Jackson!" Since I was fairly short all the way through high school, the big 'fro helped me gain some height. My first driver's license at sixteen listed me as five-foot-five inches, weighing 110 pounds. I was a twig. When I graduated high school at eighteen, I was only three or four inches taller than that. I didn't grow to my full adult height of six feet until my freshman year of college.

I played football my sophomore year in high school as a very undersized running back. I was a string bean with a lot of heart. I might have been quick and agile while wearing the red and gold colors of the Willow Glen Rams, but I wasn't strong enough to play football proficiently. Once, a defensive player wrapped me up on a running play, then carried me five yards backward and dropped me. A linebacker who probably weighed at least 160 pounds had simply grabbed me and picked me up like I was a kettlebell. It wasn't long after that incident that I decided to shift from football to track, where I could take better advantage of being quick and agile. I ran hurdles on the track team in the spring of that year. My small frame made it challenging, but I had long legs and enjoyed the high hurdles, where I was able to master the form quickly.

When not socializing at events like Homecoming or playing sports, I spent as much time as possible with Mark Mills. He lived with his mother, brother, and three sisters, but there was one aspect of his life that I found extraordinary: Mark came from a racing family.

His father, who was divorced and lived in Ohio, raced as an amateur in the Sports Car Club of America (SCCA). Mark would go to Ohio every summer to live with his dad, and he'd come back with stories about new racing techniques that he'd picked up. While still in high school, he persuaded his mother to buy a 1977 Mazda RX-3 *SP*. This two-door coupe worked as a small family car, but the Special Package designated by the SP meant it came with a front air dam and rear spoiler. Racing versions of this little pocket-rocket and its unique rotary engine were scoring victories regularly in the International Motor Sports Association (IMSA) professional road racing series. It wound up being a race car for Mark and me on the city streets around San Jose—at least, that's how we treated his car.

Mark always drove, and I happily rode shotgun. Starting from his house or mine, we would cruise to a nearby, quiet neighborhood to find a street with low traffic activity. From a standing start, Mark would accelerate the car as fast as possible, racing through the five-speed transmission, and then slam on the brakes at the very last possible moment, hoping like hell that we'd stop by the end of the block. We weren't always successful. On more than one occasion, we skidded out into the intersection and prayed for no oncoming traffic. Amazingly, we never crashed, got hit by another car, or got caught by the police.

Many times, I would follow Mark in his Mazda while driving my mother's BMW as if we were racing each other. But matching Mark's speed through some segments of the San Jose streets proved difficult. My mother's BMW carried significantly more weight than the Mazda and was not nearly as nimble. I lived for this type of adrenaline rush and never cared about or considered the consequences of my actions. I was a quintessential teenager and found out the hard way about exceeding my limitations.

One day while racing around town, Mark flung his Mazda through a corner at a high rate of speed. His car slid around the bend and completed the turn without incident. I was not as lucky. In a competitive effort to keep up with him and match his moves, I lost control of the rear of the BMW, and then overcorrected with the steering wheel while trying to catch the slide.

The car skidded off the road and the BMW ended up beached on top of a pile of concrete rubble. I was able to throw the car into reverse and carefully dislodge it from the debris. After backing it off, I got out, and saw the damage.

My blood pressure spiked—luckily, the car was still drivable, so I drove the relatively short distance back home. I was in anguish and filled with regret the whole way and terrified of my parents' reactions.

Once I got home and parked on the street in front of my house, I noticed the smell of burning oil. I already knew the steering was off-center. I had heard grinding and groaning from under the hood as I maneuvered the car back toward the house. I hopped out of the car, bent down, and looked underneath. I saw oil leaking from under the engine—I had cracked the oil pan!

Now completely overwhelmed with anxiety and fear, I wished I could reverse time and right my wrong. My mom had always put so must trust and faith in me. I dreaded telling her that I had been reckless with her prized possession, not to mention that I had put myself in danger by driving so aggressively. I wasn't quite sure how she was going to react to my news: Would she scream at me? Would she cry? Give me the silent treatment? Ground me for life?

My stomach was knotted as I entered the house.

My mother was standing over the stove when I slowly walked into the kitchen. I took a deep breath for courage.

"Mom, I crashed your car," I said with as much sorrow in my voice as I could muster.

She turned around quickly to face me.

"What do you mean you crashed my car?" she blurted out rapidly. She sounded more concerned than angry.

She knew what a good driver I was, so I'm sure she hadn't ever expected to hear me say those words. Too nervous to look her in the eye, I kept my head down and avoided looking straight at her.

"I lost control of it going around a corner, and I crashed. I was able to get it home, but there's definitely some damage underneath it. I'm so sorry, Mom."

"Oh my God. Are you okay?"

She still didn't sound angry—yet—but I had a strong feeling that once she knew I was unscathed, the parental anger would kick in.

"Yeah, I'm fine."

"Are you sure? Are you bleeding? Do you have any bruises? Is anything broken?"

"No. I'm really okay. The car is more messed up than I am."

I tilted my head up to take a peek at what sort of an expression she was wearing now that she knew I was unharmed. I feared for the worst.

"Good." Her tone grew more somber. "Where is the car?"

My insides fluttered with a renewed sense of trepidation.

"It's outside."

Moving past me, my mother walked around the kitchen table and rushed out through the front door. I followed her hurriedly. She ran over to the BMW and began to assess the damage. Her face was masked in an unmistakable show of sadness and disappointment. As her eyes continued to pan, the look of despair deepened. I remained silent, fearful of what she would say if I spoke.

Without a word, she walked back inside the house. Unsure of what to say or do, I slowly walked behind her.

My mother stopped in the family room and faced me.

"How did this happen?"

"I was following Mark in his Mazda and when he rounded a sharp turn, I tried to do the same, except I lost control and ran the car up on some rocks."

"You were following Mark? You mean you were *racing* Mark!"

It was more of an assertion than a question. We both knew the answer. There was no point in denying it.

"Yes," I admitted, almost in a whisper.

She shook her head and let out a sigh that could only mean she was too mad to even try to form words.

"You're going to pay for every repair it takes to fix my car!" she said in a voice just short of a scream.

With that, she turned, and went back to the kitchen to finish making dinner. My mother's response was actually more subdued than I had anticipated. I had expected her to verbally rip me apart. I knew how much she loved that car; however, she didn't lecture me or try to give me a guilt trip. I was grateful that she didn't make me feel any worse. I suspect that she knew how badly I felt already, and that my lesson would be reinforced heavily by the financial impact of fixing her car.

The next day, the car was towed to the BMW dealership. All of the money I had worked so diligently for, initially as a grocery store parking lot cart retriever and then as a grocery bagger, had to go to the repair bill. I had saved nearly $3,000 and my eye had been on a sleek 1969 Chevelle 396 Super Sport that I had seen for sale around town. I had spent the last few weeks dreaming of that car and how it would be mine. That dream died with my crash.

The trust I had worked so long and hard to establish with my parents over the years had also been shattered. My father was generally a man of few words, but he spoke even fewer to me after the accident. The scarce times that he did verbalize his feelings about the matter, his disappointment hit hard.

My mother gave me the cold shoulder for what seemed like an eternity. She had little sympathy for my reckless actions. The fact that I had hurt her hurt me. Seeing that BMW in our driveway every day was a constant reminder of my misstep and its ripple effect on my mother.

I learned a hard lesson about physics and car control, too, from this episode, but it did little to diminish my intoxication with cars and racing.

My passion was just as vehement as ever, but after that day, I was much more careful and deliberate with my driving. And I would never race my mom's car again.

Prior to my senior year in 1978, my family moved from the South Bay to the East Bay of the Bay Area, which meant I would graduate from a different high school. I had reservations about moving prior to my senior year but attending Skyline High School in Oakland turned out to be a wonderful experience given the substantially greater racial diversity of the student body. My father was going to head up a new research organization called the National Resource for Computation in Chemistry (NRCC), and that required us to move. Following the close of NRCC years later, he became a tenured member of the Chemistry Department at the University of California, Berkeley.

Once in Oakland, I discovered Malibu Grand Prix, where I started racing go-karts. I didn't have a lot of money and usually spent what cash I could scrape together on the karts at Malibu. These surprisingly fast karts had bodywork around the cockpit, but they had exposed wheels and tires. They looked like the cars driven in the Indy 500 and enabled me to fantasize about driving a real race car.

Since karts were released onto the tight, twisty Malibu track one at a time, drivers raced each other on the clock. A large scoreboard tracked our times using a computer and displayed each driver's lap times, keeping the day's fastest laps at the top. I prided myself on being able to show up and challenge whatever was the current, fastest time of the day. I never needed much practice. I could easily command the lead in only a few short laps. The secret was staying on the accelerator as long as possible without using the brakes. Employing an optimal line around the track permitted me to do just that.

As it turns out, almost all professional drivers love to compete in karting. The fastest karts closely mimic real race cars in terms of cornering, braking, and acceleration, but at lower speeds. Many of the guys I would compete against in professional racing later in life had competed in karts on various youth circuits from an early age, gaining not only racing experience and track time but early recognition in the racing community. I did not enjoy that privilege.

When I hit my senior year of high school, the time had come for me to decide what I wanted to do with my life. My mother and father had goals for me and expected me to earn a degree from a prominent university. I wanted to be a race car driver, but the likelihood of success still looked like a faraway dream.

After the BMW incident, I had tried hard to replenish my savings by working long hours at Burger King all summer. Still, I could not recoup the money spent on repairing the BMW in such a short period of time. But it did not stop me from looking for my dream car, which I finally found at a dealership while on a trip to Los Angeles with my cousin Darryl. It was a 1977 Mazda RX-3 SP, the same make and model that Mark drove.

I came home one afternoon and approached my father to see if he would help me buy it. I was not optimistic that he would be supportive, but it was my only shot.

"Dad, I really like this Mazda RX-3 SP I saw in LA when I was down there with Darryl and you know how much I want a car. Would you possibly consider splitting the cost of buying it with me?"

I was sure that he was going to immediately shut me down, but instead of rejecting me straight away, he looked at me pensively. I couldn't tell exactly what he was thinking, but it seemed as though he was considering my proposal.

"Why are you so interested in this car?"

He couldn't understand my attraction to the Mazda since he didn't have my appreciation for its racing prowess and performance capabilities. I went into vivid detail explaining the car's appeal, performance, and style. My father was intrigued and sat there silently, taking it all in.

What I hadn't counted on was that my father knew that I had been waiting for admission responses from Stanford and UC-Berkeley. As a private university, Stanford would be much more expensive than UC-Berkeley, which is public. He proceeded to make me an offer I couldn't refuse.

"Son, you can either go to Stanford and walk around campus or go to Berkeley and drive. If this is really the car you want, we'll fly down to LA and I'll split the cost of it with you."

My jaw almost hit the floor. He was going to help me!

"Seriously? Thank you so much, Dad!"

And just like that, I had my dream car and I knew which college I was going to attend. The Berkeley versus Stanford decision was a no-brainer. They were both great schools, so I would be fine academically at either one. And meanwhile, the dealership wanted $3,000 for this Mazda, and fortunately, I had a little over $1,500 saved in my bank account. We flew down to LA the next weekend and looked over the car. He still couldn't understand my affinity for it, but we drove it back home to Oakland together later that day.

Unlike Mark's bright orange Mazda, the one I had found was an iridescent, electric blue. Over the course of my college years, this Mazda underwent a number of transformations. I continually enhanced it with performance modifications. Not only did I improve the power, brakes, aerodynamics, and how the car handled, but my driving skills also improved. Sometimes I would compete in autocross events through a course consisting of plastic cones in a closed, controlled environment like a giant parking lot. Mark exposed me to his company's car club, which sanctioned these events. But more often than not, I would test the limits of both myself and my car on the city streets and local highways of Oakland and Berkeley. I honed my racing chops on those streets long before I ever got the chance to race on a real track.

■ ■ ■

RACING TO THE FRONT

I enjoyed *getting out of my comfort zone* with my friend Mark in ways that are familiar to many teenagers. Sometimes we took chances that put ourselves in jeopardy. And sometimes, as in the case with my mother's car, it was other people's property that we were playing games with. I learned that *getting out of one's comfort zone* doesn't mean taking stupid risks. While not scared about some of the things we did with our cars, I was definitely afraid of losing the trust of my parents. They were the two most significant people in my life. I learned a painful lesson about the importance of exercising good judgment and not overlooking the consequences of my actions.

When I lost the opportunity to buy my own car by spending my savings on repairing my mother's BMW, it hurt. This hobby of mine was such a simmering *passion* that I had allowed myself to make some very bad decisions that had serious consequences. But it did not dampen my desire to become a professional race car driver. I began to realize that maybe a little more *self-discipline* would be in order. Nothing excited me like racing, but how was I going to get there?

My father worked in the science and technology field at IBM and exposed me to the idea of obtaining a degree in engineering. It was a lucrative way to earn a living. I would be able to write my own ticket and provide the income I needed to pursue my racing dreams.

Learning to couple passion with discipline improves your chances of success.

4

Racing Through Engineering School

My two biggest passions during my college years at UC-Berkeley were driving my car around the city and working on it to improve performance. I also loved going to watch professional races at the two major racing circuits near the Bay Area, Sears Point International Raceway and Laguna Seca Raceway, where I could meet professional drivers and hang out with fellow car enthusiasts.

As for school itself, I considered an engineering degree strictly a means to an end since I really had no passion for it. I decided to pursue a career that could lead to making a decent amount of money in the shortest time possible and therefore enable me to go racing. I didn't want to spend the time to become a doctor, lawyer, dentist—anything that required an advanced degree.

School at Berkeley was no picnic. Among rankings for engineering schools in the country, Berkeley came second only to MIT. It was a tough place to get an education; I did not enjoy my collegiate experience. Most people leave college with fond memories, but I think I can speak for many of my fellow students in engineering when I say the Berkeley experience was painful.

I studied extremely hard, but not with much inspiration. I viewed it as paying my dues. Berkeley could be very demoralizing in the respect that it did not provide much support to its engineering students. In my experience, neither the professors nor the administrators really cared whether you made it out or not. Once you paid your registration fees, you were just a number.

That appeared to be the case for all the professors in the technical disciplines. They considered teaching a necessary evil. My father did research in the Chemistry Department at Berkeley, so he had to teach, too. He didn't prefer teaching: like many of his colleagues, he really wanted to do research. That was his passion. There were, no doubt, many great professors at Berkeley who had a great passion for mentoring and teaching. Unfortunately, I did not cross paths with any of them during my time at Berkeley.

At the time I attended, there were more than fifty thousand students at Berkeley and each graduating class of engineers had about six hundred students. That's a lot of students and, from my perspective, a lot of them didn't look like me. The majority of aspiring black engineers I started with got weeded out, gradually disappearing from the engineering school. They moved to the College of Letters & Science, which was a less rigorous curriculum, to pursue computer science degrees. But I was determined to finish what I had started. I stayed in the College of Engineering and earned a dual degree in Electrical Engineering and Computer Science.

At one point, I was just barely making it. I received a letter from the associate dean of the College of Engineering indicating that I was to see him in his office one Wednesday morning. Based on my GPA at that point, I already had an uneasy suspicion of what the meeting was for. When the day arrived, I went to his office and sat down across from him.

"You know this is one of the hardest curriculums in this university and it's not cut out for everyone. Based on your current grades, it might be worth considering a change in your major."

I was flabbergasted. I couldn't believe that he would actually suggest such a thing to a student. I thought deans were supposed to be supportive. There was no way that I was going to quit or give up. It wasn't in me. I was going to obtain my engineering degree despite the long hours and sleepless nights spent studying or in the computer lab.

"What?" I asked in utter confusion.

"It's not too late to transfer. Plenty of students come to similar realizations. There's no shame in changing your mind and going in a different direction."

He may have had good intentions, but his lack of faith in my ability to succeed cut like a knife. Looking back, I wish he acknowledged that I was struggling, and then said, "Look, Bill, I know it's a rigorous curriculum. What can we do to help you? What might help get you back on track?" But his seeming acceptance of my defeat only served to fuel my fire and solidify my determination to proceed and prove him wrong. I could do it. I would do it!

"No, I'm going to stay right here and I'm going to get my engineering degree from this school," I responded curtly.

I knew if I got my engineering degree from Berkeley, I could write my own ticket for employment. I was not about to give up that opportunity. I had plans and nothing was going to deter me from achieving my goals.

There were a few black and brown people in engineering, primarily from Africa, but not many. It was a very, very lonely experience. If not for the

Professional Development Program (PDP), and the Black Engineering and Science Students Association (BESSA), I probably would have flunked out. There were a few black upperclassmen in engineering who were BESSA members, and I found their mentorship necessary for my survival.

It seemed like all the white students studied together through their fraternity associations and related organizations. Similarly, all of the Asian students appeared to study together. They often spoke the same lanugages and probably felt isolated by the "American" scene in similar ways that I did. They primarily spent time with each other. The students from India comprised a third segregated faction in engineering school.

The Asian and Indian students were under tremendous pressure. If they weren't getting the job done, their families or supporters in their countries of origin withdrew funds and they had to return home. Friends I knew in these two groups made that reality very apparent to me. They told me it was like life or death for them, and the only people who could really relate were others who were under that same type of pressure. They huddled in their own silos and spent little time interacting with other groups. It seemed crazy to me!

Feeling adrift, I sought out mentoring from PDP and BESSA. I received great direction about which professors or courses to take and gained access to sample tests and sample final exams to help me better study and prepare. If I had questions my friends could not answer, I asked my mentors. The professors typically were not around for office hours anyway and the teaching assistants often only knew the bare minimum—if you could even get their time. They kept office hours, but they had so many people looking for help you could barely get to them.

I never flunked a course, but I did fail a test or two. I don't think I ever got a D in a course, but I got a few Cs. I wanted to be an A student. But Berkeley had brilliant students from all over the world, especially in engineering. I was sharp, but far from brilliant.

I worked hard because the course material often didn't come easily to me. When I began to get a little stir-crazy, I found ways to relieve the stress and unwind. When I had free time, I would take my Mazda RX-3 SP out for a joyride. I'd tear up the streets of Berkeley every chance I got. Driving was my release, my escape from the day-to-day struggles of real life. I socialized as much as I could without compromising my studies. I found time to attend parties on the weekends, play video games, or shoot some hoops after class. And like many males in their late teens and early twenties, I spent a healthy amount of time trying to get to know specific representatives of the opposite sex. College wasn't all bad.

I could not get on-campus housing as a freshman because I lived too close, so I commuted in my first year from our home in Oakland. It didn't take long to get to campus or back home with me behind the wheel, bobbing and weaving in and out of traffic. I frequently challenged myself to shorten my commute time, which made the trips back and forth more exciting and provided an escape from my academic challenges.

Living at home gave me convenient access to working on my car in the driveway whenever I decided to make upgrades. I continued to use that space even after I started living on campus. The house had a carport on the side where my mother and father parked their cars, one in front of the other. I parked my car on the driveway pad just outside of theirs, leaving mine more exposed and subject to some of the elements since the carport roof did not completely cover it. But when my father was gone, I would position my car in his larger space and work on whatever modifications I had in mind.

Although I had a full-fledged Mazda RX-3 SP in terms of the engine and suspension, my car did not have all of the racing attachments and appearance package additions of the production-based versions being raced in IMSA. The race cars had a spoiler at the back of the rear deck lid and an air dam at the bottom of the front bumper. My Mazda bore none of these additions used to improve aerodynamic handling. Instead of a spoiler, mine had a luggage rack over the trunk, clearly not the most aesthetically pleasing feature you could add to a car.

The racing version had a wide stripe and *RX-3 SP* in bold script on the side of the car to promote this Mazda model at races and in the media. I had something more like a street appearance package. An understated black and thin white stripe with no lettering ran along the roof and sides of my electric blue car. The stripes started at the nose and followed the body lines all the way to the tail. It was a very understated design compared to the full graphics version of this car on the streets, calling out for every police officer in town.

While the appearance of my car may have been understated, I made sure its function would not be. First, I put in a single form-fitting Corbeau racing seat with more padding and a sturdier build. Later, I took out the Corbeau and the other, ugly original plaid front passenger seat and installed two heavily bolstered, state-of-the-art Recaro racing seats.

"What is that you're doing to your car?" my mother questioned one day after coming outside to see what I was up to.

"I'm putting in a roll bar," I responded proudly.

My mother slowly shook her head disapprovingly. I knew the trepidation she felt every time I made high performance modifications, which was often. My mechanical adjustments became extensive. I even updated the suspension, including the shocks, the springs, and the anti-sway bars.

"Are you planning on rolling?"

"No, I'm just making it safer. I've even hung a fire extinguisher off of it just in case."

Her look now became quizzical.

"Are all of these things you're doing really necessary?"

I laughed.

"Don't worry, Mom. It's not all about increasing performance. Actually, I'd have thought you'd be happy knowing that I've taken steps to make my car safer."

What she didn't know was that the main reason I was adding the roll bar was to make the chassis stiffer to provide better handling. The safety aspect just happened to be a convenient benefit.

I went through several front spoilers over the years. Initially, I ordered and installed a factory front spoiler from Mazda, which was very thin and very low. Mounted to the bottom edge of the valence under the bumper, it directed air into the radiator and around the car instead of underneath it, which helped the handling at higher speeds. Plus, it looked cool and racy.

I actually broke the spoiler a time or two thanks to the low mounting position. I wound up becoming pretty proficient in working with fiberglass to repair the damage I incurred hitting parking stops or speed bumps. I soon began taking brand-new spoilers and building them up before even putting them on, reinforcing them with enough fiberglass to take more of a hit. I painted these spoilers in a smooth semigloss black so they almost had a professional body shop appearance.

When it came to using tools and working on cars, I owed a lot to my maternal grandfather. When I was growing up, he enjoyed getting me involved with what he was doing, whether it was tinkering in his workshop, tuning up his car, or going fishing.

My sister and I affectionately called him "Pops." Light-skinned in complexion and ruggedly handsome, he combed his hair back with a part on the side. A blue-collar guy, he was energetic and liked working with his hands.

Pops spent hours in the garage tuning, fixing, and cleaning his black Oldsmobile Ninety-Eight and later, a white Chevelle Malibu. He provided me with my first experience behind the wheel. As a young boy, he would let me steer the Oldsmobile in the alley behind the house while I sat in his lap. When I got older and taller, he also let me use the brake and gas. Once I became a teenager, he taught me how to drive in that same alley.

My grandmother, sister, and I often went fishing with him at Lake Michigan, using worms from a flower bed at the back of their house. Most of the time, I would throw the bait off the hook, because I wanted to see how far I could cast my line. Casting was the fun part for me, not catching a bass or a bluegill. I especially didn't like having to clean them afterward. Invariably calm, Pops let me do it my way without ever getting mad when I snapped a fishing line or lost tackle in the lake.

My grandfather was a miracle worker. I truly believed he could fix anything with his wide assortment of tools. He often let me assist him with projects. Most of my skill in handling tools and my ability to fix things resulted from my apprenticeship under him. When he had a mild stroke, he lost control of his right side and his mobility. Always so strong and full of vitality, it saddened me to see the change in his health. I had a hard time accepting it when he finally passed. At his funeral, I remember feeling compelled to stand and speak on his behalf. My heart was full of memories that the world needed to hear about so that they could envision him the same way that I did. Though mere words could not do him justice, I stood up and bled out my stories to a room full of tearful friends and family members. My admiration for my grandfather was boundless. Pops had always been a positive inspiration for me and I wanted to honor him as such.

Armed with the mechanical knowledge Pops bestowed on me, I began modifying my Mazda and started driving to the professional races at Sears Point and Laguna Seca. My heroes—Jim Downing, Roger Mandeville, and Joe Varde—were competing in RX-3 SPs and I actually had the opportunity to meet them! It was surreal to enter into a world that I had only dreamed of. I was also able to get an up-close look at how they modified their cars for racing. I had been following their careers in the Champion Spark Plug Challenge Series of IMSA in racing magazines. The Champion Spark Plug Challenge comprised one of the support series that made up an IMSA race weekend, which meant they competed in shorter races prior to the major event. Known for being a relatively friendly series, IMSA opened its paddock to all spectators, meaning you could walk right up to where teams worked on their cars. I tried to engage the Mazda drivers and their crews to talk about their cars. I looked at what racing components their cars had, observed the engine configurations, and found racing modifications to consider for my car.

My efforts paid off because Jim Downing and I actually became friends. I eventually bought a bona fide racing spoiler from him for my rear deck lid to replace the luggage rack. Not one to be modest about my souped-up "race car," I was proud to show off my modifications to anyone who would indulge me. Jim quickly learned how passionate I was about my car. I showed him pictures of it with the Champion Spark Plug Challenge decal banner emblazoned across the top of my windshield, like the competitors had on their IMSA cars. A fanatic about IMSA racing and Mazda's role within it, I displayed a personalized license plate on my car that read IMSA RX3.

I don't know why Jim had that spoiler readily available. It wasn't brand-new and had some imperfections in it, but I was more than up for the task of fixing it up. I applied some fiberglass to it, sanded it down, then primed and painted it. Once done, I had an authentic IMSA Champion Spark Plug Challenge rear spoiler on my RX-3 SP, which helped plant the back end of the car at higher speeds, and I was very proud of it. Eventually, I also got an engine manifold modified for racing from Jim. This simple bolt-on component gave me a reasonable horsepower increase, but didn't do my fuel mileage any favors.

Sure, I liked the more glamorous, state-of-the-art Prototype sports cars that headlined the show in IMSA, but the Grand Touring Prototypes, as they were called, weren't like anything you would see on the street. The Mazdas in the Champion series were very similar to my RX-3 SP. Basically, I had a race car I could drive on the street.

When I went to races at Laguna Seca, I parked my clean and racy RX-3 SP in the corral reserved for the newer and more expensive two-seat RX-7 sports cars, joining a proud brotherhood of Mazda owners. The people who owned the RX-7s liked my car and just invited me in. My electric blue coupe stood out among all the sleek RX-7s. Looking back, my pride in this scenario confirmed I had the mentality of a racer—somebody who liked standing out from the crowd.

Those participating in a manufacturer's car corral got to drive around the track on a parade lap, albeit at relatively low speed, in between races. So, I drove on the circuit in my RX-3 SP with the RX-7 club. I had a blast coming down the hill, through the twisty corners known as the Corkscrew, on the track where I'd first fallen in love with racing.

I had put aftermarket tires and wheels on my car, which had originally come with extremely narrow 13-inch tires. They were an eyesore and I couldn't understand why Mazda had decided on such limited performance rubber for a relatively high-performance car. I installed American Racing brand four-spoke wheels made from magnesium for lighter weight. I regularly wore out the high-performance tires I would buy since they were made from softer rubber for more adhesion.

The sticky rubber came with a trade-off. I was lucky if I got 20,000 miles on them. Due to my aggressive driving, my tire mileage invariably fell way below the manufacturers' wear warranty.

My little street racer enabled me to learn the limits of my ability, the limits of the car, and how I could modify it to handle and perform better.

I never went driving with the intent to race people on the streets. And practicing in the street was dangerous on many levels. I mainly sped my car through less populated areas that contained long, winding, hilly roads. I considered Skyline Boulevard my personal speedway for this very reason. Whenever I left from my parents' home in Oakland early in the morning, I made it a point to take Skyline Boulevard. When I returned home, I took the same route.

This stretch was a four-lane road divided by a tree-filled median, scarcely lit by street lights. In each direction, the lanes were divided not only by paint markings, but also by small lights embedded in the road that came on at night. I would often speed at night after having turned my headlights off. I relied on the moonlight and the small lights that separated the lanes as my road guides. It heightened the thrill of knowing that danger could lurk around any corner. On more than one occasion my sister unexpectedly experienced this excitement when she rode with me. It was a foolish thing to do, but I couldn't get enough of the thrill. Allison didn't appreciate it, though.

She was not the only person who experienced my indiscretions. I hate to admit it, but I enjoyed watching *The Dukes of Hazzard* on TV and devised a way to imitate the way the General Lee (the nickname for the Dodge Charger on the show) went flying through the air. One steep hill near my house had a flat landing for a side street to come in. I would speed down that hill in my Mazda RX-3 SP, hit the flat section and take off, landing on the downhill portion. Some of my cousins enjoyed the adventure as much as I did and would often tag along for the adrenaline rush, but much like my sister, not all of them enjoyed "the jump." Anyone seated in the back had to hang on tight to the roll bar. To this day, a few of my cousins still remind me of how I "petrified" them with these escapades.

I had a close friend at Cal Berkeley and, fortunately, his father was in the Berkeley Police Department. His father got me out of plenty of tickets that I acquired around the campus and the Berkeley area.

I would say to him, "Hey man. I got another ticket. Will you talk to your dad for me?"

His dad would have a conversation with the citing officer and the officer would magically fail to show up for the court date. Or the judge would merely give me a warning and say something like, "Just watch it" and my ticket would be excused. I rarely abided by the speed limit and with my Cal Berkeley friend's father's help, I didn't really need to. Without the threat of penalty, I didn't have to pay fines, suffer points on my license, or deal with an increase in my insurance plan. As a young male already in the highest rated category for insurance risk, any mark on my driving record would have proven costly to my insurance premiums. Maintaining a clean record was always a priority for me. My parents initially paid my insurance, and a bump in the premium would have signified irresponsibility and been clear leverage for them to take my driving privileges away, something I definitely did not want.

To limit my vulnerability to tickets, I heavily modified the exhausts on my Mazda in an attempt to muffle the sound. My modified rotary engine was so loud you could hear it a mile away. I didn't want the police to hear me coming. When I had the engine ports for the intake and exhaust enlarged to be more like a racing engine and produce more power, it only got worse. The "street-ported" engine in my car didn't produce the *rap-rap-rap-rap* sound of a fully "bridge-ported" Mazda racing engine, but it was pretty close.

I put in an exhaust system with six "glass-pack" mufflers, which were packed with fiberglass instead of the typical metal baffles. My rotary engine had dual exhausts, and I put three mufflers on each exhaust pipe. I had two glass-packs on each exhaust runner before the rear axle, then the dual exhaust pipes went over the rear axle into another set of glass-packs and then out the rear. It was insane!

Glass-pack mufflers weren't designed for a rotary engine due to the extreme heat the motor produced. I blew out glass-packs on a frequent basis and had a muffler shop that knew exactly what I wanted replaced every time I showed up. Despite all the mufflers, I couldn't sneak up on anybody. When I got on the gas, the noise was obnoxious. People clearly heard me before they saw me. I felt like a race car driver.

Since I needed money to feed my need for speed, I worked summer jobs each year while in college. Eventually, I made enough money to pay my way through school as well, thanks to summer internships at Hewlett-Packard.

After my freshman year, I was fortunate to fall into a job working at International Harvester making about $18 an hour, a terrific wage in 1980!

I drove a Taylor-Dunn electric cart, and picked parts in a warehouse to fill customer orders. I had a reputation for being one of the fastest with the cart (surprise, surprise) and admittedly did some crazy tricks with a Taylor-Dunn. My summer internships at H-P started after my sophomore year. I was able to work all summer making an impressive income, which I stockpiled so that when the school session started again, I was able to focus solely on my studies.

I effectively put myself through college. I had always done very well academically prior to entering college, and earned myself a Regents scholarship to start out my freshman year. With the scholarship, my parents had to commit a nominal amount for my first-year tuition. From my sophomore year onward, I paid for my own education. I could afford my street car, go to the races, and put myself through college thanks to the internships.

As mentioned, my father was a professor of Chemistry at Berkeley while I attended school. His presence as a member of the faculty provided me with a perpetual sense of support. My father had always been a positive influence on me, but our relationship grew even tighter with the close proximity. He habitually checked in on me, inquiring about how classes were going and how my grades were coming along. Though Chemistry was a far cry from the engineering degree I was pursuing, my father was always curious to know what I was learning.

If anyone ever tells you that Cal Berkeley is an easy school to coast through, you should immediately question their integrity, their sanity, or both! It was one of the toughest experiences of my life. There were often times when I was demoralized by my results not matching my efforts or my test scores not rewarding the number of study hours I had invested. I learned the hard way that perseverance and determination did not always equal good grades, but there was no chance that I was going to quit. I chose the path of engineering and there was no turning back. I pushed myself to overcome the obstacles and handle the disappointments. I spent countless hours studying. I labored many long nights in the computer lab. I employed whatever support resources were at my disposal to reach my goal. Meals were missed frequently when study groups ran long. All-nighters were pulled when exams needed to be crammed for. I did not make the Dean's List, but I made it to graduation, and for me, that's all that mattered.

The sense of pride I felt on graduation day was palpable. After four years of watching me claw my way through the electrical engineering and computer science program, I knew that my father would be present to watch me stand up and receive my diploma from the university that was so near and dear to his heart. Unbeknownst to me, there was quite a surprise in store.

I had nervous butterflies pulsing in my stomach as I sat in the audience and waited for my name to be called. My last name begins with an L, so it's right in the middle of the alphabet. I had to sit through nearly three hundred students receiving their diplomas before it was finally my turn. I was terrified that I would trip over my graduation gown in front of the whole school, so as I made my way up the steps, I kept my head down, carefully watching each step. I crossed the stage, putting my head up just in time to see the dean, who had been handing all of the other students their diplomas, take a calculated step backward. My heart dropped into my stomach.

What was he doing? Was I not graduating after all? What was happening?

Suddenly, my father stepped out from behind the dean. He was draped in a long black gown adorned with blue and red scarves, just like the other professors who were on stage. My father was not a professor of the Engineering School, so there was no reason for him to be on that stage, other than to honor me with the surprise of a lifetime.

He has been hiding the entire time off to the side, waiting for this moment. With a smile grander than any I have ever seen, my father extended his arm, presenting me with the rolled-up parchment. I was utterly speechless. Shock blended with confusion, but it only took the proud look on my father's face to tell me everything I needed to know. My father had watched me strive and struggle for four long years, and now he was going to be the first person to stand on stage in front of an auditorium full of people and hand me my diploma. A sense of immediate euphoria washed over me as I held my left hand out to accept the degree. My right hand reached forward to meet my father's firm handshake. He gripped my hand with a strength I had never experienced.

"Congrats, son. I'm so proud of you."

One of the school officials was able to snap a picture right at that moment. You can see the look of pure joy on my face. I had accomplished something many people only dream of. And my family was there to support me every step of the way.

It's a day I'll never forget.

■ ■ ■

RACING TO THE FRONT

For the majority of engineering students at UC-Berkeley, pursuing a degree required *getting out of one's comfort zone* for the long haul. Treated like registration numbers, we were taught an extremely demanding curriculum by professors who weren't typically available after class. For me, this sense of alienation was even more intense, because in the engineering department there were so few students who looked like me and who I could readily identify with.

I was determined to succeed in reaching my goal of achieving a dual degree in electrical engineering and computer science, and my *persistence* enabled me to find ways to connect with others at Berkeley, academically as well as socially. It was the beginning of my reliance on *networking* to find what I needed to reach my goals, a strategy that would sustain me throughout the rest of my career.

When obstacles become overwhelming or foreboding, persistence and finding—and embracing—a support network is a key element in moving forward.

5

Seeing Sky on Skyline Blvd.

Nothing could slow me down. That continued to be my mindset. Once out of college, I worked full-time at Hewlett-Packard while living at my parents' house. I continued to test my skills on the streets of Oakland. I might have been sublimating my impatience about becoming a full-time racing driver. Looking back, it's incredible that I did not get hurt or killed.

When you move into amateur club racing, or the professional ranks, your commitment to going faster takes place on a closed circuit with protective barriers in a car full of safety equipment. If something goes wrong, safety crews and medical personnel are standing by. Racing around on city streets is a far more dangerous endeavor. None of the safety elements present in organized racing exists on the streets. Barriers, if any, are generally not designed to catch cars traveling up to speeds of twice the posted limit. You might be wearing a three-point seat belt and sitting in a single bucket seat in a road car, but that protection in a crash pales in comparison to what's offered by a roll cage, racing seat, and six-point safety harness.

With the roll bar, four-point safety harness, and fire extinguisher, my car was as safe as a road car reasonably could be, but I knew a real race car provided far greater protection in a safer environment. Still, that didn't slow me down.

I liked testing myself, and my Mazda, on Skyline Boulevard, the stretch of road that runs through the hills high above Oakland. Regional parks border the east side of the road and more developed areas are off to the west. It was the scene of two of my crashes, including one that Mark and I were fortunate to walk away from. Much of Skyline is a divided road, with two lanes running in each direction separated by a median of trees and brush. Usually a fairly isolated stretch, police did not patrol it often. The first accident I had on Skyline turned out to be more of an aggravation than a severe consequence, which should have served as a warning.

It was a gorgeous, sunny afternoon, and I was cruising down my favorite strip of road, pushing the pedal to the metal in the usual fashion. I knew the road backward and forward and didn't think much of testing my limits on it. In a section where the road weaved downhill, a sharp turn followed by an immediate dip caused me to lose control of the back end of my car. I was carrying too much speed as I hit the corner. I tried my best to correct it with as much opposite steering lock as I could muster, to no avail. The back end became light, and the rear tires were already slipping. My heart pumped furiously as I desperately tried to regain control. I felt the car pulling away from me as I slid up onto a guard rail. My body shook with the impact and my neck jerked sideways. The thud of initial impact followed by the bone-chilling sound of metal scraping metal groaned from beneath me as my Mazda ground to a halt.

With trembling hands, I popped open the latch of my seat belt and pushed open the driver's door. I did a quick personal assessment: no pain; I was fine. The seat belt and safety harness had done their job in protecting me. Despite being emotionally shaken up, I was physically unscathed. I stepped out of the car to inspect the damage. The right rear corner of the car had beached itself over the end of the guard rail, which was sloped to the ground, emulating a ramp. The bumper was hooked over the guardrail, suspending the car in place. Overall, it didn't look too bad. There was no significant damage. The car was still drivable. Since the left rear tire was still in contact with the pavement, I was able to throw the car into reverse and slowly back off the rail.

The right corner of the rear bumper was damaged and the underside required a bit of bodywork. I needed a new section of bumper, but after priming and painting it, I was able to secure it back in place. It looked almost as good as new. By opening the trunk and pounding with the heel of my foot, I popped the section underneath the bumper back out as best I could. After carefully applying a small amount of color-matching spray paint, it was hard to see evidence of my indiscretion.

Undeterred, I was back racing on the streets in short order. Mark was still living in San Jose and was now working as a mechanical engineer at Lockheed, but when he came up to visit, it was like no time had passed at all. Mark called to tell me about a new car he had bought and wanted me to see. I knew this showing would not be complete without one of his joyrides. Mark had purchased a Chevy Monza and modified the suspension, tires, and wheels. He boasted about his new baby and was excited to show off its performance. A version of this Chevy, built especially for racing, had been very successful in the mid-1970s in IMSA competition, so the car had some pedigree.

Once again, Skyline Boulevard served as the makeshift test track. I was not worried about our test drive because Mark was behind the wheel. I was more than happy to ride shotgun. It was a day that could have easily cost Mark and me our lives.

Although he was a very skilled driver, Mark wasn't familiar with Skyline. I should have been clearer about its dangers. We were coming down a very steep part of one of the many hills. Near the bottom, there was a switchback—a very quick left–right—just before the next incline. Our speed was approaching 80 mph before he needed to brake for the zigzag in the road. The two lanes blended into one right before the windy section. The road became one lane in each direction beyond that.

Mark handled the first two-lane stretch on Skyline Boulevard with his usual aptitude. As we started on the downhill slope, I began to wonder if I should have told him that he was going to need to slow down. We were hauling along at about twice the speed limit. I had such faith and confidence in his driving that I failed to appropriately assess the situation. Mark had pulled off so many crazy stunts over the years that I naturally assumed that he could handle everything the road threw at him. In those days, we thought we were immortal. I truly believed that he could defy the laws of physics with his driving ability. I was wrong.

Mark continued at full throttle. A pit sunk in my stomach. Surely Mark knew the limits of his car. He had made and tested all of the performance modifications at length. I couldn't help thinking that either his car handled really well and he had driving abilities way beyond what I could comprehend, or we were about to be in trouble. It was too late for me to offer a warning. He was fully concentrating and committed, exhibiting a confidence that suggested he would be able to handle anything that was thrown his way.

When looking down toward the bottom of this hill, a driver is blocked from seeing what's around the turn until they're virtually in it. Your view to the left is blocked by trees and shrubbery. You can see that the road goes down and then left, but you don't know how severe that left is and you can't see that an adjustment to the right quickly follows.

Mark had no way of knowing what was beyond the bend. We came down to the first left, which he made. When he turned to the right, he lost the back end of the car. If you don't keep the car on the pavement, there's a 15- to 20-foot drop of brush down a hillside to a dirt road below. If not for that dirt road, a car could go careening all the way down a very long, steep hill and into the nature reserve.

We started sliding out of control where the road began to go back uphill, and I saw sky. It's not as if we drove off. We flew off sideways, and then we hit, and then we rolled down the dirt hillside. Our tires departed the road, sending the car spiraling into the horizon.

There was no time to be frightened. All of my senses were acutely aware that my body was pumping blood to my heart at an alarming rate. Adrenaline kicked in as the world spun all around me. It seemed like we were rolling forever in slow motion. I didn't have the presence of mind to count the number of times. The blue sky repeatedly crashed into the brown dirt, over and over until I no longer knew which direction was up. My vision shifted expeditiously between sky, dirt, sky, dirt. I shut my eyes tightly, not wanting to see what was coming next. I felt the weight of the car with every tumble. My body stiffened, bracing for each impact, anticipating that pain would soon follow. But it never did.

We must have rolled several times before finally coming to rest upside-down on a dirt road. With Mark's car planted on its roof, we were suspended in midair in our seats.

"Are you okay?" I asked Mark while dangling upside down.

Without hesitation, he replied, "Yes! I'm alright. How about you?"

"I'm not sure yet, but I think I'm okay."

After regaining my orientation, I realized popping my seatbelt would land me on my head. Bracing myself, I carefully unbuckled the seatbelt and caught my weight by extending my hand down to the roof of the car. There was no way to open the door. I was going to have to crawl out the window. I twisted my body and slid my legs out the window frame. Mark followed suit and managed to slip out on his side.

I pulled myself to my feet and Mark slowly walked his way around to where I was. My legs were shaky, but I was able to stand.

Words escaped me as I surveyed the damage to the Monza. I think we both innately understood that we had dodged a bullet. I stood back and evaluated the carnage. His car was absolutely destroyed. The hatchback had torn off and was lying up on the hill.

After flying off the road and rolling down a ravine, I would've expected to see a bone protruding through my skin. At the very least, I expected to feel some sort of ache or pain. Although we were covered with dirt, we had both come out without a physical scratch.

Mark had a strange, disoriented expression on his face. I wondered if he was experiencing some sort of shock.

"This road is crazy. I'm sorry, man. I guess I should've warned you to slow down," I apologized.

Mark didn't respond. He must have still been in disbelief.

A few cars had arrived on the scene and the police had been called.

While waiting for the officers to arrive, Mark and I climbed up the side of the hill to see the skid marks from the accident. From the spot where Mark had turned back to the right and lost the rear end, the deep black tire tracks went across our side of the road and through the oncoming lane. It was clear that had there been an oncoming car, we would have crashed into it head-on. The skid marks formed a large half-moon and then went straight off the cliff. After scrubbing off some speed, we had probably flown off the road at around 50 mph.

"I can't believe that drop didn't kill us," Mark said.

"You and me both," I mumbled under my breath.

The first officer to arrive on the scene was a tall black man in his mid- to late forties. The hardened look on his face told me that this was not the first hairy collision he had seen on this strip of road, but still, he shook his head in awe.

"I have never seen a car with that much damage after a crash where the occupants walked away. I can't believe how lucky you guys are."

I was indeed grateful this accident had not claimed our lives.

"Believe me. We are counting our blessings right about now," I told him sincerely.

The officer asked about our families and called my mom who, I understood later from my sister who was home at the time, immediately burst into tears. I'm not sure if they were tears of joy that we were unharmed, tears of fear that we kept taking chances with our lives, or tears of anger that Mark could have killed me. I never asked her.

The tow truck came shortly after the police arrived. The towing crew flipped the car over, hoisted it onto its flatbed, and towed it away. My father pulled up just before they towed the car away. The look on his face as he came over to me made it clear he was shaken by what he saw. He threw his arms around me and hugged me tighter than any embrace I had ever felt before.

"Son, are you sure you're okay?" my father gasped through bated breath.

There was no denying that he was distraught.

"I'm okay, Dad. I'm not hurt."

Once the initial relief of seeing me alive and in one piece passed, his thoughts shifted to how the accident had occurred. It wasn't hard for him to piece together the fact that we were traveling too fast. He seemed relieved that at least Mark was the one driving, and not me. I can't imagine how much worse things would have been for me if I had been behind the wheel. We soon headed home in an uncomfortable silence that meant he was too livid, too anguished, or too disappointed to even form words. It was probably a mix of all three.

To my surprise, my mother had very little to say after we walked into the house. She had already called Mark's mother in San Jose to tell her about the accident and to come get her son. I had never seen Mark's mother really mad or disappointed before but, when she arrived, she was fit to be tied, not only because of what he could have done to himself but for what he could have done to me.

This was a wake-up call for Mark and the beginning of a falling out between us. We didn't have an argument or call each other out. There was no "You're an ass" or "You're a schmuck." Nothing like that. I think the emotional, psychological, and financial impact of the incident probably diminished his interest in speed and motor sports. Maybe he held me responsible for not telling him about the road ahead. I don't know, but I also don't remember us talking about racing ever again.

As for me, it didn't diminish my interest in racing or speed at all. I was none the worse for wear. Did it give me a sense of vulnerability? No. I was determined to get back on the horse quickly—or in this case, in the car. Mark was like Superman, but all of a sudden, he had found his kryptonite.

Mark and I drifted apart. The accident had a deep effect on him. He changed toward me so much that it became a huge setback in our friendship. I'd be lying if I said it didn't bother me, even if rationally I understood. But it still hurt that suddenly we didn't have a lot in common. The bond that held us together had been broken.

I had another crash in Oakland a few years later, this one while driving my prized 1986 Mazda RX-7 Turbo. I had first seen this car on the cover of *Autoweek* magazine and thought, "I have to have that car!"

Shortly thereafter, I saw the car in the classifieds section of the magazine. I couldn't believe it! I called the seller and he told me it was still available.

Working at H-P by this time, a great friend of mine, who I met there, Mark Copeland, and I flew to Texas, where I inspected and bought the car. It had been modified with a turbocharger setup by a company called

Cartech. It rode on custom MOMO Italian racing wheels and sported a beautiful Kaminari aftermarket five-piece body kit. All of these additions enhanced its performance, appearance, and aerodynamics. Taking turns, we drove the car back home.

One evening, I was having fun showing off in the RX-7 to Shelly, a woman I was seeing who lived in the South Bay and worked with me at H-P. She came up to Oakland and we went out to dinner in my car.

The turbo on this RX-7 behaved like an on-off switch. If you weren't pointed in the right direction, that sudden power boost could bite you with an overload of horsepower and subsequent loss of rear traction. And I happened to not be pointing in the right direction when going through a short tunnel near the library in downtown Oakland on the way home.

I lost control of the back of the car when the turbo kicked in, spun the rear tires, and bounced off the concrete barrier lining the inside of the tunnel. Fortunately, no one was hurt. Over the years, I had become friendly with the owner of the Immaculate Auto Body & Custom Paint shop. John took care of fixing the car, but it was expensive. The entire right side was torn up. I had to replace two wheels, some suspension pieces, and parts of the aftermarket body kit.

It didn't bode well for my future with Shelly, since the car had hit on the passenger side. She must have been wondering if I was trying to kill her. I remember the turbo spooling up fast and the tires immediately losing traction on that cool night. I had no way of controlling that car.

I quickly lost interest in the RX-7, and Shelley quickly lost interest in me. Both of those outcomes were better than nearly losing life and limb up on Skyline Boulevard, along with losing my long friendship with Mark.

■ ■ ■

RACING TO THE FRONT

I experienced the loss of a childhood friendship that had been sustained through high school and college when Mark and I drifted apart after our horrendous crash. We shared the best and the worst of times growing up, and I was disappointed that our friendship didn't continue, despite my efforts to the contrary. Looking back on it now with the benefit of age and maturity, I can understand what might have led to our distance. I suppose that my presence could have served as a constant reminder of a traumatic event for him. Teenagers don't always readily share their emotions but it's very possible that he felt a lingering guilt as the driver. I have *gratitude* that we were both unharmed during the incident, and that it didn't diminish my *enthusiasm* for racing.

I maintained my *enthusiasm* for racing despite this crash. I would not consider being relatively unintimidated by the event an accomplishment, but it was a gut check. Having learned a hard lesson about racing on the streets, I realized the need to employ more *discipline* if I wanted to become a professional driver. That meant competing on a circuit with proper sanctioning and safety considerations. And solo in the car.

Sustaining enthusiasm under adverse circumstances helps reinforce conviction.

6

Silicon Valley Life

Right after I graduated from UC-Berkeley and started working at Hewlett-Packard, I quickly discovered that being on the fast track in the relatively early and heady days of Silicon Valley didn't hold much appeal for me. I was living for the weekends and the racing it would bring. I wanted to be on an actual track, not in an office building! It steadily became an uphill battle to get through the workweek. For two years, I raced my GT3 class Mazda RX-3 at the Sports Car Club of America (SCCA) club level. But once I won the championship that second year, I spent much of my spare time, even on work days, trying to open doors to professional racing.

I enjoyed working with the engineers at Hewlett-Packard, but I did not care for the actual work itself. The technical challenges weren't exciting to me and I didn't have a passion for developing computer diagnostics, the department where I worked and would eventually become a project manager in. I knew how to do the assigned tasks and I took care to do them well, but I wasn't exactly using my spare time at home to think about a better way to develop diagnostic tools. My heart was on the racetrack.

During my undergraduate years, I had worked as a summer intern in various areas of diagnostic software development where I predominantly wrote code. Interning unquestionably helped ease the transition from college to the working world. Since UC-Berkeley was a heavy research institution, most of the instruction I received dealt with theoretical, rather than practical, application. My courses tackled the theory behind electrical engineering and computer science, but didn't include much hands-on work, which was infinitely disappointing considering the hefty price tag that came with my degree. As a result, the internships over three summers at H-P were invaluable. Once I graduated, that experience enabled me to step right into a full-time job writing diagnostic software. After four years, I was promoted to managing a team of software developers, essentially putting me on the management fast track.

Since H-P constantly introduced new computers and devices, our department never ran out of work. I began my career working on computers located in the office laboratory, pulling boards and doing other hands-on work with the hardware. I was mechanically inclined and liked working with tools, in the same way I liked working on my car. Once I became a project manager, though, my opportunities for hands-on application disappeared.

As a manager, I had to coordinate with engineers to ensure that they had the tools and support they needed. I managed their schedules and continually asked a series of standard questions:

"Are you on schedule?"

"What are the resources you need?"

"Do you need to talk to an engineer out in the field?"

"Do you need access to a specific piece of hardware?"

My goal was to assist the engineering team in succeeding, mostly by removing obstacles; however, this was not what I had signed up for. I preferred to do the work myself. I enjoyed being part of the team that created and developed. My enthusiasm was being drained as I watched everyone else dig in and get their hands dirty. Most engineers would relish the opportunity for their career trajectory to include management responsibilities within five years of leaving school, but while I was proud of my accomplishment, I felt hollow.

My superiors were convinced that I had a bright future at H-P. I was on my way to potentially becoming a section manager, which meant multiple project managers would be reporting to me. Sure, it would have paid me more money and provided more responsibility, but I had no interest in that type of position. All the extra hours would only take me further away from my goal of being a race car driver. My priorities were firmly in place and they did not include climbing a corporate ladder to an executive position. The management "fast track" was not the type of track I was chasing.

Despite my lack of interest in the position, I worked hard to make sure the company got the results it needed and the people working under me received what they deserved. But racing was always at the forefront of my daily thoughts. My greatest gifts and natural abilities flourished behind a wheel, not behind a desk. I knew in my heart that my destiny did not include fluorescent lights and an endless row of cubicles. Software development was never going to fulfill me, no matter how many more dollars or promotions H-P threw at me. Monday through Friday consisted of biding my time, doing the grunt work required of me so that when the weekend came around, I could spring to life again. Initially, that meant racing in the

San Francisco Region of the SCCA at the Sears Point International Raceway and Laguna Seca Raceway tracks.

I didn't want to race my RX-3 SP. In case anything catastrophic happened on the track, I needed to still get to work with my street car. Instead, I bought a plain white Mazda RX-3 race car from a guy named Rick Weldon, who'd had moderate success competing with it in the San Francisco Region events in the GT-3 class. Mechanically and technically astute, Rick was a capable driver and a nice guy.

I had occasionally seen his car in competition when spectating SCCA races in college. In the market for a race car, and a Mazda RX-3 in particular, Rick was a target. In speaking with him at the track, Rick indicated he might sell the car, so I went to his house in Hayward to look at it. I bought it for $7,500, much less than the arm and a leg I was afraid he might be asking. The deal included some spare parts and an old trailer, which required new wheels and tires. I had already solidified a commitment from my friend John at Immaculate Auto Body & Custom Paint to sponsor me, and they painted the race car and rusty black trailer the same electric blue as my Mazda RX-3 SP. I was starting to officially look the part.

I had a very primitive race car, but figured I could make up what the car lacked with my driving ability. To stay within my budget, I couldn't do too much to develop this RX-3. For a car running in the GT-3 class, my primitive example had a basic chassis and drive train, and a standard body with no fender flares. Most competitive GT-3 cars ran light custom-contoured fiberglass bodies. Mine wore heavy stock-production steel.

The 13-inch wheels my car raced on were relatively small. But it fit my budget to continue with them instead of upgrading to bigger 15-inch wheels and high-performance brakes. The car had a standard four-speed transmission instead of the five-speed gearbox built by Mazda Competition. The extra set of drive shafts and rear-end differential gears I got from Rick were a meager set of spare parts compared to those held by my competitors.

My Aunt Judy allowed me to use one of the garages at the four-plex she owned in Oakland, where I was living with her son, my cousin Darryl. I had moved there from my parents' house upon graduation. Aunt Judy was so supportive. When I started racing, she often loaned me her pristine Lincoln-Mercury Cougar to use as a tow vehicle.

I did everything that I thought needed to be done to go GT-3 racing. Boy, was I wrong! My eagerness to race clearly superseded my naiveté. At the outset, the only toolbox I had was a plastic fisherman's tackle box containing off-brand tools. To prep the car for race weekends, I went to the office early on Friday mornings and tried to get back home by the early afternoon. After working on the car until late in the evening, I'd leave for Sears Point in Sonoma or Laguna Seca in Monterey on Saturday morning, depending on where the races were that weekend. The format for the weekend included practice and qualifying on Saturday, with warmup and the race on Sunday. I ran ten races in 1985, my first year of competition.

Early in the year, I met Mike Johnson, who became my crew chief. I met him through a mutual friend, Eric Hand, who I knew from my time running around the streets of Hayward. As a fellow Mazda RX-3 SP owner, Eric and I were a rare breed. When we first saw each other's cars, we immediately pulled over and started talking shop. Our mutual love of our unique cars formed an instant camaraderie between us. It wasn't long into the conversation before he told me about his friend Mike, who he said knew almost everything about Mazdas, and I mentioned I had just bought a GT-3 class Mazda RX-3 race car. He said Mike might be willing to help out, so I called Mike and just as Eric had surmised, he happily agreed to come over and inspect it.

Mike was a formidable presence. Standing about 6'2", he was tall and lean with thick, dark hair and a welcoming smile. I heard him pull up as I emerged from the garage. He strolled up the driveway and reached out his catcher's mitt of a hand to greet me.

"You must be Mike," I said. "Nice to meet you. Eric speaks highly of you. He says you are the go-to guy when it comes to Mazdas."

"Nice to meet you, too. Yeah, I've learned a thing or two over the years," Mike responded humbly.

"I appreciate you coming by. Let's check out my toy."

Mike followed me into the garage where my freshly washed race car sat sparkling.

"Nice car. This used to be Rick's, right?"

"Yup. I needed a full-on racing car for the track. I have that RX-3 SP over there, but I don't want to race it. I'm keeping it as my street car. This one here will be my track weapon."

Mike walked around the car like a shark circling its prey.

"That's smart. Rick keeps his cars in great condition. When is your next race?"

"I'm planning on running Sears Point in a couple of weeks. I could sure use your help in getting this baby ready. You already know way more about this thing than I do!" I explained.

Mike nodded his head and crossed his arms to his chest.

"I can help with you that. I can also help you with transport. That Mazda rotary pickup truck out there will come in handy."

With Mike's truck, I could relieve my aunt from subjecting her Cougar to my racing exploits.

"Oh, man. That would be fantastic. Thanks!"

"No problem. This will be fun. I'm not much for driving them, but I love working on race cars and watching them perform on the track."

From the way he spoke, it was clear that he was as passionate about his hobby as I was about mine. Joining forces would be the perfect opportunity for both of us to satisfy our ambitions and pursue our dreams: his of becoming a fledgling race car mechanic and mine of becoming a professional race car driver.

Mike did the majority of the mechanical work on my race car with occasional help from Eric. My network of race car mechanics and other drivers continued to grow. The more I hung around the track, the more connections I made and the more relationships I formed. Mike Haag was a guy I met through another SCCA Mazda racer. He initially rebuilt my RX-3 SP street car engine and joined my racing effort by rebuilding my race engine. But I was a one-man show when it came to organizing and funding my racing program. It became difficult to get through the week at H-P because I was so focused on the race weekends and being successful there. I was constantly thinking about budget, logistics, and what extra parts and equipment I needed.

Like any racer, I needed financial help and hustled to find it. In total, I brought in $10,000 in sponsorship that year. I obtained two local sponsorships, which consisted of cash and trade-outs from Immaculate Auto Body and Custom Paint, and George Oren Tire & Brake. Both businesses sat across from each other, and had provided service to my RX-3 SP, so I had become friendly with the employees and owners over the years. I persuaded a local Budweiser distributor to support me with $2,000. I even landed a corporate sponsorship from the Nippon Denso Spark Plug company by sending them my race results. The next thing I knew, they had provided me with a sponsorship package. I got free spark plugs, which was a significant perk since they were very expensive for a rotary engine and they didn't last long in competition due to the rotary's heat demands. In order to secure their product, I had to agree to promote their brand. I had a Nippon Denso banner in my pit area and decorated my car with their decals. I now had a well-prepared, full-competition car, a crew, and sponsorship; I was slowly turning into a bona fide race car driver!

In my first season, I won Rookie of the Year for the San Francisco Region of the SCCA, comprised of competition at the Sears Point and Laguna Seca tracks. I also finished second in the GT-3 class points championship. The next year, I won the GT-3 class championship. Had I not met Mike Johnson, I would have never done so. He kept me afloat. He was a stand-up guy who helped escalate my career to the next level. Meticulous and knowledgeable about every part of the car, Mike's mechanical aptitude was phenomenal. He could easily take apart the transmission and put it back together without needing an instruction manual. I did not have that same extent of mechanical wherewithal—not even close—so I was always awed and impressed by his natural abilities. He was easygoing and fun to be around, but when it was time to work, Mike always got things done.

Our pit area at the track had a rudimentary, ragtag appearance. Mike's rotary pickup truck wearing worn green paint would be hitched up to my flatbed trailer. We didn't have the enclosed trailer pulled by a big motor home typical of my competition. Most other GT-3 cars sported a more sophisticated, high-dollar appearance and were steered by far more experienced drivers. But my driving was clean and consistent. I may not have always been the outright fastest on the track, but I typically finished every race. I won the Rookie of the Year title because I was judged to have demonstrated true driving talent, and had done the most with the least amount of budget or development spent on their car.

Natural driving talent cannot be taught. It is an innate gift. Sure, anybody can be taught to drive fast, to a certain extent, but the best drivers have inherent car control and the ability to feel that edge of control without overstepping it. You have to feel the car under you and instinctively know exactly when and how hard to accelerate when exiting a corner, or when and how hard to brake when entering a turn to avoid spinning out. It is also the ability to know how hard to drive a car without wearing it out and causing its performance to diminish or fail. Driving talent also encompasses race craft, which is how to read your opponent's strengths and weaknesses, and having the ability to know how to capitalize on them during competition.

I'll always remember when I won my first SCCA race that first year. It was only my second race ever at Sears Point Raceway. It happened to be Mother's Day and my entire family was there to support me: my mother, father, sister, girlfriend Gina, cousin Darryl and his girlfriend Anitra. They all piled into the pit box along with my two-man crew, Mike and Eric, to watch the show. I looked sharp in my mandatory, recently purchased off-white race suit with SCCA and Mazda patches emblazoned on the front. My race car was adorned with a large *20* on both sides. There wasn't a cloud in the sky as I went out onto the track. It was as if Mother Nature herself was cheering me on. I could not have asked for a more perfect day. I felt anxious but ready.

Sears Point Raceway is a two-and-a-half-mile, hilly road course with a series of winding curves and bends that form a loop. The track that day was comprised of four different classes of cars and housed thirty-five competitors in total. As would become the trend in my career, I was the only African American driver in the race. Once the green flag waved, signaling the start of the race, my foot thrust hard on the gas pedal and remained committed throughout the event. Many of the other cars outclassed mine; they had far superior components: bigger brakes, more elaborate suspensions, lightweight body components, plexiglass windows instead of glass, and faster-shifting, more rugged transmissions. I had to make up for my shortcomings by relying on aggressive, flawless driving and Mike's impeccable car preparation. And that's exactly what I did. I took bold chances when passing other cars; I consistently drove on the edge of balance and control, and the car didn't skip a beat. It all paid off. For my class, I whizzed under the waving checkered flag first.

I had just won my first real race!

"Whoooohoooo! Yeah baby!" I screamed out the window.

I threw my fist into the air in celebration. After all the years of racing on the streets, I had finally graduated to a real course, and I'd won! I beat twelve other GT-3 drivers, who had likely all raced on actual courses more times than I had. The sense of elation that throbbed through my body was like nothing I had ever experienced. It was a mixture of hard work paying off, passion being fulfilled, ability being realized, and dreams coming true. I always knew in my core that I could win, and I had just proven it.

I looped the track one last time during the cool-down lap. My pulse quickened in my veins as I slowed my car to a stop on the start/finish line and let my accomplishment sink in. My family had run out of the pit box and were now jumping up and down, hugging each other and shouting at the side of the track. The flagger hustled over to my open window and presented me with the checkered flag.

"Congratulations. That was a hell of a run," he said with a smile.

My hands trembled as I proudly took it from him. Firmly grasping that stick in my fist was the ultimate sign of victory and accomplishment.

I turned my head to see my mother running toward my car.

"You did it! Baby! You did it!"

Any semblance of composure I had completely left me at that moment. Seeing tears of joy streaming down my mother's face unbuckled me. Tears burst out from within. My mother carefully climbed in through the passenger door window opening and got in. She threw her arms out over me and locked me into an embrace. I hugged my mother back as best I could while still confined in my racing seat.

"Mom, hold on to whatever you can!" I told her while she crouched down on the passenger side floorboard. "It's time to take our Victory Lap."

With that, I dropped the clutch and slipped the car back into first gear and slowly proceeded up the straightaway into Turn 1.

"You won! Baby, I'm so happy for you. I'm so proud of you," Mom yelled as she waved the checkered flag out the window for all the flaggers and spectators to see.

Hearing her words of praise was everything I could have wanted in that moment. There are times in life when all you need is your mother, and this was one of those moments. She shared my bliss in a way that only a mother truly can. She knew how badly I wanted to be successful in racing. She had suffered with fear and anxiety during my street crashes. And now, she was here, experiencing my moment of glory right alongside me.

"I knew I could do it! But I can't believe it! I actually won!" I yelled over the noise of the motor in an unusually high-pitched voice.

"I always knew you could, baby," she said, gripping the roll bar tightly as if she was clinging on for dear life. "Bill! Slow down! You're going too fast," she shrieked.

"We're barely even moving. We're practically crawling."

"Bill, please. Slow down," she insisted.

"You're safe, Mom. I promise. Just hang on to that flag!"

Taking one last lap around the course without having to worry about other cars on the track was magical. I gracefully swept through the turns and over the hills with all the confidence of a champion. I owned the road.

It's important to note that my mother was a stylish, classy woman who exuded poise and refinement everywhere she went. She always held herself with the highest of dignity and grace. For her to jump into this loud, dirty race car with no seatbelt and ride the course with me showed just how much she loved me. Since day one, she has always been my biggest fan.

"Happy Mother's Day, Mom."

There are not enough words in the English language for me to accurately and justly explain how much my mother means to me. She is a fiercely intelligent woman whom I love and respect with every fiber of my being. She always spoke with a flawless command of the English language, not surprising for a former teacher with a degree in English. It's no wonder that I would be either complimented or harassed for being so "well spoken," depending on the environment I was in. I remember many episodes of being teased for sounding "too white" among my black friends, or seeing the surprised look on the faces of white people who finally met me after only having talked with me previously on the telephone.

My mother was respected as a strong advocate for education and worked for the local office of an organization called A Better Chance, which fostered college opportunities for minority youth. She was also a charter member of the local chapter of the Links, an organization that brought together black women of distinction and supported social responsibility, economic development, and community service.

She partook in the proverbial "mom duties" like running me around to Pop Warner football activities and cooking dinner each night. Her culinary talents were extraordinary. She would often introduce our family to a wide variety of exotic dishes even though spaghetti or burgers were just fine with me. She was always loving and affectionate to my father, my sister, and me. I couldn't ask for a better mother. But I definitely put her through her paces over the years.

Since I was often rebellious and always rambunctious, my mom struggled to keep me in line at times. While proud of me and my ambition, she wasn't always pleased with my decisions and actions. And it wasn't just cars. When we had conflicts, it often revolved around my approach to dating. I was fairly popular and found that women responded well to my advances. I was young, considered attractive, and took advantage of it. I wasn't looking to settle down in my early twenties, so I often played the field. She didn't exactly approve. But her largest point of contention was my need for speed. Here I was now, at a legitimate racetrack, celebrating my first win as a race car driver, with my mother supportively sitting beside me with the proudest smile on her face. Life had finally come full circle.

In my championship season of 1986, I never set any track records, but I finished all my races due to smart driving and Mike's staunch preparation. The title resulted mostly from running quick, consistent laps, avoiding accidents, and from the reliability of my car, thanks to Mike. I finished second in the first six races and won the season-ending seventh.

I also raced that year at the legendary Riverside International Raceway outside of Los Angeles before it got shut down and converted into a housing development. Riverside races were run by Cal Club, a separate region, so I didn't score any San Francisco region championship points. But I enjoyed watching the professional races held there and just loved the high speed and prestige of that legendary track.

When we went to Riverside, Mike, Gina, and I towed the car down with Mike's truck. It was cramped with three of us in the cab, but we had a great time together that weekend. I rented motel rooms for us and left the car on the trailer in the parking lot under a car cover, hoping nobody would mess with it. Luckily, no one did.

There were two races being run for our class that weekend, a double-header, and I scored two third-place finishes against a pretty decent group of GT-3 cars, despite not having prior experience on the Riverside track. This affirmed my love of racing on a fast track, since I hit higher speeds there than on Sears Point or Laguna Seca. The track had a back straight that was so long it necessitated running a taller rear end gear to avoid over-revving the engine. That back stretch led into a sweeping right-hand Turn 9, which had an intimidating concrete wall bordering the outside. It demanded respect because hitting that wall could easily destroy any car on the track. While Riverside presented a formidable challenge, racing on it was a huge rush for me and deepened my thrill of driving at top speed and my resolve to continue down this path.

■ ■ ■

RACING TO THE FRONT

To succeed in any competitive professional endeavor, *sacrifice* is a necessary element. I initially learned this watching my father pursue his career. He gave up family time to succeed. As a result, I learned how to *sacrifice,* too, because I had to accept that his time with me was limited.

Working a full-time job at H-P to pursue the career I really wanted required a huge *sacrifice* of my time. At an age when others pursued their racing careers on a daily basis, my limited access meant I had to pave my own way. I knew I had the talent and the desire and certainly was willing to *persist*.

Fortunately for me, a day eventually arrived when I could afford to risk leaving my job. When I took a leave of absence from H-P to pursue my career full-time, auto manufacturers were starting to look for minority race car drivers. It was a matter of preparation finally meeting opportunity.

Sacrifice becomes justified when it helps achieve one's goals.

7

The Influence of Willy T. Ribbs

Race car driver Willy T. Ribbs became one of the greatest influences in my early motor racing career. I was incredibly fortunate that he lived right down the freeway in San Jose, my old childhood hometown.

About the time I launched my racing efforts in the amateur category, Willy began winning races regularly in the SCCA Trans-Am Series, a full-blown, factory-backed professional tour and one of America's top road racing shows. Willy was an African American driver who had raced Formula Ford cars in Europe as well as Formula Atlantic cars back here in the States. He had been racing in the SCCA for a few years at that point and had even been named the SCCA Pro Rookie of the Year for his prowess in the Trans-Am Series. He was making a name for himself on the racing circuit. There were very few black race car drivers, and even fewer who were consistently winning races. If a black driver like Willy could win races and compete for championships with major teams, then there was no reason to believe that I couldn't do the same. It encouraged me to keep pressing forward. I was invigorated by his success and hopeful that I could follow in his footsteps.

Starting in 1983, when he broke into driving in the SCCA professional ranks after a couple of false starts in open wheel racing, Willy won eighteen Trans-Am races over the course of four seasons. He had an incredible winning percentage before switching to the IMSA series, where he continued his winning ways while driving for the famed All American Racers team owned by Dan Gurney.

I met Willy by blind luck. I was going through SCCA Driver School at Sears Point Raceway in Sonoma. With a focus on safety, these schools teach you the procedures and rules of engagement before you start racing your car. This involves entry-level instruction where you learn how the races start and end, how flagging and corner workers operate, and how to safely enter and exit the track.

I was on the track at Sears Point learning how to minimize my time through the corners and around the race course when Willy happened to show up. The year was 1984 and Willy was in the middle of his second year of stardom in the Trans-Am Series. An imposing physical presence, he had become one of the winningest drivers in American–road racing in just two years, basically an overnight sensation.

I was set up in the paddock area, preparing my car for my next on-track session. I had no idea Willy was there until he walked up to me. I saw him approaching with his friend Eric in tow. Eric was a large Scandinavian guy who had a solid, athletic build, and spoke with a strong accent. I think Eric was his bodyguard. Willy was a few inches shorter than me, with deep set eyes and a strong jaw.

"Hey. I'm Willy T. Ribbs. This is my friend Eric," he said, extending his hand for a handshake.

My jaw nearly dropped to the ground when Willy introduced himself. He didn't need to. I had been closely following his career. He had become a hero of mine because of the strides he was making in a sport that didn't typically see men with our skin tone.

"Man, I know who you are!" I announced excitedly. "I'm Bill. Bill Lester."

"I've been watching you. You got what it takes to make it in this sport," Willy said slowly in his deep voice.

His unsolicited pronouncement floored me. It's not like I asked, "What do you think of my driving?" No, he had gone out of his way to seek me out and applaud my skill. It was one of the most impactful compliments I had ever received.

"Really? You were watching me?"

I was in sheer disbelief. This man was a well-known professional racer, and yet here he was at a driving school watching a bunch of amateurs. And not just any amateur: me! And complimenting me on top of it.

"You've got a lot of ability. I was impressed," he proclaimed in the same melodic way I had heard him speak in interviews.

Hearing these words come from the mouth of someone I admired so much was both amazing and surreal. The massive grin smeared across my face could probably have been seen from outer space.

"Man, you don't know how much that means to me coming from you!"

I was over-the-moon ecstatic. It took everything I had not to start jumping for joy like a little kid at Christmas.

"Talent should always point out talent. And you've got it," he said with an approving head nod.

A disciple of Muhammad Ali, Willy presented himself with an emphatic confidence. Unlike Ali, who was never at a loss for words, Willy tended to use few words to express himself. He need not have said a thing to me that day, so his words left a deep impression.

"We should get back. They're probably waiting for us," Eric piped in, pointing back toward the main building.

I didn't want to end the conversation that quickly. I knew I had to find a way to create a line of communication between us.

"I'd love to pick your brain about racing. How can I stay in touch with you?" I asked.

To my pleasant surprise, Willy gave me his number. I called him for the first time shortly after I passed driving school—with flying colors, I might add. We immediately became friends. I had already been watching everything he did as far as his races were concerned. I quickly began spending whatever free moments I could find with Willy because he lived not far from my job, and we were easily able to forge a friendship. I would skip out of work for an hour at lunchtime and go to his house during the week. I would borrow one of H-P's company cars, which were not necessarily for casual use, and drive to Willy's. That's how I learned what it was like to be a professional driver. He was the only person in professional racing whom I could identify with. His father, Bunny, owned a successful plumbing business and they had lived on Ribbs Lane before Willy's stardom enabled him to get his own home in the San Jose hills.

Hanging out with Willy was like sitting at the feet of the master. I spent a lot of time with him and learned as much as I could by just being his shadow, absorbing everything I could like a sponge. He probably didn't realize how much I was watching and listening. I think he enjoyed the mentorship role that he provided. Maybe he wanted to help me progress in my career because there weren't many African American men in the sport of race car driving. We were an anomaly, and because of it, we were kindred spirits trying to break through a glass ceiling. Because I was still up-and-coming, I didn't pose a threat to his established career. He stood at the top of professional motor sports, and I was merely trying to scale that same mountain, from quite a distance behind.

I genuinely valued his time. I always called in advance to check his availability and was conscientious not to overstay my welcome when I visited him. Willy was fun to be around. He was often outlandish, in a way that was vastly different from my more conservative upbringing at home. I may have done some wild things in my life, but I was somewhat reserved in my temperament, especially compared to him. Willy threw caution to the wind and was unapologetic about it. I typically flew under the radar and was conflict averse, whereas he was front and center and rarely gave a damn about what anyone thought of it. I tried to blend the best from both worlds: the sturdy, reticent foundation my father embodied and Willy's outspoken, extravagant demeanor.

During my lunch breaks, I attempted to get inside his mind and understand how and why he thought the way he did. His wealth of experience could only benefit me. When I asked questions, he didn't pontificate. He simply told me what he thought I needed to know. We didn't shoot the breeze much. He didn't have the time. He seemed to live on the phone, dealing with either sponsorship matters or car performance issues with his team, but I learned immensely from the stories he told me. He was often guarded with the extent of what he shared, probably to avoid detailing all his extracurricular social activities. He was fond of the expression, "Loose lips sink ships."

Sometimes I was an eyewitness to his lessons. I once rode with him to the airport in Los Angeles to pick up his wife Suzanne before a race. He had a Lincoln Town Car, one of the privileges of being a Ford factory driver in Trans-Am. We were already late and got bogged down with all the cars trying to get into the curbside pickup area. Willy started ranting and raving about the car in front of us not moving. He decided to do a vigorous brake stand, which meant flooring the accelerator with one foot and holding the brake with the other. It created an inordinate amount of burned rubber, giving rise to mountains of billowing smoke. I couldn't believe he did that right there in the open for everyone to see. But I guess the message got across, because the car in front of us moved. Willy had a way about him that couldn't be silenced or surrendered, and when he wanted to be heard, people listened.

I was privy to countless phone calls that Willy made throughout his professional career. Some were with his team to discuss car setups or how to improve the car's speed. Most of his calls were to his business manager and other associates, trying to acquire more sponsorship. Up until I met Willy, I thought the driving itself was the hard part of racing. I discovered from him that getting behind the wheel and putting the helmet on was the easy part. Obtaining sponsorship was the hard part. Being able to find and secure funding to race was so much harder than I could ever have anticipated. It became abundantly clear that you had to have money to get anywhere in the world of racing. Willy taught me that networking came first, money came second, and driving talent third.

Willy maintained the same approach on the phone as he did in person. When calling to look for sponsorship he would start off with something like, "It's Ribbs here" or "It's your favorite race car driver."

His deep voice was a staple of his persona. Willy's voice was probably three octaves lower than mine. His brash attitude was one thing I always admired about him, although I often wondered how the person on the other end of the line received it. Big and solid, Willy also trained as a boxer. He was a commanding figure. Conversely, I weighed about 150 pounds soaking wet.

Willy and I came from different backgrounds. He grew up blue-collar and I grew up in a white-collar environment. I had attended a reputable college and worked in corporate America, and I found it difficult to color outside the lines the way he did.

He once said to me, "Les, I grew up on a farm and I didn't want to get into the family plumbing business. I wanted to race!" "Les" was how he addressed me. I didn't let anyone else do so.

He wasn't worried about going to school and getting a degree. He craved the adrenaline rush of racing the same way I did. He also wanted to prove himself and beat people on the track, but my parents had instilled in me that a degree was the key to my future. We were opposite sides of the coin in that respect.

I may have had a college degree, but Willy's dad Bunny had given him an excellent racing education, which was typical of how many professional drivers got their start. Willy got his by going to the track with Bunny, who was a local club racing legend in the San Francisco Region of the SCCA. When Willy decided to pursue a professional career, his father's flourishing plumbing business funded his move to England to compete with Formula Ford race cars in the entry level Dunlop Series.

After some success in England, he learned how to make his own way when he returned home. Typical of Willy, he got involved in a promotional stunt while trying to break into NASCAR. He drove the wrong way down a one-way street in Charlotte, North Carolina, which led to a police chase through the city. He earned himself the nickname, "Wrong Way Willy." Willy lived in the fast lane.

I was not cut from the same cloth. He often did things I just wouldn't do. Sometimes I would cringe when I heard about or witnessed some of his controversial antics. I always took the path of least resistance, the opposite of Willy's approach. He pursued his career his way and didn't take crap from anybody. That meant using the "chrome horn" or pushing someone out of the way on the racetrack if he thought he was being blocked. It sometimes meant altercations with other racers off the track.

After winning five races in his 1983 debut season in Trans-Am, his team owner Neil DeAtley fired him prior to the next season's first race—Willy punched Bob Lobenberg during a disagreement in the Road Atlanta paddock over something that had happened during track practice, and that was the end of that. Willy then switched to the team of Jack Roush and proceeded to win four races that year. In IMSA, he once punted leader Scott Pruett off the track on the final lap of the Miami Grand Prix. Two years later, he became the first driver ever suspended for fighting in IMSA after he punched Pruett following an incident on the track.

Even when winning, Willy was eccentric. To celebrate Trans-Am victories, he danced the "Ali shuffle" atop the roof of his car in Victory Lane. Like Ali, fans either loved him or hated him, but the driving talent was irrefutable.

A few years later, in 1988, Willy got hired by DiGard Racing to drive in the NASCAR Cup Series. I didn't care about NASCAR at that time. I had no affinity for NASCAR, primarily because of the Confederate flags I'd seen on ABC's *Wide World of Sports* broadcasts as a young boy. I couldn't bring myself to support a sport that was so overtly racist, so I didn't follow stock car racing at all when Willy was involved. It didn't go well for him anyway, in what appeared to me to be an underprepared car, and the whole effort with DiGard folded before the end of the first season. If Willy had been doing well in NASCAR, and if he had talked about it when we'd get together, the situation might have been different. I don't remember him saying anything about NASCAR, maybe because it wasn't his forte, or maybe because he knew how much road racing meant to me.

Willy later helped me prepare for my first pro race a few years later, in 1989. Prior to that, I had been racing in the SCCA GT-3 class at the amateur level with my Mazda RX-3, whose rotary engine had about 250 horsepower and a four-speed synchronized transmission. A production-based race car sitting on relatively narrow 13-inch-tall tires, the RX-3 didn't even have a real racing gearbox. But looking for a way to move up the ladder and race professionally, I decided to enter an IMSA race at Sears Point in the GTO class. At the advice of Willy, I rented a race car from a friend of his.

This car ran on wide 18-inch tires and a racing gearbox made by Weismann, with straight-cut gears designed specifically for racing. It made shifting gears possible without using the clutch. The engine produced somewhere between 650 to 700 horsepower! This car was way different from what I had been driving, but Willy helped me with the transition. He taught me how to shift a gearbox with straight-cut gears. You had to shift it much faster so as to not damage it.

At first, I was so inexperienced that I didn't know what was going on with the transmission. Once I left the pits and was on track, Willy could clearly hear that I was struggling with the shifts. After I came in, he decided to climb into the car and get behind the wheel in street clothes. The powers that be at Sears Point would have never let any driver out on the track without wearing a fire-resistant Nomex driving suit and a helmet. But Willy marched to his own beat. He jumped into the driver's seat without giving it a second thought. I climbed in on the passenger side, which had no seat, and hung on to the roll bars. At least I had a helmet and fire suit on, because I had just finished my practice laps.

He gave me an eye-opening lap around Sears Point.

"Les, this is what it's like," he yelled over the roar of the engine.

Wearing jeans, a short-sleeve shirt, and no helmet to drive a lap at full racing speed—it was unbelievably unsafe and totally insane! But Willy always let his actions speak at least as loud as his words. In this case, he performed an extraordinary act of friendship and a ride around Sears Point that I'll never forget.

■ ■ ■

RACING TO THE FRONT

Forging a friendship with Willy T. Ribbs was not my first professional effort at *networking*. During my internships at Hewlett-Packard I continued to develop interpersonal skills through the mentoring programs that I was a member of. But Willy was by far the most important influence on my early and untried racing ambitions. Was I out of my *comfort zone* initially pursuing a friendship with him? You bet. Willy cast a big shadow; he was "The Man." Initially, that was somewhat intimidating to me. To my great satisfaction, Willy reciprocated the friendship. And I was as eager to learn from him as I was to enjoy his company.

Pursuing an important relationship by getting out of one's comfort zone accelerates success.

8

Moving Up to the Pro Ranks

With some guidance from Willy, I decided to test myself in the professional racing ranks by renting a car to compete in the GTO class at a Sears Point IMSA race. During one weekend in September of 1989, I made the satisfying discovery that I did have the ability to compete at the professional level in road racing. The revelation was also painful, because I found out it would take more than one professional race for others in the sport to recognize my potential.

My affection for racing grew with every race. What started as a hobby had evolved into so much more. I was putting in the work and yielding the desired outcomes. I felt like I was on the precipice of something great. Propelled by my boundless racing aspirations, I refused to be derailed by obstacles. I just didn't realize how many there would be.

I had proved myself at the club racing level and kept looking for a way to break into pro racing. I doubled down and followed up the IMSA race with two entries in the Trans-Am Series the following year, again trying to establish enough credibility in the racing community to earn a full-time opportunity to race at the professional level. These events ultimately led to added frustration since the phone still didn't ring. After those two races, I received an opportunity to participate in a tryout with a Ford-funded program three years later. But little else resulted from my initial—and relatively expensive—professional forays. I was frustrated and disappointed, so I tried to focus elsewhere for the time being.

My family's support helped to keep things in perspective. Though my parents stood by me, racing was not what they wished for my future. I understood their perspective; I had fought hard to earn a degree from a competitive university, and they didn't want to see it go to waste. They also had a hard time imagining that racing could manifest in a viable career. Even if they could envision it, they didn't want that life for me. Aside from their concerns about how dangerous racing was, it was unpredictable, whereas engineering was steady and stable. My day job was a consistent paycheck that would keep a roof over my head and food on the table. My father once said to me, "You must be crazy, but we love you. We support you. But you're pretty much on your own with racing."

I couldn't help but laugh.

"Dad, this is what I want to do. I haven't found anything else in life that makes me feel this alive. I'm good at racing and I love doing it. Why would I be given this gift if I couldn't see it through?"

My father always looked at me quizzically whenever we talked about my racing desires.

"I know it's what you love doing, son, but why can't it just be what you do on the weekends for fun? Why can't you keep your job at H-P and race on the weekends like you've been doing?"

I was never able to fully put into words how stifled I felt in an office environment, or how my soul came back to life when I pulled onto the track. I couldn't make them understand that a part of me was dormant five days a week.

"It's in my blood, Dad. It's the only thing I've ever wanted to do, and you know you're partially to blame. That Can-Am race you took me to at Laguna Seca set the hook, you know!"

"Okay then. If it makes you happy. I want you to live your dreams, but try to keep racing in perspective."

Other friends and members of my family also thought that I was crazy for trying to do something so "foreign." Racing was completely unorthodox to them, leaving me on an island by myself. Despite the fact that my family didn't fully understand my voraciousness for racing, they still accepted it. My parents actually stepped up in a major way when I decided to test the professional waters. They knew the expense associated with my goal of racing in the Sears Point IMSA GTO event and suggested a friends-and-family fundraising effort. They contributed seed money and suggested close friends of theirs to contact who might be willing to donate.

Having grown up in a mildly affluent area, many of my neighbors and family friends were financially well-off. I was lucky enough to get financial support from two of my parents' friends: Dr. Ralph Melton, a urologist, and Don Sutton, owner of a furniture business. They were both successful, upper-middle-class African American men who were well established in the community. I approached them just that once for support and never asked again, but at the time, their backing was huge. They could have easily rejected my request, but instead they chose to take a chance and offer a generous financial boost to my budding career.

I also received smaller contributions from other friends of my parents and extended-family members. The financial assistance helped me cover the major expenses, like renting the car and the race entry fee. It also helped with the smaller costs that weren't as much individually, but added up over time. Buying tires and racing fuel, and maintaining a three-man crew quickly depleted my wallet. Racing is one of the most expensive sports to participate in, but I was figuring out how to manage my way through it.

Having Willy in my corner helped me steer the course much more easily. He gave me access and credibility. If Willy T. Ribbs was speaking on my behalf, people listened. He helped me locate a suitable car to rent. I wouldn't have known where to begin, but Willy was right there to lead the way. Perhaps most importantly, he made the initial contact with the car owner, Larry Less. At the professional level, you don't drive street cars on the track. This meant that I had to rent a professional race car.

Once rental arrangements for the car were completed, Willy employed his racing experience to accelerate my transition from an amateur racer to a professional. A few weeks before the race, he came to the track to observe my driving performance while I engaged in the one test session I could afford. While the track was familiar to me, the GTO car was anything but. Willy bridged the gap. He taught me how to properly use the Weismann racing transmission the car was equipped with. He also tutored me on Sears Point track logistics and its subtle speed secrets. By sketching diagrams of specific sections of the track, he helped to confirm what I believed were the fastest lines and proper shifting points, both of which are critical to fast lap times.

The IMSA schedule called for a GT race of fifty laps during the Sears Point weekend. This preliminary GT race included GTO-classified cars like my Camaro and a GTU class for cars with smaller engines and less horsepower. Our GT race would run prior to Sunday's GTP class 75-lap feature consisting of the fastest, most technologically advanced prototype cars, in which Willy would be competing.

For the GT race, GTO "factory" entries came from Audi, Lincoln-Mercury, Pontiac, and Nissan. Most notable and celebrated among these eight entries were the remarkable all-wheel-drive Audi Quattros driven by world-class drivers Hans Stuck and Hurley Haywood.

My personal goal was to be the fastest of the non-factory entries. My race crew consisted of the car owner and three mechanics, crew chief Grant Ingram and crewmen Dodge Riedy and John Martella. We may have been a glorified amateur program at a professional race, but when the checkered flag fell denoting that I had qualified, we had achieved our goal. I qualified ninth, first among the non-factory entries in the GTO class. Our lap time was just four-tenths of a second behind the factory Pontiac Fiero that came in eighth place on the grid, and we had another four-tenths of a gap over our closest independent competitor in tenth place.

Qualifying answered my question about pursuing pro racing. Any reservations I may have had up until that point were immediately laid to rest. I loved driving cars with big horsepower and apparently was pretty good at it. Going through the amateur ranks, I had won Rookie of the Year followed by a championship. At my first pro race, I was the first non-factory driver, ahead of veteran independent drivers with bigger budgets and better equipment.

The day of the big race came and I had an entourage to cheer me on. My parents, a few of their friends, including Dr. Melton and Don Sutton, some of my cousins, and quite a few of my friends all came out. For many of them, it was their first time at a race. They were about to step into my world and finally see what I could do firsthand!

We set up our own hospitality area in the pits, where we housed a small camper. It served as a landmark and headquarters for the team. My mother and sister took on the hosting duties, preparing lunch and drinks for everyone while they waited for the adventure to begin.

The excitement on race day at the track is tangible. You can feel it in the air. Spectators share in the intoxicating rush and become part of the experience. And there's nothing quite like being in the pit area where all the action is. It's an interactive front-row seat that comes equipped with all the perks. The ground shakes as the cars roar past. The vibration feels like a rolling earthquake that comes in waves. The sound is almost deafening. You have to scream in order to be heard over the commotion of the cars speeding by. Oil, gas, and burnt rubber form an aroma that permeates the atmosphere. Towering, oversized electronic scoreboards erected at various locations around the track keep tabs on the leaders, while sponsor billboards line the track. If you can't actually be out on the track racing, it's the next best place to be.

I wanted my team to be the first non-factory team to finish. For the first thirty laps, our plan held up. I maintained ninth place. Nobody farther back on the starting grid could catch me. But my luck ran out. While driving through the Esses, a series of high-speed left and right turns, my car suddenly jolted to the side. Through the sweeping right hand turn, the car pulled hard to the left. I had to react quickly in order to keep myself on the track and out of the barriers. I immediately suspected what had happened. The suspension had broken.

I took to the radio to notify my crew.

"Guys, I think my suspension failed. But the car's still drivable. I'm coming in."

"Copy that. We'll be ready for you."

I limped the car back to the pits. But the lead I had built through the first half of the race was gone and my morale was deflated. There was no way I could make up for the time lost coming into the pits. Even if I could get the car fixed, I was not going to win the race. And there was nothing I could've done to prevent it or get the time back after the fact.

Once in the pits, the crew quickly diagnosed a broken left-side A-arm component in the front suspension. They fixed it and got me back in the race. But the time it had taken for repairs meant we ended up twelve laps behind the winning Audi of Stuck. The disappointment was overwhelming. Mechanical error stood between me and my goal. I'd had just that one shot, and it was gone.

The race was covered by the newspapers, but there was no mention of me in the recap. My Dad showed me a copy of a letter that Dr. Melton had written to the *Oakland Tribune* about a strong performance by a local rising talent—me—at Sears Point. I was touched by the gesture.

When I decided to have another go at a professional race and chose to run a Trans-Am race in 1990, my grandfather was there to support me. He was a retired postal worker who lived in Chicago, but despite the distance, we were fairly close. Both sets of my grandparents lived in Illinois. My parents would take my sister and me to Chicago to stay with my mother's parents on the South Side every year. I was accustomed to the perpetual warmth of California, so the freezing cold temperatures of Chicago's winter were difficult to get used to. Perhaps worse was the sweltering heat and humidity of the summer. During those vacation visits, we would go to the nearby house of my paternal grandfather, who took particular pride in me being William Alexander Lester III.

He was a stern, strict, and intimidating man who was notorious for being tight when it came to money. One day, we were on the phone catching up. He asked me to explain the financial breakdown of racing so that he could better understand what it entailed. I walked him through the cost of renting the cars, gear, crew, parts, gas, maintenance—you name it. He was flabbergasted.

"Bill! How can you afford that?" he asked incredulously.

"I can't really. That's why I have to try to get sponsorship, but it's hard finding companies with deep pockets who believe in me."

The line was silent for a moment and I could hear him breathing heavily. I could tell that he was taken aback by the figure.

"Would $10,000 help you?"

I was utterly shocked.

"Are you serious? It would make all the difference!"

His generosity bowled me over. He was not an overly wealthy man and he was known for being frugal. I was stunned that he was willing to provide me with such a large amount. I think it was his way of indicating that he was proud of me and believed in me. I asked him a few times if he was absolutely certain, but in the end, I gratefully accepted his offer.

My grandfather was a man who had aged well and carried himself confidently. He was opinionated and not afraid to express himself with authority. He demanded respect and got it. He was not particularly affectionate, which intimidated me when I was younger. I would always be on my best behavior around him and did not want to draw his ire. It was hard to be myself, though because I was always on guard.

As his only namesake, I had a distinct responsibility to uphold his legacy and make him proud. On more than one occasion he would say, "The Lester name dies with you." Talk about pressure for a youngster! The comment obviously left the desired impression, because I named my firstborn son William Alexander Lester IV.

Sadly, that same year, lung cancer claimed my grandfather's life. My father inherited his Rolex with our initials, WAL, engraved on the back. I was honored when my father passed it along to me. So many of my father's character traits came from his dad, including his staunch values and no-nonsense approach to life. But like my father, my grandfather knew how to enjoy life and the trappings of success that he had worked so hard to achieve. He was an avid golfer who, for as long as I knew him, drove a Cadillac Fleetwood—upgrading to new and improved models over the years. It was a statement of his accomplishment. I suppose a healthy appreciation of fine cars runs in my blood. I'll always cherish the memories I have of my grandfather.

The Trans-Am Series maintained a high profile in US road racing, but it had a different format from IMSA. Instead of multiclass racing, only one class of cars raced in the relatively short events without pit stops. Trans-Am seemed like a more level playing field, because more parity existed between the front-line teams and the independent entries. This was an important criterion—equipment not being the determining factor—especially for someone trying to break in, like me. The driver had a lot more input in the outcome of the event. Just as importantly, some of those front-line teams made additional cars available as rentals.

In 1990, Willy helped me land a solid rental ride, this time with the Rocketsports team owned by Paul Gentilozzi, whose cars could be expected to contend for victory. I would race a plain white Oldsmobile Cutlass. But my race at Portland International Raceway, where my first Trans-Am race was held, turned out to be a bit of a bust. Luck was not with me that day either.

Gentilozzi, as I always referred to him, entered four Olds Cutlass race cars powered by V-6 engines. His primary driver, Darin Brassfield, qualified second and would eventually win the 53-lap race and set the fastest race lap. Gentilozzi started fifth and finished third. No doubt, the team's cars were competitive.

I had the fifth car entered by Rocketsports. As one of the team's older cars that had a V-8 engine, it didn't have the improved weight distribution and development of the newer, better-developed V-6 cars that Paul and Darin drove. Plus, I had never raced at Portland before and had to learn the track in practice and qualifying before the race. My qualifying performance on Saturday in the Cutlass was mediocre, but as I became more familiar with the track, I grew more optimistic about Sunday's race. But that didn't last long.

On race day morning, while tuning the engine, a crewman accidentally dropped a wing nut from the air cleaner down the throat of the carburetor and couldn't retrieve it. While the part might have possibly passed through the combustion of the engine without damaging it, we anticipated the higher probability of comprehensive engine failure and decided to park the car.

Paul was both displeased and embarrassed by this engine mishap and returned most of my rental fee of $22,500. I was determined not to let that stand in my way. I entered a second Trans-Am race with the Gloy Sports team owned by Tom Gloy later in the 1990 season. A former Trans-Am champion, Tom raced Chevy Berettas and had a shop at Sears Point. Again, Willy helped me broker the deal.

After many years as a factory team associated with Ford, Gloy created his own independent program. I was helping him keep the team afloat financially as a paying driver in return for his helping me get some experience and exposure in Trans-Am. It was the same deal I had with Rocketsports. Gloy and I agreed to a race together in September at the Mid-Ohio Sports Car Course.

I raced my unsponsored yellow Beretta, but unfortunately, I didn't have the greatest result. Mid-Ohio was another new track for me. I qualified twenty-eighth out of forty-one cars and gained nine positions in the race to end up nineteenth. We definitely didn't set the world on fire that day, though we weren't exactly stinking up the show, either. I just never found a good pace or rhythm on the twisty track. To this day, I don't like Mid-Ohio, and I don't dislike many tracks. A lot of drivers love the place, but it never appealed to me.

The only thing to evolve from my one IMSA race and two Trans-Am events was an invitation to a professional driver search competition conducted by Bob Bondurant. A former pro driver, Bob had created the PRO-search program to promote his driving school at the Firebird International Raceway near Phoenix with backing from Ford. At stake for the winner was the opportunity to drive a Mustang in three Trans-Am races during the 1993 season in a car prepared by Gloy Sports.

During the event, we were competing for the best lap times in the school's Mustangs. It had now been three years since my last Trans-Am race at Mid-Ohio, so to call my skills rusty would have been an understatement. The fastest way around a track is always the most precarious. During my run, I overstepped the limits of the car and spun out. Had it not been for this mishap during my segment, I might have gotten the deal. At least that was the indication given by the lead instructor, Bill Cooper. It made me feel slightly better—but only slightly. It was my last chance and I'd blown it.

After that, my prospects were dismal. I had hit too many snags too many times in a row, and I was out of options. My dreams of going professional had come to a screeching halt. Although most of what had happened was out of my control and were unavoidable pitfalls of the sport, it didn't stop me from feeling the gravity of the situation. I sat on the sidelines with my only connection to racing being on the TV set. I was no longer a race car driver with a promising future; I had transitioned back to a spectator, and I was miserable. My funds had completely dried up and sponsors were nowhere to be found. I didn't have any more money.

Fortunately, when one door closes, another opens. My silver lining came in the form of Cheryl, my future wife. She was my saving grace and a welcome pursuit.

■ ■ ■

RACING TO THE FRONT

Being able to pause in moments of high stress and evaluate the situation rationally, practically, and devoid of emotion is a trait that professional drivers need to learn early in their career. Keeping a level head is not easy when your adrenaline is pumping and the world feels out of your control, but I always tried my best to take a step back and keep my cool so that the moment didn't engulf me.

It can be hard to overstate the significance of family support. The pushback and setbacks I received in racing—in many ways the nature of the beast—were frustrating and, at times, demoralizing. But knowing I had the support of my family helped me endure. If it wasn't for my family serving as a support system and a sounding board for all of my disappointments and frustrations, I might have easily unraveled in the high-pressure moments that embody the sport of professional auto racing. My family's lack of knowledge about motor racing and how far afield it was from anything in their experience meant an even deeper sense of *gratitude* for their affirmation. Could I have gone forward without their support? I was glad I didn't have to try.

Gratitude for support received from others can be an excellent source of motivation.

9

Love and Happiness at Home

Cheryl and I were both UC-Berkeley graduates, but I finished four years ahead of her. We first met in 1990, when I was working at Hewlett-Packard. Cheryl was the volunteer director of the university's Black Alumni Mentorship Program. Our first encounter was not exactly love at first sight—or sound.

I was home one evening watching an NBA game. The Chicago Bulls were playing and I was a huge fan of Michael Jordan. I was so immersed in the game, I'm not sure why I even picked up the phone after I heard it ring. When I did, there was a sweet-sounding female voice on the other end of the line.

"Is Gil there?"

"Who?"

"Gil Lester," the voice replied.

My game was being interrupted by someone who didn't even know my name!

"No, but this is Bill Lester." I replied indignantly.

"Oh, my apologies. I'm so sorry. Bill, this is Cheryl from the Alumni Mentorship Program at UC-Berkeley."

Realizing the call was not just some sort of marketing solicitation, I turned my attention to what she had to say. I softened my tone.

"Hi, Cheryl. What can I do for you?"

I reached for the remote and turned the TV down so that I could hear her more clearly.

"I'm terribly sorry about messing up your name," she continued to apologize. "I'm calling because Angela Johnson suggested that you would be a good mentor for a current student within the engineering program. As I'm sure you know, the engineering program is a very difficult one and students are extremely grateful for any extra help and support from the alumni who have already been through the curriculum. I was wondering if this is something you might be interested in?"

I knew from firsthand experience how beneficial programs like this were. I had often utilized the services of BESSA during my time in the engineering school. I was honored that this organization thought highly enough of me to ask me to partake in their program. It was a worthy cause. I was keen to give back and help the next generation.

"I don't know if I would've made it to graduation day if it wasn't for mentorship. I'd be happy to help out. Sign me up."

"Great! Thank you so much. I really appreciate it."

"Sure thing. How does it work?" I asked.

"We will assign you a student to work with one-on-one. You can set up times with your mentee that work best for your schedules. We also ask that you attend monthly meetings."

Cheryl told me that she would send me all of the information I needed. We hung up shortly after that and I went back to watching the game without giving it another thought. I had no idea that I had just spoken to my future wife.

I first met Cheryl at one of these Saturday morning meetings. She had long, full, curly hair that swept over her shoulders. She exuded confidence and intelligence. Although I found her to be attractive, I didn't immediately look at her as a viable dating option. I considered her entirely too young for me. She was four years younger than me, and at the time, I had been dating older women. I didn't really put in much effort to talk to her or spend time with her at the Saturday morning meetings held on campus. Once they ended, I would quickly exit and rush over to the nearby gym to play basketball.

I started attending the meetings in the fall and the program went through most of the academic year. I saw Cheryl regularly at these meetings, and while we would have an occasional conversation, there was no epic love-at-first-sight moment. She was a beautiful woman who I enjoyed seeing at the mentorship gatherings, but I didn't consider it to be anything more. But Cheryl had other ideas and she wasn't afraid to act on them.

One afternoon, after the Mentorship Program had ended and I had returned home from basketball, I got a surprise call from Cheryl. After a few minutes of small talk she got to the point.

"I have some tickets to a jazz concert next weekend and I was wondering, would you be interested in going with me?"

I was taken aback. I was accustomed to being the one to make the first move with women, so I was flattered that she had taken the initiative. I had never looked at her in that way, and I'd certainly had no idea that she had interest in me as anything other than one of the mentors at the weekly meetings. But she was a smart, gorgeous young woman who clearly was confident and assertive enough to go after what she wanted in life. I was impressed by—and attracted to—her boldness. Had she not made the first move, we never would've gotten together. I am definitely grateful that she had the desire and fortitude to pursue me.

I readily agreed and became glad that I did. Cheryl has a radiant spirit that touches everyone she interacts with. It's hard to be anything but happy when she's around. She has an uplifting way about her that is contagious.

The next weekend, I picked Cheryl up for our first date. I had washed my car specifically to make a good first impression, but the weather didn't cooperate. There was a downpour only an hour after I wiped the car down. My clean car wasn't clean for long.

As if that wasn't frustrating enough, I was also sporting a bum leg due to an injury during a basketball game I'd played earlier that morning. I had scored on a layup and then been pushed by a defender on the way down, causing me to twist my ankle and land hard on my rear end. Pain shot through my leg for the rest of the day, but I tried, unsuccessfully, to tune it out. So I showed up to our first date with a dirty car and gimpy leg.

Cheryl didn't mind letting me lean on her as a crutch as I limped along through the parking lot of the Woodminster Amphitheater.

"Man, I can't believe how much it still hurts."

I had one arm wrapped around her shoulder as we walked toward the entrance.

"You poor thing. Don't worry, I won't make you dance," she said with a smile and a flirtatious wink.

With this incredible woman on my arm, we ventured inside to see Dianne Reeves and Gerald Albright. They were two of the most prominent jazz musicians at that time. Although I liked jazz, I didn't love it the way Cheryl did. She preferred smoother, more sultry music to the more up-tempo hip-hop and R&B that I usually listened to. But just being with Cheryl that evening meant it almost didn't matter what we went to hear.

The theater was an outdoor facility in Joaquin Miller Park that was large enough to house a decent-sized crowd, but intimate enough that every seat had a great vantage point. Cheryl and I took our seats near the front. We enjoyed the music almost as much as each other's company.

After the concert was over, we went to the Claremont Hotel in nearby Berkeley for drinks. We talked about our shared love of music, sports, our lives growing up, our dreams for the future—no stone was left unturned. Cheryl was as funny as she was charming. It was a perfect evening.

We began to date regularly. She supported my passion for racing from the very beginning. Things were going so well that by our fourth date, I took her to my race in Monterey at Laguna Seca. She didn't know much about racing, but I was all too happy to give her a crash course. But words can only go so far. I wanted her to experience it firsthand.

Cheryl was excited to have me accompany her to her first race. I showed her around the track and proudly introduced her to my crew. She had no problem hanging out in the pits with a bunch of guys she had only just met while I competed on the track. Although I didn't win that race, having Cheryl there with me made me feel like a winner.

Cheryl came to a number of other races, including a four-hour endurance race at Sears Point where she saw me co-drive to victory. I considered her interest in the sport a huge plus since I planned for racing to play a significant role in my future. I don't think I could have ever made it work with a partner who didn't support me and my passion for racing.

Although we both enjoyed each other's company immensely, Cheryl and I only dated casually for the first few months, both still seeing other people. But I always came back to Cheryl. Eventually we became a couple. After three years of dating, we had a disagreement and decided to part ways, but I soon realized how much I missed her. I dated other women for a while, but it just wasn't the same. They weren't Cheryl. I realized she had a hold on my heart, and I simply wanted her back.

Luckily, Cheryl had not closed the book on our relationship. She happily agreed to give us another chance we committed to being exclusive. Our relationship progressed slowly over time, but I think that's what made it so strong. We didn't rush into things. We took the time to really get to know each other before coming to the realization that we both truly only wanted to be together. Eventually, after Cheryl completed her MBA at Stanford, I proposed.

We were married in the Stanford Memorial Chapel in September of 1994. On the day of our wedding, Cheryl looked as radiant and beautiful as I'd ever seen her. She was spectacular in her white gown with a long, flowing train. I don't know what I'd done to deserve her, but I was thankful that we had been brought together.

Focusing on our relationship was a welcome distraction and helped soften the disappointments of racing. Cheryl became the focus of my life. We were later blessed by two sons. My personal life was in order. To this day, my family is my greatest accomplishment.

On the racing side, I had spent a lot of money, but hadn't been able to climb the racing ladder like I had expected. Disenchanted by the fruits of my labor—or lack thereof—I tried my best to let go of the frustration and resentment, but it always found a way of creeping back in. My inability to acquire sponsorship support from corporate America was a permanent source of angst. Despite being as good as other racers, or even better than most of my competitors, the deep wallets weren't able to see past the mechanical errors from the races that put me behind the curve. Even when I was winning races and earning titles like Rookie of the Year, sponsors were not willing to take a chance on a black guy from California who wasn't born into the racing world.

Aggravated with the trajectory of my racing career, I decided to quit racing for a while. I considered that maybe I was too obsessed with racing, since it seemed to have consumed me. I decided that I needed to shift my priorities and put my focus solely on my family and my engineering career.

I needed to see if the passion to race would gradually disappear if I stopped chasing it every waking moment.

It didn't.

I came to the conclusion that I needed to find a way to make a living racing cars, come hell or high water! I had proven that I had the skill and desire to be successful and I didn't want to give up. I came back to the fray in 1996 when I got an offer from a local team to race in one of the SCCA's pro series, called the World Challenge.

Brian Richards, who owned and operated a repair shop called Mostly Mazda in the Bay Area, decided that he wanted to build Mazda RX-7s based on the car's third-generation body style and enter them in the World Challenge competition. I had been bringing my third-generation RX-7 street car to Mostly Mazda because Mike Johnson, my former crew chief, worked there. Brian and Mike built beautiful turbo Mazdas for the World Challenge. I saw this as an opportunity to begin racing again and scraped together some money to get back behind the wheel.

While beautiful works of craftsmanship, these cars were raw in terms of having any racing development. They had not been tested. But we did extremely well for a new team. In my first race, I finished fourth at Road America in Wisconsin and then in the next race, I finished third at Watkins Glen International in New York, two classic road courses I had not driven on previously.

I stood on the podium at Watkins Glen with Kermit Upton, who drove a BMW, and Lou Gigliotti, who raced a Ford Mustang. Both of those cars were factory-backed with support. I received my trophy alongside those guys after having driven a non-factory-backed Mazda RX-7. I'm sure my unexpected results raised a lot of eyebrows. Up against these programs, we had no business being so competitive, especially since I had not raced in five years and had never been to either of these tracks.

"Man, I still love it and I'm still good at it," I thought to myself as I held up my trophy.

I drove in two more World Challenge races that year: a race on the streets of Reno, Nevada, and the other at Sears Point, but I did not achieve podium finishes due to mechanical issues I experienced with the car during each race.

Cheryl supported my decision to drive in the World Challenge. She knew me well enough to know that something was missing for me. The sparkle in my eye had faded since she had first met me. She knew I had become complacent and stagnant, and she didn't want that life for me. She fully backed my decision to get back behind the wheel.

I wasn't happy with my corporate job, and Cheryl knew it. I complained about work. I didn't look forward to the things H-P paid me to do. Though my heart wasn't in it, I still made sure my work was satisfactory. The employees I had charge of worked well under my leadership. I charted courses that they believed in and we all pulled in the same direction to achieve desired results. But I was unfulfilled.

My thoughts were elsewhere as soon as I left the office. When I woke up in the morning, I was thinking about racing. I led a dual life for a long time, living for the weekend and doing what I had to do through the week to maintain income for our household.

But my heart begged, "How can I go racing?"

Cheryl saw that racing dominated my state of being. She could tell that I was doing both my own career and the people under my direction a disservice by not being fully engaged. And emotionally, I wasn't getting any easier to live with, either.

One evening, after we had finished dinner and were relaxing on the sofa watching TV, Cheryl gently took the remote from my hand and clicked it off.

"Honey, we need to talk."

ABOVE: My mom and dad enjoyed a loving relationship. BELOW LEFT: Three generations of William Alexander Lester at my grandfather's house. BELOW RIGHT TOP: It's hard to believe at age 16 I stood only 5-foot-5 when I got my first driver's license. BELOW RIGHT BOTTOM: My Malibu Grand Prix license. Often called 'Billy' in the family, my formal signature has always been William A. Lester III.

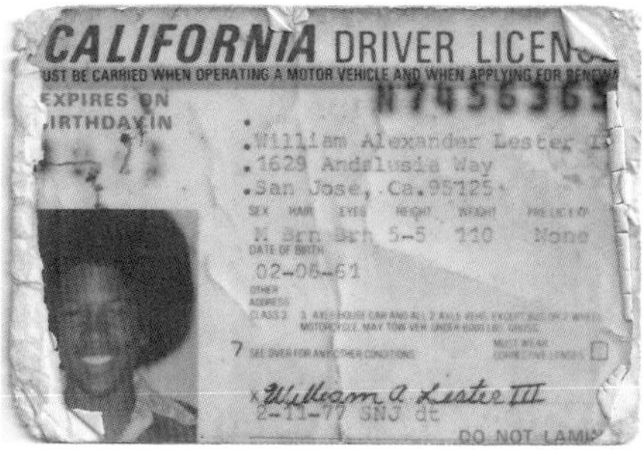

ABOVE: My race-modified RX-3 SP helped get me into the Mazda RX-7 corral and onto the track for the group's parade lap. BELOW LEFT: My dad surprises me at the last second by presenting my UC-Berkeley diploma. BELOW RIGHT: How to tell a young SCCA amateur racer from the pros—the driving suit has very few sponsor logos.

ABOVE: Mike Johnson played a big role in my 1985 Rookie of the Year title for the SCCA San Francisco Region. BELOW: After my first ever win in 1985, my mom joined me for an emotional victory lap on Mother's Day in an SCCA race at Sears Point.

TOP LEFT: It looks like I couldn't believe my eyes and just closed them when Willy T. decided to test drive my IMSA GTO Camaro in his street clothes. It was amazing for him to help me this way. TOP RIGHT: My sister Allison models a Bill Lester Racing t-shirt during my pro debut weekend at Sears Point. CENTER: My first professional start came at the age of 28 in a rented Camaro at Sears Point in 1989. BOTTOM: After this Trans-Am race at Mid-Ohio in 1990, I suffered a long drought. My next pro race didn't occur until 1996.

ABOVE: Celebrating a big win with a big trophy after an SCCA 4-hour endurance race at Sears Point. BELOW: A welcome return to racing: when competing in the World Challenge Series in 1996 on board a Mazda RX-7, I was on a mission.

RIGHT: For my second Rolex, I rented a seat in a Porsche 911 RSR along with four co-drivers. We gained eight positions to finish 10th in class. BELOW: At my first Rolex 24 in 1998, I backed this Mazda RX-7 into a tire wall before finding the right pace. Although fifth in class, we were running at the finish, which is always a victory in the Rolex.

ABOVE: Pressure was on: Ed Rensi took me to a short track in Anderson, Indiana to drive a "heavy car" for the first time during an ARCA test. RIGHT: At Watkins Glen, Cheryl and I are ready for my debut in the NASCAR Busch Series. BELOW: I was on my way to a Top 10 finish in the closing laps at Watkins Glen in Bobby Hillin's Chevy in my first Busch Series race before another driver's spin took me off the track.

ABOVE: Following my race at Watkins Glen, Chevy tested me for their driver development program in a car normally driven by series regular Todd Bodine. BELOW: The crew was all smiles after testing in Cicci-Welliver Racing's Chevy for General Motors—probably because I didn't wreck it!

ABOVE: Our very fast Amick Corvette had the Rolex 24 field covered—until it hit the guard rail in the closing hours. *Photo courtesy of John Brooks.* RIGHT: My good friend Mark Lewis created this distinctive helmet design during my Dodge days. BELOW: A happy day at company headquarters for the announcement of Dodge's factory drivers.

ABOVE: Strauss Discount Auto Parts was a rare primary sponsor on my Dodge factory-backed truck. BELOW: At Daytona with my good friends and track employees, Mark Lewis (right) and Andrew Booth (left).

ABOVE: Notice any resemblance? In addition to having my image on the boxes, the community outreach program with the Honey Nut Cheerios brand was an enjoyable experience for me. RIGHT: I became the first black driver to win a pole position in the Truck Series at Charlotte in 2003 during my second full season in NASCAR. BELOW: Bobby Hamilton, in the high groove, did his best to help me learn how to drive short tracks.

ABOVE: The arrival of my son Alex added a fourth generation to the W. A. Lester name. LEFT: Representing Toyota and Bill Davis Racing in the Truck series was a good experience, but unfortunately it had an abrupt ending. BELOW: It was always good to have family at the track supporting me. Alex and Cheryl join me in pre-race ceremonies at the Nashville Superspeedway.

LEFT: Back-to-back poles in 2005 and three poles overall confirmed my speed in the NASCAR Trucks. BELOW: There were always two heroes in my corner. Here, Mom and Dad join me at Richmond International Raceway.

ABOVE: Getting congratulatory autographs from NASCAR President Mike Helton, Atlanta track President Ed Clark, champion drivers Jimmie Johnson and Jeff Gordon, and car owners Jack Roush and Richard Petty were a welcome sign. BELOW: Ready to qualify for the Cup race in Atlanta – a proud but nerve-wracking occasion.

TOP: The Rock Valley Oil team pauses for a team photo with our Daytona Prototype. They were a fun group of guys to be around. CENTER: Here with Jordan Taylor on the top step of the podium following our win at VIR in 2011. Yep, the trophy was a radio made to look like a generator! That didn't stop us from smiling. BOTTOM LEFT: Over the years, Dad enjoyed my racing career too! BOTTOM RIGHT: I made it all the way to the Grand Finals representing TeamUSA in Portugal during a belated, one-season karting career in 2012. *Courtesy of Studio 52.us.*

ABOVE: While I enjoyed exposing my sons to racing, my wallet is relieved that neither of them was bitten by the racing bug. BELOW: I'm so fortunate to be blessed with such a wonderful family.

This is never a sentence that anyone wants to hear. I looked at her with puzzlement and turned to give her my undivided attention.

"Oh, no. What did I do?" I asked, half joking, half serious.

"Baby, you can't keep doing this to yourself. You're miserable," she said gently.

I shook my head in agreement.

"Tell me something I don't know."

Cheryl has the patience of a saint. She wasn't deterred by my crass response.

"Bill, splitting your time between racing and the office is not a very efficient way to be successful at either endeavor. You're never going to be able to give 100% to one as long as the other is in the way."

We'd had this talk a few times over the years and we were always in agreement about this point. But there was something about the way she was looking at me that told me this conversation was different.

"Agreed. There just aren't enough hours in the day. I already do everything I possibly can with the amount of time available to me, and it's still not enough. When it comes to racing, I've given so much and still haven't gotten where I want to be."

Cheryl inched closer and lovingly squeezed my hand.

"I know you have. You're not going to get where you want to go if you don't entrench yourself in where you want to go. You have to be completely committed, especially if it's something that's very hard to achieve. If you're just going through the motions and don't completely dedicate yourself to it, you're not going to be able to achieve your goal and you're going to eventually falter at work."

Cheryl was my always my sounding board when I needed to talk through an idea or gain perspective on my thoughts. But I didn't understand exactly where she was steering this conversation or what she wanted me to see.

I looked at her quizzically.

"Okay. What do you suggest?"

"You need to devote all your time and attention to see whether or not you can make it happen. Or give it your best shot and see that it wasn't meant to be."

"Wait. You aren't saying you think I should quit my job and pursue racing full-time, are you?"

Surely, I must have misinterpreted her words. There's no way a wife would tell her husband to give up his six-figure job to pursue a passion that was extremely expensive and may never lead to an actual paycheck, especially when they had two mouths to feed and a mortgage to pay.

"That's exactly what I'm saying. Baby, you're not getting any younger. If you're going to do this, you need to really do this. You'll never make it if you only do it halfway. I think you should talk to your boss about taking a leave of absence from H-P."

A blend of pure excitement and utter terror ran through me at the same time. She was serious! But was it actually feasible? Could I walk away from my job to pursue what most people would consider only a hobby?

"Hon, I would love to do that, but how can we afford it?"

I was brought up with the traditional mentality that the male should be the household breadwinner. Contemplating the idea of being unemployed was uncharted territory that would set me off balance.

"We're doing fine. I'm able to provide. You've done extremely well putting away the money that you've made, invested, and saved. Let's give it a timeline. Take a six-month leave of absence from H-P and at the end of that period, we'll take stock and see where you're at. If nothing is happening, then you go back to project management. But at least you'll know that you did everything you possibly could. At least you'll know you really tried. You won't have any regrets. But if you make it—think about it, baby, if you make it!"

She was right. I did well at H-P, but I had not relied on that alone. I also did very well in the stock market, because I knew the tech sector and had invested wisely in it. We had a healthy nest egg.

Cheryl worked in marketing and had been employed by McKinsey Inc. and a number of prominent Silicon Valley–type jobs. She worked for a company called Vicinity, which provided online driving directions for Yahoo! and all the major search engines and websites at that time. She held the head marketing position for a teeth-whitening company called BriteSmile. She was always successful when it came to creating opportunities for herself. As an only child, Cheryl became very self-sufficient. As such, she was perfectly comfortable taking the financial reins for us.

We spent the rest of the evening discussing how we were going to make it work. I acquiesced and agreed that her plan was brilliant and worth a try with the provision that if I couldn't gain significant traction in the motor sports industry in six months, I would have to return to my day job. That deadline provided ample incentive to succeed because the prospect of returning to the tech sector was extremely unappealing.

In January of 1998, I took leave of absence from H-P.

It was the best decision my wife has ever made. Next to agreeing to marry me, of course.

■ ■ ■

RACING TO THE FRONT

The most important and resolute decision of my professional life came back to the most important decision in my personal life—marrying Cheryl. Her advice and counsel as well as my trust and faith in her enabled me to become a full-time professional race car driver. I had done all the preparation possible, but without her perspective and guidance the next giant step might not have been visible or available to me. To say I was *grateful* for this support would be an understatement. It made me even more determined to succeed.

When inspired by someone you love,
gratitude becomes an even greater motivating factor.

10

First Rolex 24, Meeting Ed Rensi

Once I had the full-time opportunity to break into the professional ranks, good things started to happen. Through both networking and hustling, I finally got into positions where my skills could be recognized and my ability to represent manufacturers appreciated. Initially, I proved myself by paying my own way to race, and then going to tryouts, but all of these efforts were rewarded when my driving skills finally started receiving a closer look by the industry.

Within a year after leaving H-P, I competed in sports car racing's single biggest race at Daytona, established a factory relationship with Chevrolet in NASCAR, and succeeded in an open wheel test. Manufacturers were beginning to see the value of having a black race car driver. It was a silent, behind-the-scenes movement that would eventually influence NASCAR and its diversity program. After fifteen years of trying to promote myself into the pro ranks, I was finally positioning myself to break through. None of it could have happened if I had remained employed full-time.

This first season of racing in 1998, however, began inauspiciously when I crashed during practice for the twenty-four-hour race at the Daytona International Speedway. Early in my first trip around this world-famous track, I tried to go too fast too soon and spun in the chicane at the end of the back straight, putting my team's Mazda RX-7 into a tire wall. I slid a long way and damaged the bodywork. I felt like a complete amateur and, to add insult to injury, the team owner made me pay for repairs. But a race car driver has to be like an NBA player who misses the winning shot at the buzzer or an NFL cornerback who gets burned for a long touchdown pass. You shake it off, learn from your mistake, and reboot your confidence.

The opportunity to rent a seat for the Rolex 24 race in the GT2 class resulted from my success in the World Challenge in 1996. Brian Richards, my team owner in the World Challenge, had recommended me to Pettit Racing. After renting a seat for the race himself on the Pettit team, Brian wanted me to be one of his co-drivers.

Despite not initially realizing just how fast I could charge the relatively high-speed left and right turn chicane nicknamed the "Bus Stop," the race turned out well. The world's icebreaker race after a long winter's layoff held at the end of each January, the Rolex 24 was a race I had always wanted to do. The drivers of the winning car took home special edition Rolex Daytona watches along with the prestige of a victory in one of the world's most famous races. The race attracted some of the world's best manufacturers, teams, and drivers. I had been watching it on TV for years prior to ever competing in it.

Fans and drivers alike love 24-hour endurance racing, because after a Saturday afternoon start it's a never-ending carnival of visual and aural excitement featuring a large field of GT and Prototype sports cars. Getting behind the wheel of the RX-7 for the first time, I jumped directly into the middle of this carnival and was living my dream on North American road racing's big stage.

The late winter sunset was throwing a golden glow over the broad expanse of the Daytona track. During my opening stint I was anxious about succeeding but excited, too. As the race wore on, I found a relaxing tranquility while running in the dark. The radiant red exhaust glow at the back of the Porsches, the flames shooting out of the back of the Mazdas, and all the brake rotors lighting up from dull red to bright orange as cars arrested their speed entering the corners, inevitably caught my attention even while concentrating on driving.

All drivers had to keep a strong pace, but another key was staying consistent in lap times and out of trouble in the unending offering of different classes of cars racing at varying speeds. We didn't win a Rolex timepiece, but after starting ninth, we finished fifth. If nothing else, I gained confidence about succeeding in the sports car ranks, where gentlemen team owners regularly paid professional co-drivers to help their chances of success in endurance races. I wanted to be one of those co-drivers.

Not long after Daytona, my relentless networking brought me what turned out to be my best opportunity to become a full-time professional driver. I received an invitation to an inaugural event held by the Urban Youth Racing School (UYRS) in April, an indication that I was beginning to get some recognition. Based in Philadelphia, the UYRS exposed black youth to Indy car racing. The organizers wanted to use racing as a carrot for kids to perform better in school, to encourage them to think about careers in racing, and to realize the skills they would need to develop to pursue this direction. It became a long-running, highly successful program with plenty of testimonials from those urban youth who it benefited.

The inaugural meeting featured the presence of Michael Andretti from nearby Nazareth, Pennsylvania, who was performing extremely well in the Indy car series. That's where I met Ed Rensi, a former president and CEO of McDonald's, and a major benefactor of the UYRS who had since become a NASCAR race team owner after retiring from business.

After Ed and I were introduced at the event, we enjoyed a long conversation. While he was clearly an industry titan, my years in corporate America at the management level kept me fairly calm during our exchange. I found him to be engaging, though strongly opinionated and confident in his views. Ed spoke with conviction, like someone who had seen and done it all. I believe he was interested in me since he probably had not met many thirty-seven-year-old black guys who had left a corporate engineering management job to pursue a racing dream.

"Bill, I know you're a race car driver and you've been driving those little sports cars," Ed began. "Have you ever driven a heavy car?"

I didn't understand what he meant. I had never heard that term before.

"What's a heavy car?" I asked curiously.

"A stock car!"

"No, I've never driven a stock car."

Ed paused and looked at me intently, deep in thought. I wasn't exactly sure what he was thinking, and he wasn't quite ready to elaborate.

"Oh, okay, well, let me give some thought to that."

We exchanged information and agreed to stay in touch. I headed home that evening wondering if he had an opportunity in mind. I was hopeful, but I wasn't expecting anything to come to fruition. He was one of the most powerful men in the business world and I didn't really think that he was going to continue to think about me after we parted ways. But he did.

That evening, Ed called me up and got right to the point.

"I want to test you in a heavy car. We're going to go to this track in Indiana and put you in one of my cars to see if you can drive it."

It was a defining moment in my career.

He took me to a quarter-mile short track in Anderson, Indiana. When we got there, I couldn't believe what I saw! I was used to driving on multi-turn road courses two to four miles in length.

I looked at this place and thought, "What's this? How can you race such big cars on this itty-bitty bullring?"

I had no experience on an oval prior to this test, which turned out to be a race weekend, not a private test like I had naively assumed. It was an Automobile Racing Club of America (ARCA) series event and all of the top drivers, like champion Ken Schrader, were entered. Ed's team showed up and unloaded a painted car for his regular series driver and a primer gray backup car for me.

As if he was merely telling me to run to the store for a gallon of milk, Ed said, "Okay. Let's see what you can do."

After getting over the shock of the circumstances, I got into the backup car and ran some laps on a track occupied by all the drivers practicing for the race. Despite never having been on a short track in a stock car before, I acclimated myself to the conditions and began to push the car. After pitting and asking for setup changes to improve performance, I continued to gain confidence and speed behind the wheel. The crew told me that if my practice time had been posted during qualifying, I would have qualified in the Top 10. They were impressed by my speed and my solid feedback about how the car performed.

Before leaving Anderson, Ed indicated there were no promises, but he'd try to work something out for me to race a stock car. As it turned out, I would have to wait until the following season, but I had already waited thirty-seven years to get here; a few more months wasn't going to kill me.

■ ■ ■

RACING TO THE FRONT

It was not by chance that I appeared at the inaugural Urban Youth Racing School event where I met Ed Rensi. From the beginning of my efforts to race, I recognized that race car drivers could play a role in inspiring others, particularly young people. It was fulfilling to respond to and influence kids who saw race car drivers as role models.

But I also recognized that to be successful, I needed to meet the right people in racing. That was a matter of climbing every mountain and pursuing all opportunities. Connecting with Ed Rensi, on the surface of it, might have been a chance meeting. But it wasn't by chance that I was in Philadelphia at the first event for the UYRS, a program I would continue to support for many years. And it wasn't by chance that I established footholds in sports car racing, NASCAR, and Indy car racing in just one year. It was a matter of *networking*, getting myself in front of people in a way that was mutually beneficial—the proverbial win-win situation.

Once networking creates an opportunity, it's important to be prepared to take advantage of it.

11

CART Calamity, Shifting to NASCAR

After establishing a relationship with Ed Rensi, I was invited to a completely different challenge. It was a tryout sanctioned by Championship Auto Racing Teams (CART). The biggest and richest series for open-wheel cars in the United States, CART agreed to work with a company, Miller Racing Group, to put together this audition for black talent called the African American Driver Development Program. The Miller Racing Group was a small, black-owned organization. CART wanted to see if a black driver was ready to compete in their Indy car series. The program had been created not long after Willy T. Ribbs made headlines at the Indy 500 driving in the rival Indy Racing League. CART took notice of the immense publicity his effort generated and realized they could be missing out on an expansion opportunity of their own.

Ironically, I went through the back door to get the opportunity to test. CART officials had commissioned the Miller Racing Group to find the talent and to help administer the test. But that organization wanted me to sign an exclusive agency representation agreement for a period far longer than I felt comfortable with, agreeing to pay them what I believed was an unreasonable percentage of my earnings. I firmly declined.

Since I wouldn't sign a contract, they excluded me from further consideration. I made it a point to attend the CART race at the Laguna Seca track that year, where I sought out and spoke directly to the CEO of CART, Andrew Craig, in a private meeting. I told him about my qualifications and why I should be a candidate.

He agreed.

"You're going to be CART's selection to participate in this program," he told me.

After having to talk my way in, things eventually got worse. Once I proved to be the fastest driver of the three assembled for the tryout, and was declared capable of competing in any Indy car, I got hoodwinked again.

The first test in the program took place at the Buttonwillow Raceway in California in a Formula Atlantic car, one of the developmental series that led to Indy car. I had never driven a lightweight Formula Atlantic car before and with its impressive power-to-weight ratio and aerodynamic capabilities, it was far more responsive than any other car I had driven. My neck muscles were sore for days after the test from trying to keep my head from falling over in the corners and under braking. During the test, I acclimated quickly to both the car and this new track and smoked the other two guys who were invited. As a result, I got to drive in a separate individual test hosted by Team Kool Green, a top CART team that also fielded an Indy Lights entry—the last stepping-stone to an Indy car. I drove their Indy Lights car at Firebird Raceway, the same track where I'd come close to winning the Bondurant PROsearch tryout to get a Trans-Am ride five years earlier.

While again having no experience driving an Indy Lights car, I proved I could turn competitive lap times and was only fractions of a second off the baseline time established by their full-time driver, Jonny Kane. Needless to say, they were highly impressed. The team manager, Nick Harvey, was interviewed on camera and confirmed I did everything well and was ready for competition.

I expected I would have at least an opportunity to race an Indy Lights car and maybe even a potential Indy car ride. That was what I'd initially been led to believe by CART officials at the beginning of the program, who then told me after the test:

"Okay, bring us a million to 1.5 million dollars, and we'll put you behind the wheel of an Indy Lights car."

CART wanted me to bring money! There had been no prior communication that I would need to bring sponsorship. Had I known from the beginning that these resources were required, this program would have held little interest for me. Since I had none at my disposal, the program quickly terminated. All I got in the end was a piece of paper that I could take to a team, which indicated that I had the talent to compete at the Indy Lights level. I was so disappointed that I turned my back on open wheel racing, deciding to focus on NASCAR instead.

Though I had never felt drawn toward NASCAR before, I now felt optimistic about pursuing a career in NASCAR after my initial conversations with team owner Ed Rensi. Crowds at NASCAR races had been growing significantly throughout the 1990s and its premier Cup Series also offered the biggest purses compared to any other racing series. Succeeding in NASCAR, I believed, would put me on the big stage, allow me to make a name for myself, and position me to enjoy some financial rewards as well.

Most important, I would achieve the goal of competing against some of the best drivers in America.

But driving in NASCAR meant facing a couple of drawbacks, which included driving stock cars and living in the South. NASCAR's hub was located in North Carolina, and many of the drivers lived in that area. And as Ed informed me, the Cup Series used heavy cars. Compared to the more familiar sports cars I'd raced or the open-wheel cars I'd tested, stock cars were not nearly as nimble or responsive. And almost all of the racing took place on ovals with only the occasional race on road courses—my comfort zone.

Knowing my road racing background, but believing in my ability after our test at the ARCA race in Indiana, Ed decided he wanted to put me into a stock car on the Watkins Glen road course. After confirming my skills on an oval, I think Ed saw me as a potential asset for his team and thought a black driver had a good chance of standing out in the eyes of a manufacturer and possibly some sponsors. Ed liked me and realized he was in a position to help me reach my goals and aspirations. He must have also known he could make a profound social statement by being the catalyst behind my involvement in a sport consisting primarily of white participants.

Ed owned and operated a team in the Busch Grand National Series, the understudy to the Cup Series. Not surprisingly for a retired corporate CEO of a fast-food chain, Ed liked the business of making a deal. He did well when it came to selling and he consistently tried to pair the right drivers with sponsors for his cars in the Busch Series.

In 1999, Ed had enough sponsorship money from the Dura Lube company to back a second entry at Watkins Glen. He made an agreement with fellow team owner Bobby Hillin Jr. He wanted me to replace Bobby as the driver in his Chevy Monte Carlo for this one race. It was a customary practice in NASCAR to substitute drivers with road racing experience, known as "ringers" on road circuits like the Glen. The "ringers" often produced better results than drivers who raced primarily on ovals. In this case, Bobby needed sponsorship and Ed promised Bobby he'd also back him in an oval race with Dura Lube if he stepped aside for the Glen event.

For this 200-mile Busch race in June, my Chevy, prepared by Bobby's team, carried the Dura Lube sponsorship provided by Ed, whose own team also entered a road racing specialist at the Glen. In an event where six drivers failed to qualify for a starting position, I qualified twenty-fourth out of fifty entries. In my first race driving a stock car, I drove my way into the Top 10. With the finish of the race almost in sight, a car spun in front of me in a section called the Inner Loop, forcing me to take evasive action. This unavoidable incident, which forced my car off-track, dropped me to a disappointing twenty-first at the finish, but still on the same lap with the winner, Dale Earnhardt Jr.

This break led to another. Despite the race result, my driving performance at the Glen had generated attention. I received an invitation from Chevrolet to test the Busch Series car usually reserved for driver Todd Bodine, a circumstance confirming Ed's recognition that manufacturers were interested in black drivers. This Chevy offer came through Gary Claudio, the marketing director for GM Racing and the Chevy brand. After I had tested Bodine's Chevy at Concord Motorsports Park in North Carolina and he liked what he saw, Claudio began looking for opportunities to put me behind the wheel of a Chevy stock car. That situation didn't materialize, but Gary set up a co-drive with Chevy factory driver John Heinricy in an entry-level professional road racing series called the Motorola Cup, where we were successful racing a virtually stock Corvette.

When the 2000 season began, I returned to Daytona for my third consecutive Rolex 24-hour race, the twenty-four-hour-long race comprised of individual racing teams, usually made up of four drivers. Each driver drives a stint, so as to not exhaust themselves. My co-drivers and I would take turns behind the wheel while the other three drivers rested. Most of the drivers, me included, would have a motor coach, where we could lie down between stints. I usually tried to get three or four hours of sleep, but it was hard because of the excitement happening all around me. The adrenaline would never really subside long enough for me to actually fall asleep. We would each drive somewhere between forty-five minutes to an hour before switching off to another driver. The number of stints a driver runs before handing off to the next driver is dependent on a number of variables: weather conditions, the driver's speed, driver fatigue, fuel strategy, caution flags, etc. The complexity of the race is dynamic. There are engineers and race strategists who are experts in planning these types of races with precision. The driver is in constant contact with the pits and the strategist via the radio.

A twenty-four-hour race has its own unique challenges. Simple daily functions like eating, drinking, and using the bathroom all become strategically mapped-out points of the day. I realized early on that it was important to eat well before the stint began, but I would have to be careful what I ate and when I ate it so that I could perform at my peak. Staying hydrated was also crucial to being able to remain alert so that I could operate at a high level. As far as using the bathroom, that's typically the last thing the driver does before strapping into the car. There are no bathroom breaks, and nobody wants to get behind the wheel after someone who can't hold their liquids. Going to the bathroom in the seat is a cardinal sin.

The twenty-four-hour races are a totally different format than any other type of race. There are no other sports that have competitions that last for twenty-four straight hours. It is an experience for the fans as well. Many spectators will park campers and RV's in the infield camping areas so they are able to bounce back and forth between viewing the race from different vantage points around the track and their home on wheels. They can take breaks for food and sleep, the same way we drivers can. Other spectators may rent hotel rooms in the area and will head there overnight. But everyone shows back up to watch the end of the race. For this particular race, I shared a car with Heinricy and drove in a funded ride for Chevy instead of hunting around to pay for a seat behind the wheel. It was a difficult twenty-four-hour race due to a persistent power delivery problem with our Corvette, but I was being paid by a major manufacturer in road racing's most prestigious event, a big step forward from my first Rolex 24 two years earlier. The drive shaft on our Corvette routinely broke. A production part, the stock drive shaft couldn't handle the additional horsepower from a race engine. We completed just 261 laps after breaking every replacement drive shaft put into our car. Including one other factory driver, R. K. Smith, and team owner Jeff Nowicki, we as drivers performed far better than our car. Frankly, it was maddening. I remember the car being up on jack stands in the garage area more than I remember driving it or seeing it circling around the track.

I came back with Chevy again the following year for my fourth Rolex 24 in 2001. This time, I had a serious chance to win one of the prized Rolex Daytona watches. The watches are a tradition and a symbol of success and achievement. Every year Rolex comes out with a new design that is more impressive than the year before.

As with any athlete, I was mindful of what I put into my body to make sure it was working as efficiently as possible. I prepared with my signature meal: grilled chicken with pasta and a side of broccoli. This enabled me to get an equal amount of protein and carbs, and a small portion of a light vegetable that was easy on the stomach. I was fastidious when it came to ensuring that my body was performing at its best.

This IMSA program was another put together by Gary Claudio on behalf of General Motors. I drove for Bill Amick, a team owner in both ARCA and NASCAR's Busch Series who had decided to give the Rolex 24 a try due to a new class called American GT (AGT). Amick wanted to put his sons, Lyndon and David, behind the wheel with two veteran road racers.

Lyndon had driven regularly in the Busch Series, and his younger brother David was testing the waters of a possible professional driving career.

This class was based on tube-frame race cars with full-on racing modifications. The Amicks were chicken farmers from South Carolina who had ample resources and had decided to stuff an unrestricted ARCA-spec Chevy V-8 under the hood of their brand-new, tube-frame Corvette, making it a rocket ship. This AGT-class car was so stout that our top speed was as fast as some of the cars racing in the top-level Prototype class. We hit 190 mph through the tri-oval section of the track in front of the main grandstand. Not surprisingly, our lead professional driver, Joe Varde, drove it to the AGT class pole during qualifying by a considerable margin over our competition.

Our Corvette had the widest 18-inch tires I had ever seen on a race car with a body resembling the production version. Coupled with our horsepower, nobody could touch us in our class. None of the competitors came close to the Amicks in terms of what they'd spent and the resulting quality of their car.

I was part of a four-person team, alternating stints. Joe was the most experienced driver and was also charged with managing the team. Before the race began, he gave us the obligatory motivational pep talk.

"We are going to go out there and win this race, boys! Our team is far superior to the others in our class. This is our race to win—or lose. Some of us may pull a double stint, but I don't foresee any triple stints being run. Our driving talent is too good and I want to make sure we all stay fresh behind the wheel. Stay focused. Stay sharp. Keep the car on the track and do not be afraid to radio in if you need a break."

With Joe having qualified the car, the race started with him behind the wheel. When I wasn't out on the track, I spent most of my time sitting in the pits watching the race from the monitors and listening to the conversation between the drivers and the race strategist over my headset. I made sure to stay hydrated, but not so much that I would have to use the restroom during my stint. I ate modestly so that I would not be full or sluggish while driving. I tried to rest for a few hours in the camper, but it was pointless. I never could get a proper power nap in during twenty-four hour races.

When the last three hours of the race came around, our team had a commanding lead. We consistently ran fast lap times, so much so that no one could touch us. We were poised to win. The vibe in the pit area was one of enthusiastic anticipation. Joe had been behind the wheel for a double stint when our race strategist called him into the pits.

"Joe, come in next time by for tires, fuel, and a driver change."

"Actually, I'm going to stay in the car. I'm feeling pretty good," he responded confidently.

I couldn't believe what I had just heard and I looked over at our strategist on the timing stand who was in communication with Joe.

"This will be your third consecutive stint," he said cautiously. "We've got time to switch drivers, Joe. We're in the lead."

"No, I'm good. I'm doing another stint."

It wasn't unusual for race car drivers to be behind the wheel for more than two hours at a time in a normal race, but when you've been awake for well over twenty-four hours with nothing more than catnaps in between, it's exhausting, both mentally and physically. That many back-to-back hours of exertion and concentration take a toll on your body. It's damn near impossible to maintain acuity when you're racing on the edge for that long.

Joe brought the car in and the crew went to work switching out the tires. The wear and tear exerted on tires during a race is considerable. They need to be changed out regularly to keep the car in optimum working condition. There is a huge difference between racing on new, cold tires, and hot tires that a driver has been running on for multiple laps. They perform completely differently. Unlike street tires, racing tires do not generate sufficient grip until they have achieved a reasonable operating temperature. The new tires installed on our car were cold and lacked any grip, but Joe had been used to running around on hot tires for the last two hours.

"Are you sure you don't want to switch drivers?" the strategist asked one last time.

"Negative. I'm okay," Joe confirmed.

The decision was made and there would be no further argument since Joe was team manager. His word was final. When the pit stop was finished the strategist radioed to Joe that he was ready to go.

"All clear."

Joe briskly pushed down on the gas pedal and took off out of pit lane. Everything seemed normal as he made his way down pit road, but there was a hard-left turn just before joining the track. The raw, cold tires wouldn't comply with what Joe expected of them when he turned the wheel. He was going too fast for the conditions. But by the time Joe realized that the tires had no traction, it was too late.

Instead of turning left, the car went straight and glanced off the concrete wall that separated the pit lane from the racetrack. Almost every year, someone hits the pit out concrete wall in this race. This time, it was Joe who committed a cardinal sin—he wrecked exiting pit lane on cold tires, something all drivers are warned about by their teams. Joe called it in to the strategist who informed us that Joe had crashed, but we didn't know the severity of the crash and if the car could be fixed quickly enough to return to the race. We were all in a state of shock. The somber mood the team felt was immediately evident, but we held out hope that we still had a chance. Once we saw the car on the hook being towed back to the garage, I knew we were in trouble. Even if we got the car fixed, we wouldn't win the race. I was definitely not the only one holding my breath as we all anxiously waited on pins and needles.

Fortunately, Joe was okay but the car was not. The right front tire and wheel were damaged and could have been replaced, but the real problem was that the impact had been so severe that the suspension pickup points on the chassis frame were damaged beyond repair. Once our car left the racetrack, it did not return. We would not be able to finish what we'd started. We retired the car and were eliminated from the race.

This race had been ours; there was nobody in contention with us for the win. All we could do was beat ourselves, and, unfortunately, that was exactly what happened.

There are so many variables that go into racing, and so many things that can go wrong along the way that it feels almost impossible sometimes to have everything go right. One small misjudgment or incorrect calculation, and you're done. Sometimes it's a technical difficulty, sometimes it's human error, sometimes it's inclement weather, and sometimes it's just plain bad luck. There are so many things that can go wrong along the way, especially in a race that is as grueling as the Rolex 24. Rarely does it all line up. But when it does, and you win, there's no greater feeling in the world. In our case, there's a reason why you'll often hear the phrase, "That's racing."

But every time, it hurts just as much, if not more, than the time before. You never get used to it. There are so many of us that work together, pouring our heart, soul, blood, sweat, and tears into preparing for the races that when it falls apart at the last minute, it is demoralizing for everyone.

As one of the racers who was set to take the wheel next and could have easily avoided this debacle, I felt totally dejected. I was gutted. We all felt it, but no one dared say it. The look of remorse on Joe's face said it all. His resigned demeanor indicated that he knew the blame fell squarely on his shoulders. He didn't need us pouring salt into the wound. We have all made mistakes in life, and no good could come from beating someone up who was clearly beating himself up enough already. None of us wanted to make him feel worse.

Joe apologized profusely, immediately owning up to his mistake. We all did our best to assure him that it was okay, but only for that day. After the initial sting wore off, I made sure to tease him about it for years to come, much to his chagrin.

"Hey, Joe! Have you got my Rolex?" I would ask every time we saw each other.

He always took it in stride with a smile.

Despite not running in the final three hours, the number of laps we had already completed was good enough for third place. That was how dominant a race car we had.

Missing a Rolex and the opportunity to win in America's biggest road racing event was painful. I said to myself, "I'm done with sports cars. I'm going NASCAR racing. Without any co-drivers, at least it will be on me when it comes to results."

I was considered to be under the Chevy umbrella, but about this time the Dodge diversity program came along and offered me a test drive with a team owned by renowned NASCAR driver Bobby Hamilton. I had a conversation about accepting the Dodge offer with Chevy's Gary Claudio, who was clearly disappointed by the proposition of losing me. But Gary acknowledged that Chevy didn't have a NASCAR ride for me and, to his credit, he didn't want to stand in my way. Ed Rensi also gave me his blessing to pursue the Dodge program.

The opportunity from Dodge was the one I had been hoping for. If successful, I would earn a full-time ride in the NASCAR Truck Series, a stepping-stone to the Cup Series. The sponsorship was already in place. I wouldn't need to do anything except bring my helmet and my determination to succeed.

■ ■ ■

RACING TO THE FRONT

I experienced success in acquiring opportunities to drive in several different series once I started to pursue professional racing full-time. But once in the cockpit, and on the track, most of the initial results were nothing to write home about. In CART, I received a piece of paper for being fast enough to compete in one of the world's foremost open-wheel racing series. What could I do with that, given the same old problem of not having enough financial backing?

In NASCAR, I got an opportunity race in the Busch Series—only to become subject to another driver's error, which ruined my result. In sports cars, a co-driver wrecked our car in the closing hours of the Rolex 24 at Daytona with Rolex watches virtually in sight.

The odds against winning are always high, so *persistence* is mandatory. It's no wonder drivers and their teams celebrate so much in Victory Lane. That promised land proves to be elusive for all racers, despite one's best efforts, and more than a few very talented and hardworking drivers never get there. Adaptability is also a facet of *persistence*. The willingness not just to keep trying, but to try different things along the way. I was always willing to try new cars, styles of racing, and different avenues to my goal, instead of only focusing on Indy, sports, or stock cars. I worked to adapt to any opportunity that came my way.

Without persistence and the willingness to try again (and again), that elusive trip to Victory Lane will not happen.

12

Trucking with Dodge

When racing team owners and manufacturers want to identify the best candidate to drive one of their vehicles, they often organize a tryout, an audition, or what we often refer to as a Gong Show. A group of invited drivers gathers at the same track and are tested against each other using the same equipment to determine who performs the best and gets the ride.

When I received an invitation from Dodge in late 2000 to compete for an open seat in a diversity-based NASCAR Truck Series team owned by Bobby Hamilton, I already had a fair amount of Gong Show experience. I had won the driver search organized on behalf of CART and almost won the Bondurant PROsearch tryout associated with Ford. In this case, Dodge offered a career-changing opportunity for a minority driver: earn this ride and get paid to go racing full-time in the NASCAR Truck Series.

After receiving a false promise from Bobby after the audition in 2000, I prevailed after the 2001 Gong Show and got the coveted Dodge factory ride for the 2002 season. But little did I know what lay in store for me with my relationship with Bobby Hamilton Racing (BHR), which at times turned surprisingly ugly. Only after my second season ended did I find out the effort certain members of the team put into making sure my results were not the best I could achieve. That's a very rare situation in motor racing and I doubt Dodge knew anything about it.

It all started in late 2000. Dodge and BHR hosted two days of tryouts for a handful of minority drivers, most of them black, at the Atlanta Motor Speedway, the one-and-a-half-mile high-banked track where I would eventually make my Cup Series debut. The configuration of the track played to my strong suit of high speed, but I had raced only twice in NASCAR vehicles: once in a NASCAR Busch Series race at Watkins Glen in 1999, and once in a Truck Series race at Portland International Raceway in 2000. Each time, I raced on a road course, not on an oval track.

For the Dodge diversity program, all of us aspiring drivers were tasked with getting up to speed as quickly as possible, then completing five laps and meeting with the crew chief, team owner Hamilton, and a factory representative afterward for a debrief to describe the handling of the truck. One of the other candidates was my longtime friend and mentor Willy T. Ribbs, who was taking another crack at NASCAR. I knew nothing of his attendance until later because each day hosted a unique group of candidates. He and his group had tested on Saturday, while I tested with my group on Sunday. Willy had moved from racing sports cars to Indy cars, a career change that didn't produce satisfactory results due to lack of funding.

Nevertheless, he had name recognition due to his overall impressive racing accomplishments.

Each driver's lap times were kept strictly confidential, so I didn't know where my times stood. But I thought I had earned the ride because once testing concluded late Sunday afternoon, Bobby Hamilton pulled me aside. He indicated that I was his choice and asked me to consider my salary requirements. The people at Dodge had other ideas; they preferred Willy to me. Since Bobby considered me a better prospect, he made a separate arrangement with me, offering a five-race program for 2001. That program consisted of racing a BHR-built Dodge truck for a team owned by Wayne Day under the latter owner's team sponsor, 31-W Insulation. In effect, Bobby owned the truck and paid Wayne Day to enter it and provide a crew for me.

Since I never saw the lap times in the Gong Show, I can't be certain if Bobby considered me the faster driver, or if he thought my personality might be a better fit with his team—hopefully both. By entering me five times in 2001 with Wayne Day, Bobby groomed me to replace Willy, presumably by spending some of the Dodge diversity budget earmarked for him. Being pitted against Willy in this manner, after learning so much from him during my earliest days in racing, left me feeling slightly conflicted—Bobby considered me a future full-time driver for his team, and I wanted the job. Besides, Bobby offered me the job first before having to rescind it, resulting from being overruled by Dodge politics.

During the five-race stint in 2001, I qualified faster than Willy twice and finished ahead of him once in the Wayne Day truck. At the end of the season, I was offered a chance to participate in another Gong Show, which took place because Bobby and Dodge were dissatisfied with Willy's results. After the conclusion of the second Gong Show, Bobby told me I had finally secured the job driving the factory-backed truck Dodge had designated for a minority driver for the following 2002 and 2003 racing seasons.

Willy and I did not talk a great deal during those five races in 2001. It was awkward being at the racetrack together with both of us suspecting that I was being groomed to replace him. Once Willy's contract ended and he vacated the #8 Truck, we did not speak again. I focused on performing my best in those races and although we were competitors, I never said a bad word about Willy, despite the best efforts of the media to bait me into doing so. While I watched Willy struggle, I continued to admire him and believe he understood how much it would mean to me to become a full-time professional race car driver the following year. We were both competitors and racers first and foremost. We understood and respected each other. I would never want him to give less than his best against me and he knew I would never give less than my best against him.

Losing the Dodge ride essentially meant the conclusion of Willy's professional racing career. He turned to rifle shooting competitions where he continued to take advantage of his outstanding eyesight, dexterous hands, and coolness under pressure. He also began to compete in vintage races, but those were just for fun. For me, my advancement meant the end of a relationship with an important mentor and a painful way to lose a friend and hero, especially after all we had been through.

Another difficulty loomed: Cheryl and I had to make a decision if we were going to move to a location closer to the Bobby Hamilton Racing shop in Mt. Juliet, Tennessee. I knew we had to come to the Southeast if I was going to be serious about racing in NASCAR. So, it became a process of elimination as to what city would be most attractive. Cheryl and I talked about places in North Carolina and Tennessee before deciding on Atlanta. We moved in August of 2001, a big step because I was not yet contractually bound to Dodge for 2002 and had already been surprised and disappointed by the Gong Show outcome the year before.

My wife and I wanted to live in the biggest metropolitan city we could find in the Southeast. Cheryl grew up in San Francisco, and I was raised in San

Jose and Oakland. I didn't feel comfortable with the idea of being in a small, rural town. Although racism still existed, it wasn't as prevalent in more urban areas. We decided we would make the adjustment from the West Coast to the South most easily by living in Atlanta. The largest metropolitan area in the Southeast, Atlanta was also the home of the civil rights movement. I had familiarity with the city, having visited it on occasion while working for Hewlett-Packard. I had experienced Atlanta up close with a cousin who was living there at the time. Atlanta had culture: museums, theaters, botanical gardens, historical sites, fine dining, and parks. It was everything we wanted.

Atlanta was also the best career opportunity for Cheryl. She was still anchoring us with her steady work. If we moved to North Carolina, she would have been confined to the insurance and banking industries in Charlotte. We didn't see any opportunities for her in Tennessee. I wanted to be in a position where I could easily drive to the BHR racing shop in Tennessee and see the team regularly. Atlanta worked in this sense. If I pushed it, and I always did, I could drive to Mt. Juliet from Atlanta in about three hours. It was the perfect solution for us.

As a guy coming to the Southeast from Northern California, Bobby was a completely different type of character to me. He was the epitome of a good ol' boy, unlike anybody I had ever worked with in racing up until this point. Bobby had an interesting work ethic.

"We're going to work hard," was his mantra, "and we're going to play just as hard, if not harder."

Bobby was basic in terms of how he spoke, how he thought, and how he wanted to communicate. When seeking guidance and trying to learn the NASCAR ropes, the questions I would ask him drew responses that made me feel like I had overthought everything. I had the analytic mindset of an engineer. I was constantly trying to strategically apply the principles of mathematics and science to come up with solutions to technical problems. Bobby just wasn't built that way. He liked to keep things plain and simple.

When it came to work, he was all business and matter-of-fact in his manner. But when not at the track, he just wanted to have fun, drink beer, and talk about women. Because he had so much experience in the deep waters of Cup racing, the fundamentals of truck racing were familiar to him. Understanding how to drive the trucks and running the team seemed to come easily. And as soon as he finished with the day's work, it was playtime.

"Okay, let's go out and have some fun!" He would say, inviting us all out for a beer.

Bobby made his Cup Series debut in 1989 under some unusual circumstances, driving a car loaded with cameras to get film footage for the movie *Days of Thunder* during a race in Phoenix. The movie starred Tom Cruise and included a fair amount of actual in-car footage.

Bobby dropped out of school at age thirteen, but that didn't prevent him from going on to greatness. Bobby had undeniable driving talent, eventually winning four Cup races. In 2003, my final season with his truck team, he switched his focus to driving in the Truck Series full-time for his own team, and eventually won ten races and five poles over the years, including a victory at Daytona in 2005.

I'm not convinced Bobby was the greatest businessman, but he had the right people around him. Both his wife and his general manager were very sharp at running the day-to-day tasks of the office and the team. He did not worry about the business side of things or stay up late working on the books. He stuck to what he knew. All he concentrated on were the driving aspects of racing, and what would make him money.

I don't think he was driven to make strides in the way of diversifying the sport or his team. I think the financial benefit he would receive is what piqued his interest in working with Dodge to run an additional truck for a minority driver. He undoubtedly knew how lucrative it would be to have that program. Since he already had an established team, any additional race entry carrying full-season factory funding notably bolstered his team's finances.

Bobby sometimes had a unique way of combining humor with inspiration. Early in my truck career with BHR, we were flying in on Bobby's private plane for a test on the fast oval at Atlanta Motor Speedway. When we flew over it, I saw a little cemetery between the airport and the track.

"There's a gravesite next to the track!" I exclaimed.

"Yeah, that's where the guys end up who don't make it through Turn 1," Bobby said.

That's just the type of guy Bobby was: quick-witted and almost always good for a laugh.

I would think: "Oh, God, don't let me end up there!"

Bobby did try to help me on short tracks, where admittedly I faced several challenges. I grew up on long, winding road courses that had left and right turns and were typically two-to-four miles in length. When I got on a short, half-mile oval, it was like a completely new experience. The techniques I had accumulated over the years just didn't apply to this type of a track and proved to be detrimental: I always over drove these bullrings. I never backed off the brake when going into the turn to let the truck's suspension work. I always tried to hustle the truck too much by carrying speed too deep into the turn.

Bobby would chastise me for my driving technique on short tracks during testing.

"You're always driving it too deep into the corner—until you see God." He said. "These things don't work that way. They can't turn on a dime. They're 3,400 pounds. It's not a 2,800-pound sports car with big tires and big brakes. This thing's got a small tire with small brakes, and it's heavy. You can't drive it that deep into the corner, stand it on its nose, and expect it to turn."

I heard the message. And I tried to follow it. But that method never became second nature to me. If I felt pressure from somebody catching up to me on the track, I always reverted back to my old ways and ended up driving in too deep. I was my own worst enemy sometimes. At that time, I simply couldn't rewire my innate impulses, not even with my teammate's help.

The team focused on three primary areas: testing, developing the trucks as a result of testing, and racing. We went testing (practicing) as a team, and all of us contributed to enhancing the performance of the trucks by trying various parts and mechanical approaches.

The testing program really helped me get much-needed seat time in unfamiliar vehicles on tracks that were new to me. It was a steep learning curve, but I wanted to be fast in testing and I usually achieved that goal. Testing helped my crew chief learn how to set up the truck to suit my driving characteristics.

I didn't really like just running a lot of consecutive laps—a problem for me that I didn't recognize initially.

I thought, "Okay, let's go fast, try different things, and see if I can go faster."

We never really focused on long runs. To my detriment, I just wanted to run the fastest single lap possible and didn't push for the consecutive lap sequences that would simulate race conditions. The other drivers really never did long run tests, either. The emphasis fell on finding speed by running short stints in testing and developing the trucks mechanically.

Because of the experience they had, my teammates and their crew chiefs could better anticipate what might happen to their vehicles over the course of a long green-flag stint during a race or over the entire length of a race. What I didn't fully understand was how much the balance of the truck changed as the fuel load burned off. The handling characteristics also changed due to more rubber being put down on the track surface or a change in prevailing conditions, such as cloud cover or temperatures dropping at night. The varying demands put on the truck's suspension when racing also caused the handling to change over the course of a race.

Other drivers that I raced against were often aloof in their interactions with me off of the track, but they were aggressive on the track. I believe more yellow caution flags were waved because of my being spun out than any other driver that year. I was the prime target on the course. How it worked was another driver would come up behind the left rear corner of my truck and lightly push it with the front right corner of their truck. At those speeds, and already being on the edge of grip, the smallest nudge forces the vehicle to lose control and spin out. No matter how seasoned the driver, if you are rubbed in that way, you're spinning.

There is a saying: "Rubbin' is racing." As long as you aren't trying to hurt the other driver or destroy their car, it is perfectly legal and an acceptable practice. Many rookies have their merit tested when they first start. It is universally felt that rookies need to earn their place and prove themselves. That year, I was the obvious target. I wasn't from a legacy racing family. I didn't come up racing on dirt tracks in the South like they had. I was a middle-aged, black college graduate from California who was invading their territory, and my competitors didn't hide their contempt. But I kept my wits about me and continued to race as hard as I could, hoping to eventually win their approval and respect. Thankfully, none of the other drivers were outwardly rude toward me. By the same token, I couldn't consider many of them friends.

My results showed improvement during my first full season in 2002. I qualified eight times in the Top 10 and four of those Top 10 starts came in my last six races. But I had trouble maintaining my pace over a long stint. I usually had my truck running when the checkered flag fell, but only finished three of twenty-two races on the lead lap. I was up against guys who had been oval racing pretty much their whole lives. Together, these drivers and crew chiefs knew how to set up a truck for longer runs before the races started. They also knew far better than me what chassis adjustments were needed during a race and at what point they needed to make them.

For me, it was usually a matter of running a few strong laps, then fighting with the truck for balance once its handling began to fade.

"Just bring it back to me, and we'll make some adjustments on our next pit stop," the crew chief would say over the radio.

The changes to the track surface and behind the wheel of the truck were so dynamic. I didn't have the experience to know how to process all these variables and determine what I needed at a given track at a given time of day. Although circle tracks look fairly similar, they were all very different. Trying to conquer them was like feeling my way around in the dark. I gained respect, not only by how well I qualified on the fast tracks, but by often running in the front pack early in races. Unfortunately, I wasn't always able to sustain my speed and position, and there wasn't much advice being offered to me on how to remedy this problem. I found this situation of falling back in races extremely frustrating.

My second season at BHR showed improvement. I qualified in the Top 10 eight times and ran the fastest lap during qualifying on the 1.5-mile track in Charlotte. In doing so, I made history as the first black driver to win a NASCAR Truck Series pole position. I also finished on the lead lap seven times. But despite the fact that I was close on several occasions, I only managed to achieve one Top 10 race result.

I continued to make history that year when I became the first African American driver and first Truck Series driver to appear on a cereal box. I was completely caught off guard when Scott Hayes, the representative from General Mills, approached me with this once in a lifetime opportunity. Scott was in charge of the brand strategy for Honey Nut Cheerios. He was at the track one afternoon and approached me to ask if I would be interested in forming a Personal Services Agreement (PSA) relationship with Cheerios.

A PSA meant that I would sport the Honey Nut Cheerios branding on my suit and polo shirt and appear on the front of the cereal box along with my truck. It's different than a typical sponsorship agreement because they did not put much money toward my race vehicle and only occasionally sported their logo on the Truck. But it was fantastic exposure for me, which I hoped would lead to more sponsors and opportunities down the road.

There are only a handful of athletes who have had the honor of being on a cereal box. I was touched that, out of all of the drivers they could have selected, they were interested in me. Cheerios is one of the biggest cereals brands that has ever existed and they literally could have chosen anyone, but they chose me. It might also be fair to assume that this was a rare example where being the lone black driver in the sport proved to be an advantage. Whatever their reasons, it didn't matter to me. Honey Nut Cheerios was already a staple in my household, so it was a perfect pairing that I was proud to be a part of. I was elated and gladly jumped at the offer.

Once the cereal box hit grocery store shelves, I was eager to see it displayed. As I walked down the cereal isle of my local Walmart, I noticed that there was a middle-aged, African American woman standing there holding a cereal box. She was studying the box closely. As I got closer, I realized that it was my Honey Nut Cheerios box and she was looking at me!

With a mischievous grin, I hurried my pace and stopped right next to her. Standing shoulder to shoulder with this woman, I joined her gaze and looked at the box in her hand. She must've been wondering what kind of a person would stand so close to a complete stranger because she quickly retracted her arms defensively, as if I might take her cereal.

The look on her face bounced back and forth between surprise and confusion. She looked at me, then down at the box, then back up to me, and then back to the box again. I can only imagine what was going through her head at that moment: *Had the person on the package magically leapt out into real life?*

Finally, she gasped, pointing at the picture of me smiling in my red racing suit.

"That's you!" she exclaimed.

I couldn't help letting out a laugh as I nodded in agreement.

"Would you like me to autograph that for you?"

She definitely didn't know who I was, but she was excited that some sort of "celebrity" was having some fun with her.

"Yes, please. Oh my goodness. This is crazy! Nobody's going to believe this. Here I am shopping and minding my own business and then this man comes out of nowhere and happens to be on the very box that I'm holding!"

We both had a good laugh. I happened to have a Sharpie pen in my pocket—maybe a small part of me hoped that this very situation may arise—and I happily signed her box with my name and the number eight. I wonder if she still has that box.

To my pleasant surprise, Honey Nut Cheerios extended my contract for the following year as well. Being privileged enough to grace the cover of one of the most well-known cereal boxes twice is one of the highlights of my life.

During that year, I decided to take the cross-country trip with my hauler driver in his eighteen-wheel tractor-trailer. At the professional level, typically the drivers would fly to the races and let the truck drivers transport their cars from track to track, but I wanted to immerse myself in all aspects of racing. It was an experience like no other: I ate and showered at truck stops, I got to listen to the communications on the CB radio between truckers and learn their lingo, and I was able to bond with my hauler driver and form a friendship that would last years after I completed my run with Bobby's team. But not everyone was as welcoming of me as he was.

My teammates and crew members at BDR were all accustomed to a different way of life than I was. Many of them had grown up on farms with vast acreages and rolling fields. I was from a suburb of Oakland, and I was as close to a "city boy" as they had ever seen.

It was important for me to try to build relationships with them. We came from such different backgrounds, but I wanted to bridge the gap in our differences and fit in with the guys. There was a definite learning curve when it came to understanding their dialect and local slang, which sometimes made it tricky to keep up with. During everyday conversations, I often found myself completely clueless as to what they were saying.

There was one afternoon when I was sitting outside the shop on a picnic bench eating lunch with a few of the other guys. I was unpacking an apple and a sandwich from a paper bag when I heard a few of the other guys at the next table discussing something that caught my attention.

“So, I don’t know what the hell is wrong with this Cub Cadet. I’ll be damned if it won’t run right for more than a minute before shutting down!” Chris said. He was one of the mechanics on my team, and a guy I had not gotten a chance to know well.

“You make sure you’re running the choke until it’s completely warmed up?” Dale asked.

My curiosity was piqued. I had no idea what they were talking about, so I leaned over toward their table.

“What are you guys talking about?” I asked incredulously.

Both men stopped chewing and looked at me like I was from another planet.

“My Cub Cadet!” Chris repeated louder, as if he was sure I merely hadn’t heard him.

“What in the world is that?” I asked.

Chris and Dale both looked at each other in confusion.

“Are you serious man? It’s a riding mower.” Dale explained.

Chris let out a loud belly laugh. “Ol’ Yankee Bill don’t know what a Cub Cadet is! I guess they don’t have grass in California. But down here, you can’t maintain thirty acres of field with a regular old push mower.”

“Ha!” I exclaimed, “I guess you can’t. I’ve just never heard that name before.”

“You guys have soda out there, but down here we call it a Coke.” said Chris, taking a bite into his sandwich. “I’ll bet you don’t know what flat meat is, either.” He said through a mouth full of ham and cheese.

"Flat meat? Sounds like something you guys ran over out on the street." I blurted out jokingly.

Chris pointed down at a piece of ham that was dangling out from between the wedges of bread. "Flat meat: Ham, salami, roast beef, turkey . . . you know, lunch meat!"

"Oh. You mean cold cuts!" I said, excited that I was able to figure out the translation.

"Yeah, yeah, city boy. Cold cuts. But 'round here, we call it flat meat."

Living in the South was a bit of a culture shock for me. Many times, it really did feel like we were speaking completely different languages.

Sometimes I went out to Cracker Barrel with the guys for breakfast before a long day at the track. Some of them were vulgar and derogatory when they would talk about women. I was not accustomed to dudes so casually referring to women in such harsh terms, but I kept quiet for the sake of not rocking the boat; however, it was the blatant, racially charged jokes that they told in my presence that were the most disturbing. The "n-word" came out of their mouth with unsettling frequency, without any regard for that fact that they were in the company of a black man. They weren't directing the word at me (not to my face anyway), but they were so cavalier about using the most abhorrent, racist word in the English vocabulary. Their lack of remorse spoke volumes of how little they respected me, if at all. It was shocking to say the least, and unbelievably uncomfortable. I had never been a situation before where a white man had used that word so naturally.

I am always down for a laugh, but these guys would take it too far. Sometimes they would realize what they had said and would unapologetically say something like, "No offense, Bill."

No offense. They thought that by saying those two words they were granting themselves immunity. By saying, "no offense" they thought they were impervious to a negative reaction from me, no matter how disgusting the words they spit were. They didn't even try to imagine how their words affected me. Perhaps they could convince themselves that it was just a joke and they weren't really bigots if they used the get-out-of-jail-free words afterward. But really, I think it's that they just didn't care what they said, how they said it, or who they offended. They showed their true colors in those moments and I saw them loud and clear. But I couldn't help but wonder, if that is what they were willing to say in my presence, what were they saying behind my back?

The problem was that my life was in their hands. They were the ones working on my truck, fitting it with safety equipment, and ensuring that it was running properly so I didn't go spinning into a wall at 180 mph, and if I did, that I was going to live to see another day. One wrong twist of their wrench, and I could end up as a blood stain. These were not people who I wanted to piss off or pick a fight with. I was in no position to effect change other than being who I was, where I was. This was years before the Black Lives Matter movement. There was no HR department to file a complaint with. There was no media to garner support from. This was just how it was, and I was realizing that many members of my crew were racist. I was expected to deal with it, or leave, which might have also suited them fine. But I would not do that.

It became obvious that some guys in the team didn't expect me to win. Only after the season ended did I learn that BHR did not develop and update my truck chassis like the crew did for my teammates' trucks. I was told—on good authority from a crew member whom I was close to—that my truck didn't get some of the upgrades that the others received. I was informed that the crew would come back to the shop later in the evening to make modifications and upgrades on the other trucks, but they did not perform them on mine.

I don't care how good of a driver you are, if you don't have the right equipment, you can't win, or, in my case, improve. My teammates' crews were improving their vehicles, so for me to be the one driver without those key modifications or components meant I was being set up to fail. I may have been factory-sponsored when it came to financing, but my Dodge truck did not get equal treatment. My truck had the nice shiny paint job but, underneath the skin, it didn't have everything that was necessary to be fully competitive. Paint doesn't win races. Drivers win races and cars win races. I am only able to bring one of those aspects to the table; I had assumed that my team would fulfill their end of our partnership and provide me with everything needed to be successful, especially if that's what they were providing for the rest of the team. It's unfortunate that they deliberately hindered my chances of winning, and only *my* chances, and conveniently omitted it from our conversations.

I had heard disparaging remarks from many team members surrounding their 2001 season with Willy and how relieved they were when he left, but Willy's race craft had been on the decline. He was no longer in his prime. I was driving considerably better and had greater future potential. Bobby saw that. I had also made a sincere effort to befriend the guys on my team. Willy was a known brawler while I always tried to get along with everyone and anyone, having always been conflict averse. I didn't anticipate the same sentiment from my team would follow me. I thought I would win the team over. I was wrong.

It was only after the program ended that I found out the level of disdain many in the BHR team had for me. I had one close friend who was appalled by what he witnessed and felt compelled to tell me. One evening, some crew members—though I was not told how many or exactly which ones—partook in burning a doll of my likeness in effigy. Specifically, they took a lawn jockey, one of those patently offensive yard decorations of a small black man, painted it red with the number eight (my truck's number) on it, and set fire to it in front of the shop. They torched it. Hearing that this group of white men had the audacity to set flames to a black doll that resembled me made me sick to my stomach. That grotesque act confirmed that the diversity program's effort to include drivers of color was not going to be accepted by all of the teams. I'm sure there were crews out there who would never have condoned my team's disgraceful actions, but unfortunately that was not my experience.

I never found out if Bobby Hamilton participated in the burning of the lawn jockey. I'd like to think that he didn't, but I have my suspicions to the contrary. Bobby's no longer with us, so I suppose I'll never really know for sure. I ended up with a lot of animosity toward him though, especially after he began to build a larger race shop during the season. I wondered how much of my Dodge sponsorship went into funding that building. Bobby could be funny, engaging, and instructive about racing, especially about how to drive on short ovals, but he wasn't the best guy around. He was not necessarily known for being the most trustworthy individual, either. I surely didn't get the level of support I deserved from him or his team.

I learned the same lesson that Wendell Scott learned over the course of his entire career: not everyone in NASCAR was going to welcome a black man, especially if they felt he could win. Black men dominated in sports like football, baseball, and basketball, but racing was still a white man's sport, and they weren't relinquishing their grasp on it without contention. Anyone who looked different was treated differently. Diversity was a battle that was clearly being fought off of the track.

■ ■ ■

RACING TO THE FRONT

My experience at Bobby Hamilton Racing taught me about maintaining focus. It wasn't until after I had moved to Bill Davis Racing that I learned about the deliberate efforts by certain members of the BHR team to undermine my racing success. But once aware of this, and the unceremonious demonstration that represented the end of the No. 8 team, I didn't let it slow me down or deter me. I shook it off because I refused to give them the satisfaction of knowing that they affected me. I remained focused on my *passion* and the goal ahead and continued to conduct myself as a professional in pursuit of Victory Lane, optimistic that better fortunes lay ahead.

Sometimes it's easy to take your passion for granted until a reality check arrives that truly tests conviction.

13

Toyota Transition

After leaving Bobby Hamilton Racing and Dodge, I moved to Bill Davis Racing (BDR) and Toyota. BDR was a step forward, where I enjoyed a more supportive environment.

At the outset, I had to prove myself with a tryout, once again, to land the job with BDR. I got that opportunity after meeting Jim Press, the president of Toyota Motor Sales, USA, at an annual awards program in Detroit. Hosted by *African-Americans on Wheels*, a magazine geared toward a black readership that covered street cars, the auto industry, and racing, I felt it an honor to be a part of the proceedings.

NASCAR President Mike Helton accepted an award for NASCAR's diversity efforts and I was there along with fellow NASCAR driver Kyle Busch to present it to him. Out of sheer luck, I was seated next to Toyota USA's president. I knew I needed a new place to race in 2004, and had admired Toyota's prior success in sports car racing, so I introduced myself to Jim.

"Hello. My name is Bill Lester and I raced for Dodge in the NASCAR Truck Series," I said. "I understand Toyota is coming into NASCAR."

"You're right. We are. I'm Jim Press," he responded cordially.

I had nothing to lose and everything to gain by inquiring about a position on his team.

"Would you consider me as a driver for Toyota in the Truck Series?"

"Well, that's not really my responsibility, but I can put you in touch with the person who makes those decisions," he replied.

Toyota had decided to start competing in NASCAR with a Truck Series program and would later step up to the Cup Series in 2007. Press put me in contact with Jim Aust, the head of Toyota Motorsports.

Jim called and we had a preliminary conversation on the phone, but I didn't really know if they were interested in moving forward with me. It wasn't long before my phone rang again. This time, it was Mike Brown, general manager of BDR, with an invitation to test one of their trucks on a short track in Lakeland, Florida. After already having had two full seasons in truck competition with BHR, I tested well enough to become part of Toyota's first season in the NASCAR Truck Series in 2004 with BDR. I landed on my feet and was both excited and relieved to know my racing career would continue.

Many NASCAR fans were apprehensive, fearful, and just plain bitter about a Japanese manufacturer coming into the domain of the Big Three US manufacturers. As I had already learned during my stint with Bobby's team, the NASCAR community was not a very welcoming bunch and didn't take kindly to outsiders. But this time, it was the fans who were making the most defamatory statements.

"Nobody wants to see those rice burners race," I heard one spectator say in an interview. The sentiment among most spectators was acutely pro-American.

But I was jazzed when I first heard Toyota was coming and then very happy to be racing with the company and BDR. NASCAR had been comprised of the same manufacturers with drivers of virtually the same ethnicity since its inception, and it was about time that they shook things up a little bit and broadened their constituency. The exclusive bubble that had been racing for the last fifty-five years needed to burst, and I was thrilled to be able to partake in pushing the boundaries on more than one front.

During this timeframe, Toyota Motorsports had been very successful in the United States, winning IMSA championships in prototype racing and winning the Indy 500 in open-wheel competition. Toyota had also been racing in Europe for several decades and it was the natural next step for them to expand into NASCAR. Toyota had the technology, expertise, and budget (based on tremendous US passenger car sales) needed to be successful. I was excited about them bringing those capacities to NASCAR, because I believed they would be winners, and I wanted to be a part of it.

Bill Davis, who had been a longtime Cup competitor and a winner of the Daytona 500, had three separate operations in High Point, North Carolina. He had a long-established headquarters for the Cup program, a newly established truck shop across the street, and a separate engine-building operation across town.

Bill did everything first-class. He had fresh parts and pieces on the truck each time we raced. Bobby Hamilton had done everything at the level of a Truck Series team owner, whereas Bill Davis did everything at the level of a Cup Series team owner. At BHR, truck components had been left on the vehicles and raced for as long as possible, whereas at BDR they were frequently replaced. Whether it was a new chassis, body, or items like brakes, wheels, and suspension pieces, everything at BDR was first-class for each race.

Bill Davis was an imposing figure who carried some extra weight and stood well over six feet tall, but he was a gentle giant. He was reserved and quiet and did not directly interact much with his teams—especially his Truck teams—and even less with me. I never felt as if I had a chance to really get to know Bill. I was never at ease around him. When we spoke, I thought twice about every word I said. Though his office occupied part of the Cup shop that sat directly across the street from the Truck shop, Bill rarely came over to see what was going on or talk with the crew. His directives were always executed by one of his general managers. In fact, when I would visit the Cup shop, I hardly ever saw him outside of his office. Bill was the kind of guy who listened a lot but only spoke when he really had something to say. I never knew what he was thinking or how he really felt about me.

While the Truck program had its own shop and administration, we followed the same processes and procedures as the Cup program. But whenever I went across the street to the Cup shop, I was still awed by the fluidity and magnitude of their operation. There was twice the footprint compared to the Truck program in terms of size and expense. It was a well-oiled machine: Everything was managed more meticulously and with greater care than any other shop I had ever seen. All their people, managers, and offices were remarkably organized and everything on the shop floor was kept fastidiously clean. It was the nicest shop I had seen at that point in my racing career.

My Truck program, unfortunately, was underfunded. Toyota provided engines, technology, and parts for my truck, but BDR and I had to make up the remaining operational budget by finding sponsorship.

Ironically, I had experienced the opposite scenario at BHR, where I had a huge budget from Dodge, but then again, I am not convinced all of that money went into improving me as a driver or into my truck. By fully funding my truck, Dodge stated that diversity and inclusion were important to the sport, and they called the bluffs of other corporations both inside and outside of NASCAR who also dared to share the same sentiment but failed to back up their words with action. Few companies other than Dodge came to the table. No one else was willing to put significant money where their mouth was. After three years, the Dodge diversity program had run its course.

When Toyota began its efforts to participate in NASCAR, the sanctioning body decided to work closely with the Japanese company, perhaps with the failings of the Dodge experience in mind. From 2004 to 2006, most of the sponsors that appeared on my Toyota truck while I competed for BDR resulted from NASCAR's efforts to encourage its corporate partners to back its diversity program. Toyota may have been spending huge sums on its Truck program in preparation for the move into the Cup Series in 2007, but it was mostly parts and pieces, not direct cash infusions to its supported teams.

My truck entries were kept afloat mainly through NASCAR's efforts to help Toyota keep me behind the wheel. NASCAR would contact management among the corporations participating at the Cup level. Many of those companies wanted to also be official sponsors of NASCAR and the NASCAR executives used that as leverage. They would insist that in order to be an official sponsor of NASCAR, the sponsor had to peel off some of their Cup-level spending to support their diversity efforts. NASCAR took an alternate approach with existing official NASCAR sponsors and convinced them that some of their general funding should be diverted into diversity efforts. I didn't care what method they enacted as long as sponsorship support appeared on my truck so I could race. If I could just get to the track, I knew I would not disappoint.

It made sense to many of the sponsors to oblige this direction from NASCAR. The US Army backed me. SunTrust Bank, Allstate insurance, and

Checkers & Rally's restaurants were other companies whose paint schemes adorned my truck. They all did a great deal of business in the minority community. In addition, Hot Tamales, Husqvarna, Office Depot, and Old Spice made guest appearances. On my end, I would perform typical driver obligations to help the sponsor promote its brand, such as appearing at special events off the track and in hospitality areas at the track prior to races. One of my favorite sponsors was the Crown Royal whiskey brand. They supplied me with several cases of their product and a uniquely designed purple driving suit that I am still particularly fond of.

This relationship between NASCAR, Toyota, BDR, the corporate sponsors, and me benefited all of us. We were helping NASCAR reach some of the stated goals of its newly created Drive for Diversity program, which included having more minorities competing behind the wheel, creating a more diverse fan base, and increasing participation of minorities on race teams, in the offices of the sponsors, and in the sanctioning body itself.

At BDR, while no expense was spared on the preparation of the trucks, there was not enough operating budget to further my development as a driver through testing. However, another tier was added to Toyota's commitment when it came to winning races—as expected from a company with a proud motor sports history. Former Cup Series drivers Johnny Benson Jr. and Mike Skinner were hired and arrived midway into the 2004 season.

Mike drove trucks fully funded by Toyota and its Tundra truck brand, not surprisingly, since he had already won sixteen truck races for Chevrolet before arriving at BDR. His truck carried a regular Toyota white, orange, and black color scheme that was decorated with fiery flames along both sides, whereas my truck was sometimes plain white, except for my number in red. Johnny's truck would often be adorned with a Toyota scheme, although a battery sponsor and Toyota-affiliated XM Satellite Radio more regularly occupied signage on his truck. I think they both were allotted more truck testing than I was, but I can only speculate, since I was living in Atlanta and commuted to High Point only if they needed me. They definitely received more direct support from Toyota than I did. Even if I did not experience a deficit with testing, my relative lack of racing experience compared to them remained a disadvantage for me.

In my first season, I had an outstanding crew chief in Jeff Hensley. Jeff arrived at BDR the same time I did. A member of the Hensley family from southern Virginia, which had long been competing in oval racing and NASCAR, Jeff was a variation of a good ol' boy. Although deeply steeped in NASCAR racing tradition, he surprisingly didn't speak with a heavy Southern accent. Jeff was all business and didn't waste much time goofing around. I liked him and had tremendous respect for him and how much he helped me.

Sometimes Jeff would call me Bill, but most of the time I was "Hoss." He would often tell me—just like Bobby Hamilton had—that I overdrove the corners on the short tracks. Granted, I still had trouble there, but I was very good on the one-and-a-half-mile intermediate-length tracks and on the super-speedways when it came to finding speed. These fast tracks were my comfort zone.

Jeff imparted his experience and wisdom regarding how to race the trucks over the course of the season. All his efforts were directed toward giving me the best truck he possibly could. Unfortunately, BDR and Toyota were both new to the Truck Series and Toyota was new to NASCAR, so that first year we didn't produce many successful qualifying or racing outcomes, even after Mike and Johnny joined the team. NASCAR was keen to not let a brand-new manufacturer to the series come in and dominate it, and ensured that the rules under which Toyota competed reflected that.

Prior to the start of the 2005 season, Jeff moved over to Mike Skinner's truck and it was decided that the new chief, Doug Wolcott, would work with me. This was a management decision that was likely made to shake things up a bit. I had reservations about this decision that led to subsequent anxiety. I was apprehensive about making this major change, especially since I had built such a great rapport with Jeff. However, I soon enjoyed working with Doug, a former NASCAR Modified Series driver himself, and we built a strong bond. In our first year together, he led the crew that fielded the trucks I drove to back-to-back pole positions at the intermediate speedways in Kansas and Kentucky. Winning the pole position means you ran the fastest time in the qualifying session, which awards you the best starting position in the actual race. It gives you a clear advantage over the other drivers. You don't have to worry about overtaking anyone for the lead. You start at the front of the field. Winning the pole position two races in a row is an impressive feat, but unfortunately, it does not guarantee that you can sustain the lead in the race.

Trucks handle differently in qualifying configuration than in the race itself. The way the truck is set up for the two events is also not the same. Since qualifying is only comprised of two laps, there is less fuel in the truck, which changes the weight distribution and therefore affects the handling balance. Also, during qualifying, the radiator grill is often duct-taped closed. You couldn't do this during the race because the motor would overheat, but for a couple qualifying laps, it's perfectly fine and helps the truck's performance. By sealing off the radiator air, you are producing less drag in the truck because you're allowing less air to go into the engine compartment. Instead, the air flows over the truck, making it more streamlined and creating more downforce. These adjustments maximize the truck's handling during qualifying, but make it very different from how it handles in the race itself, with the tape removed and a full fuel load. So, despite the fact that I performed extremely well in qualifying, the team and I weren't able to adjust enough to the handling of the truck in race trim to maintain the lead in either race.

In the Kentucky race specifically, my truck sank through the field like a stone right after the green flag dropped. That's how poorly it was handling. I kept getting passed and never recovered. When Doug and I had the fastest Toyota truck in qualifying at those two tracks, it didn't seem to bother my former crew chief Jeff Hensley. But it did seem to agitate Mike Skinner. As a former Truck Series champion, and as one of the two designated Toyota factory drivers, he was expected to be at the front in qualifying and in the race.

I came closest to a Truck Series victory in 2005 at the Nashville Superspeedway. The team had begun to learn how to transition from our two-lap qualifying setup to our distinctly different race setup in order to accommodate my driving style, and I was ready to take on this event. David Reutimann, who drove for Darrell Waltrip's Toyota team, was also looking for his first win in the Truck Series. David Reutimann, Mike Skinner, and I spent the majority of the race fighting for the lead. And what a fight it was.

Nearing the finish, with only seven laps to go, Skinner was running in first place when Tracy Hines spun out and wrecked, leaving debris and oil on the track. As Skinner went into Turn 3 of that lap, his right tires drove over the oil, causing him to slide sideways up the track and scrape against the wall. With the field now under caution, I drove up alongside Skinner's truck and radioed to my crew that his front fender was pushed in, which can severely affect the car's downforce and handling. That message was then relayed to his team. Skinner had not had a win in nine years and had just one NASCAR Craftsman Truck Series title from back in 1995. He was determined to keep chasing first place, even if it meant having to take bigger chances and fighting even more aggressively to make up for his truck's damaged body work.

After the caution laps were completed and the track was cleared, we were back to top speed, racing for the finish. There were three Toyotas out in front. Skinner was holding first place, Dave Reutimann was in second, and I was in third, but Reutimann was challenging Skinner's claim on the victory. With the damage to Skinner's car, it was becoming evident that he was not going to be able to hang on to the lead, and I was in a strong position to fight for the front.

It was only moments later that Ricky Craven, who was in a three-wide battle through Turn 4 further back in the field, spun out, causing the ninth caution flag of the race, which was a record for the Nashville Superspeedway. The two trucks that had gotten under Craven (on the inside of him) had taken the turn too wide, forcing him onto the dirty line and causing him to lose control. You never want to go into a turn on an intermediate-length track like Nashville with three trucks side by side, because there's not enough room. It's a recipe for disaster.

My adrenaline was pumping and tension was mounting with every caution that kept me further away from the finish line. Having to keep pausing so close to the end, when I was fighting for a possible win, was frustrating. All I wanted to do was stay focused and maintain momentum to the checkered flag.

The green flag waved again and we were back underway. There were only three laps left to go as Reutimann continued to run the inside of the track. The inside line is typically the fastest way through the turn and is almost always the most advantageous. Gaining the inside line is where drivers are the most likely to overtake one another. Reutimann got inside and pulled up alongside of Skinner as we went down the back stretch and briefly managed to pass him, but Skinner regained the advantage by driving deep into Turn 3. However, he overdrove his truck and slid up the track, allowing Reutimann to become the new leader. They were nose to nose coming off Turn 4, and I was riding right behind them, hoping to establish the inside line to pass them both.

As we were about to pass the white flag, indicating that we were going into the last lap, I was looking to move into second place. After following him briefly, I dove to the left of Skinner on the inside line to get under him. But he wasn't having it. Skinner drove down to the bottom of the track in an attempt to block me and forced me onto the track apron.

The apron is the flat part of the track before the banking begins. You can drive on the apron if you have to, but you have to be careful if you race or pass on it because it's usually dirty and there's no banking, and without the banking, you don't have as much control. You can easily end up spinning out, but when another driver is trying to aggressively cut you off, sometimes you have no choice but to drive down onto the apron to avoid an incident.

This was the start of the last lap of the race and, despite Skinner's move, I wasn't lifting. Fortunately, I did not lose any momentum on the apron and was able to continue to fight Skinner for second entering Turn 1. Reutimann now had a commanding lead. The likelihood that Skinner or I were going to catch him, let alone pass him in the short amount of time we had left, was slim. Neither of us was in a position to win the race, yet Skinner was still driving like there was no tomorrow. He wanted to at least keep second place.

I managed to pass Skinner for second entering Turn 1, but we both ran wide in the center of the turn and Ted Musgrave, who had been lurking behind me for a couple of laps, also passed Skinner. Coming off Turn 2, Musgrave drove to the inside line and pulled up alongside me so that we were side by side going down the back straight for the last time. With Musgrave taking the inside line, I was moved up closer to the wall. Musgrave and I were two trucks racing side by side heading to Turn 3 when Skinner used our draft and dove down to the very inside of the track and pulled up next to us. We were now three-wide going into Turn 3. Skinner was carrying too much speed to keep the inside line and make the turn without crashing into us. You can't take the turns at full throttle at this track and maintain the same level of control as you can on the straightaway. You have to ease up in order to negotiate the turn. To Musgrave's credit, he saw that Skinner was going too fast and backed out of the throttle, otherwise Skinner would have harpooned him in the side. If one of us didn't relinquish our line we were going to crash, the same way Craven had just done, and Skinner clearly wasn't about to. With Musgrave relenting, that left just me in Skinner's sights. His excessive speed entering the corner forced his line to widen, and since I didn't want to get hit, it forced me to adjust my line, pushing me up into the dirty outside part of the track where I quickly lost momentum.

Skinner's banzai move proved pointlessly brazen and dangerous, particularly since none of us were legitimately vying for the win at that point. Reutimann was gone. Skinner had completed his pass and gotten ahead of me, but because he had gone so far up the track, he'd allowed two other drivers to pass us. The time it took me to get back on the racing line and regain speed cost me two more positions at the finish. Skinner dropped to fourth and my truck fell back to seventh place.

Near the end of a NASCAR race, there are no rules, and a driver must learn to anticipate how other drivers will race under those circumstances, and it can get grimy. Skinner was determined to take second place at any cost, even if it meant pushing his teammate down onto the apron or risking a crash in a three-car battle through a turn. It showed a clear lack of respect for me, so in turn, I lost a lot of respect for him.

My first truck win was so close, yet so far. I never would have dreamed that my biggest adversary would be my own teammate. I learned the hard way how Skinner raced in the closing laps and vowed to meet his aggressive style of racing next time so that it would never happen again. In any other sport, teammates display camaraderie, support each other, collaborate, work with one another, build each other up, and take turns in the spotlight all in an attempt to bring the entire team to a unified victory. But in racing, even among teammates, it's every man for himself. In so many ways, the sport is Darwinian: the survival of the fittest. If thirty-six guys are starting a truck race, thirty-five of them are destined to be losers. There can be only one winner, and the closer you get to the finish line, the more animalistic the behavior. The claws come out and it doesn't matter whose back they sink into, as long as it results in a ride down Victory Lane.

Racing is a crazy sport, isn't it?

■ ■ ■

RACING TO THE FRONT

It's often said in racing that you have to learn how to race at the front before you learn how to win.

While I had led races on numerous occasions, I was definitely out of my *comfort zone* racing at the front of the field near the end of a NASCAR race for the first time. I got there after a lifetime of pursuing my *passion*, but that wasn't enough. I got close to winning, but learned the hard way about competing against one of my teammates. Despite not getting the win, this race gave me more confidence and confirmed I had what it took to win in NASCAR, but everything had to line up perfectly for that to happen.

Getting out of one's comfort zone is a learning process that does not come easily or naturally.

14

Preparing for 2006

There are three national touring series within NASCAR: the Cup Series, which demands the highest budget in order to compete and hosts the largest audience and number of races; the Xfinity Series, which requires the second-highest budget and number of races run; and the Truck Series, which needs the lowest budget for the least number of races. I was ready to fish in a bigger pond. I decided to pursue my Cup Series ambitions for the 2006 season. When I'd gotten into racing, my goal had always been to compete at the top against the best drivers, and I wasn't getting any younger. I now was forty-four years old, and didn't have any more time to waste. I had to find a way to move up to the top level, but there were going to be obstacles to overcome first.

The sponsorship budget for the Cup Series far exceeded that of the Truck Series that I had been racing in up to that point. Since the day I'd decided to race on an actual track, as opposed to street racing, I had struggled with the dilemma of how to procure enough sponsorship to secure a race car and a team. Virtually all drivers have to overcome this hurdle during their careers, but because I was not the typical race car driver, I found it even more difficult. I had "only" needed to secure roughly $3.5 million of funding in the Truck Series, but the Cup Series required a sponsorship budget of roughly $20 million. Mind-blowing, I know!

My relationship with Toyota was not as strong as I would've liked. I had not won yet, and I could not close the performance gap between myself and my teammates, Mike Skinner and Johnny Benson. It was likely that continued financial backing for the upcoming 2006 season might not be forthcoming from Toyota.

I put a substantial amount of pressure on myself to drive hard and bring home results, but I may have shot myself in the foot in the process. Charlotte Motor Speedway was a track that I gravitated toward because of how well I consistently performed on intermediate-length tracks. When it came time for qualifying, I didn't just want to qualify for the race; I wanted to hit it out of the park and start out the weekend by nailing the pole position.

I had been known to thrive at Charlotte, having won the pole here in 2003, and was considered a strong contender in the field. The crew was really looking forward to this event on the calendar and there was a lot of excitement within the whole team, including those members who remained back at the shop. I wanted to make everyone proud and bring home pole position in qualifying and a win in the actual race.

Charlotte is home court, the unofficial headquarters of NASCAR, where almost every race team is based, so the grandstands brim with their families and friends in addition to the heightened spectator numbers. Bill Davis was there along with plenty of his friends and associates, who were eager to see three of his trucks race.

When my turn for qualifying came, I was primed and ready to go. Once on the track, in my fervor to start the race at the front, I pushed the truck hard—harder than I should have. The truck lost rear grip coming off the corner and I wasn't able to save it. I lost control as I sped off of Turn 4, causing me to spin out. As soon as I felt the rear of the truck begin to slide, I knew it was over.

When you have more than a full field of trucks entered for a race, if you wreck or spin out, you fail to qualify and thus fail to make the race.

My overzealous ambitions had worked against me. I'd been so hell-bent on capturing the pole that I had lost sight of the bigger picture, making the race, and it had cost me dearly. I was disappointed in myself, but even more disappointed that I'd let my team and sponsor, SunTrust Bank, down.

Bill Davis's demeanor was no longer cool and indifferent. Though he didn't look angry, it was quite clear that he was not pleased that I had failed to qualify.

Bill rarely gave me the time of day, so when he approached me with a stern look on his face after qualifying ended, I knew I was in trouble.

"Bill, I'm sorry I messed up. I went too hard into the corner and didn't back off. I really wanted to get us the pole," I said quickly, trying to explain the obvious, apologize for my misstep, and diffuse any anger he might have had.

Bill was not interested in sharing sympathies with me.

"All you had to do was make the show. That was your only job today."

His words were few, but they cut like a knife because he was right. Instead of preparing for the race, I was watching my crew load my truck back onto the hauler, and I had no one to blame but myself. If I could have gone back and done it all over again, I would've done so in an instant.

It was slowly becoming evident that Bill Davis Racing was not going to continue our relationship going forward. I saw the writing on the wall and knew I had to make provisions for what that might mean for my career. I had no idea where the sponsorship would come from if I continued in the Truck Series, but I really had no clue where I was going to find sponsorship if I moved up the ranks to the Cup Series. It was a daunting task, but I was up for the challenge. My reprieve came with the help of Ardy Arani, president of Championship Group, a sports marketing firm based nearby in Atlanta.

I first met Ardy after he invited me to his office for a meeting. Since my race truck sometimes showed up stark white on the track, it was a clear indication there were sponsorship issues with my program. Ardy couldn't understand why I was struggling with funding. He said I had everything corporate America was looking for: I was educated, well-spoken, attractive, and had natural racing abilities, but he also knew that sponsors almost always supported the more successful drivers. It was a catch-22, really: It was hard to win without strong sponsor support—their money paid for the best personnel and performance parts—but sponsors weren't interested if you weren't winning. And you couldn't win if you couldn't race, and you couldn't race if you didn't have sponsors. Quite simply, money buys speed and the winning drivers typically have the most sponsor money.

Ardy was an upstanding guy who refused to believe that the color of my skin was the intangible barrier that was standing between me and the money I needed to race at the top level of NASCAR. Even though Toyota was behind my Truck team, and despite the statement Dodge had made with its diversity sponsorship of my truck, I never completely felt that corporate America could envision the NASCAR community spreading its wings and expanding its horizons enough to fully support a black driver. I was barely making it in NASCAR's Truck Series, and after what I had seen with Bobby Hamilton Racing, I had no illusions as to the reason why. My battle had been an uphill one since the moment I'd decided to enter into a sport that was dominated by white men. Talent alone was not enough, there were social norms working against me, but I was thankful for guys like Ardy who were willing to help pave a new path.

Ardy picked up the phone and invited me to his office because he wanted to figure out what the sponsorship issue was.

"I'd like to meet you in person to make sure you don't have two heads or something," he said, laughing.

I must've made a favorable impression with him that day because after we talked for a while, he was in my corner.

"Listen, Bill. We'd like to help. I have no interest in your Truck program but we'll see what we can do to move your Cup agenda forward."

I instantly liked Ardy. He had a great sense of humor, the gift of gab, and was extremely intelligent. He knew auto racing front to back and was clearly a successful marketer—as evidenced by the many examples of corporate promotional campaigns displayed around his office. He had everything he needed to assist me to get to the Cup level, including experience running corporate programs in the Olympic Games.

Ardy quickly made progress by leveraging my ongoing relationship with Waste Management, which had first backed my truck in 2004 at a race in Phoenix. Ardy teamed up with Carlton Yearwood, a black executive in charge of corporate affairs and diversity and inclusion at the company. Since Waste Management would be appearing on my Toyota truck six times in 2006, starting with the third race of the season in Atlanta, Ardy and Carlton pitched the company on leveraging this relationship with three Cup races in key markets that same year.

Waste Management already had a full-time program in the NASCAR Cup Series with the MB2 Motorsports team and driver Sterling Marlin, a two-time Daytona 500 winner. Jay Frye, the co-owner and manager of the MB2 team, and Sterling Marlin probably didn't like the idea of their sponsor spending money that would make the field even more competitive for them. Additional money almost always translates to increased speed in racing, so all drivers want their sponsor's money to go to their vehicle alone. The more money that goes to another car, the greater that car's chance of winning, and as I learned with my Toyota team, drivers can also be cutthroat. Racing is just as competitive off the track as it is on the track, and everybody in racing understands that. All participants use whatever competitive advantage they can to get ahead.

Getting this additional Cup program approved by Waste Management would be far from easy, but I had two strong proponents in my corner: Ardy would present his expertise and company's impressive track record as an outside consultant, and Carlton, with coaching from Ardy, would work as an advocate within the company.

Carlton didn't have the full budget in his own coffers and had to secure buy-in and utilize resources from other departments to make it all work. It wasn't as if he could unilaterally write a large check. He had to convince high-level executives and the president of Waste Management to spend money based on the value and exposure the company would receive. They would be making history that they could promote, capitalize on, and profit from. I would be the first African American driver to compete in the Cup Series—NASCAR's top series—in twenty years, and that was a very big deal.

There was some pushback from the sports marketing department at Waste Management because there already was an established racing program that they sponsored with the MB2 team, but Carlton really put his neck on the line for me and I'm forever appreciative. He was successful in convincing the company to extend their racing spending and sponsor me for three Cup races in Atlanta, Michigan, and California. Carlton was committed to creating more opportunities that advanced diversity and inclusion objectives for Waste Management, and I admired and highly respected him for his efforts.

Carlton was an easygoing, positive individual who was extremely supportive of me. He was proud of what I had accomplished and genuinely wanted to see me reach my full potential. He was older than I was and there were times when people actually thought he was my father. He was about my height, with salt-and-pepper hair, and we began spending a great deal of time together at the track. There were times when I was in the garage area and someone would call over to me.

"Hey, Bill. Your father is here."

I would correct them.

"No, that's not my father. That's Carlton, my sponsor."

Considering how few black people there were in racing, I chalked it up to a reasonable assumption and an honest mistake.

Once Championship Group struck a three-race Cup Series sponsorship deal with Waste Management, Bill Davis agreed to field the cars.

Bill's team was in transition in 2006. He had ended his official relationship with Dodge, which didn't want to partner with him any further since he was gearing up to run Toyotas in the Cup Series the next year in 2007. That was when the Japanese company would make its debut in NASCAR's top series. Not receiving any factory help from Dodge meant BDR had to be self-sufficient and provide its own financial resources when it came to funding its operational budget.

With a three-race deal from Waste Management, Ardy and I helped to bridge the budget gap for BDR's transitional season before they moved to Toyota.

A test in a Cup Series Dodge prior to the 2006 season was an important part of our program. But one big hurdle loomed. NASCAR strictly controlled where and when Cup teams were allowed to test in order to help all teams keep costs in line and maintain a level playing field. Ardy came up with a unique solution.

We took our Cup Series car to a test at the Kentucky Motor Speedway organized by the ARCA Series late in the 2005 season. Since the ARCA stock cars were similar to Cup cars, especially in appearance, the goal was to slip our car into the mix under the NASCAR radar—even if our higher horsepower engine configuration and our Goodyear racing tires did not fit the rulebook at ARCA, which required teams to run on Hoosier brand tires.

Due to Ardy's relationship with Ron Drager, president of ARCA, we participated in the test with the other teams while working around NASCAR's testing rules, and raised eyebrows with our very visible Goodyear tires. I was focused on learning how a Cup car would respond on a one-and-a-half-mile track that was the same length as Atlanta's, and didn't spend much time worrying about being out there in a Cup car during an ARCA test.

I got my first taste of working with my Cup Series crew chief, Ricky Viers, who was a great guy. Ricky was from Maryland and did not fit the good ol' boy mold, either. He didn't have a drawl or a Southern accent like the majority of those on the NASCAR circuit. We communicated very well together and, thankfully, he was very patient with me. My lack of experience made it difficult to provide accurate feedback to him. For example, he needed me to tell him what a change in the left rear spring meant in terms of the handling of the car, or how the car responded entering a corner after an adjustment to the air pressure in the right front tire. Accurate observations in these areas did not come easily to me due to my lack of familiarity with Cup cars. With the increased speed and power of the Cup car, not to mention the unique handling characteristics, I focused primarily on just not wrecking it. But the more laps I could run in testing to familiarize myself with how the car performed, the better I'd be able to drive it.

As for the crew, we were more like acquaintances. My Cup program was mostly manned by second-tier guys at the BDR race shop who wanted to be primary guys. (A second-tier guy is a crew member who is not as proficient or experienced as a first-tier member.) Since these guys worked in the Cup shop, I didn't know them that well, but they were very professional, and had a great deal of competence. They were just looking for their shot to move up. I was pleasantly surprised by how hard they worked in support of me. We all had a shared ambition.

Following the test at Kentucky, the car, team, and sponsor were in place. Championship Group next put together our promotional campaign that would lead up to the race in Atlanta. I wasn't just going to quietly enter the 2006 season in a Cup car with Waste Management on it. Ardy and his team put a full-blown media campaign in place called "Driving into History," which highlighted and celebrated the fact that I was the first black driver in two decades to race in the Cup Series.

We were going to arrive on the scene with a splash. I participated in a huge press conference to announce my three-race Cup schedule. Personally, it was important for me to bring awareness to the need for diversity within the sport and to create exposure for other African Americans who may start watching racing now that someone who looked like them was suited up behind the wheel.

"I think I can be a catalyst for change. Every time I bring a friend to the race, they immediately become a fan. It blows them away. It's never something they think they would like. But as more people of color realize there are drivers out there, as they are exposed to it more, things will change," I stated during the interview.

The substantial media campaign was based around our entry and it virtually assured that everybody in racing would know about it. It was an honor and a privilege to help gain exposure for a sport that had been overlooked by minority communities, especially compared to stick-and-ball sports. Professional racing is costly and many underprivileged kids growing up in urban communities may never even imagine that they could enter into such a financially prohibitive sport, but perhaps I could help to open some eyes and some wallets, for the next generation to come. If NASCAR and corporate participants were looking for a driver to help promote diversity in a sport that had precious little of it, I was ready and willing.

All eyes were on me once we got to Atlanta. That historic night, despite the immense pressure, I qualified an extremely respectable nineteenth out of fifty-two in my first attempt at a Cup Series race. I had out-qualified notables such as Dale Earnhardt Jr. and Cup Series champions Tony Stewart, Matt Kenseth, Martin Truex Jr., and Dale Jarrett. Even more gratifying was out-qualifying my BDR teammate, Dave Blaney, and Waste Management teammate, Sterling Marlin of MB2 Motorsports—not a bad way to start!

Next up was the race itself.

■ ■ ■

RACING TO THE FRONT

My *passion* was the key element when it came to sustaining my racing career long enough to get to the Truck Series. That was where all my efforts to make it to the top tier of racing started coming together. My Truck Series ride gave me a direct connection to a Cup team owner, Bill Davis, and introduced me to Waste Management. It then led to meeting Ardy Arani and Championship Group. These were the key relationships that enabled me to step up to the Cup Series.

There were many obstacles that manifested during my time in the Truck Series; unfortunately, sometimes I was the problem. In the case of the Charlotte race, I wanted too much and pushed too hard, and it backfired. It was a mistake that I learned from and tried hard to never replicate. Coming into professional racing so late in life meant that I didn't have the luxury of time to make many mistakes, so the pressure on me was magnified. But having enough self-awareness to acknowledge my faults and correct them is what helped me evolve into a more dynamic driver who was able to compete in a wide variety of race cars. Every mistake is an opportunity to learn and grow.

Passion, and pushing through challenges, helps create opportunities that lead to positive outcomes.

15

Racing into History

The race did not go as planned. Once it was over, I was still trying to reconcile how my high after Friday's qualifying results had become such a low after the actual race. But with racing, there are so many variables that can go wrong along the way—few of which you can control. Trying to navigate your way through them and maintain a positive attitude despite all the upsets is almost a sport unto itself.

As race day approached, I was enthused by the thought of seeing 100,000 avid NASCAR fans in attendance to watch me race on Sunday afternoon. I knew that when I made it to the Cup Series, I would be racing on the biggest stage in American motorsports. Sure, the Indianapolis 500 was a larger single-day event, but the average attendance at a NASCAR Cup race dwarfed the crowd size of a typical Indy car race. Leading into the weekend, the prediction was for rain, but I was cautiously optimistic that we would race regardless. Lord knows, the weathermen were not always right, and conditions could change in a heartbeat. I wasn't ready to give up hope.

On Sunday morning, I awakened in my motor coach to light rain and overcast skies. The weather forecasters had been right. With a scheduled mid-afternoon start, I prepared to compete, as I always did, with my prerace routine, which included a light meal of lean meat with plain pasta and continuing to stay hydrated. NASCAR went through the usual motions, giving every indication that indeed we would race. I had mentally prepared to compete that day. The cars were brought out of their garages and lined up along pit road. Prerace rituals like the Driver's Meeting and the Driver Introduction ceremonies were conducted. Everyone had to be ready when, or if, the opportunity to race arrived. This meant being stationed at or near our race cars along pit road. I remained hopeful that the rain would let up before we were set to start. If it didn't, NASCAR would officially call a rain delay in the hope that the weather would eventually come around and we would race later that day.

Cheryl, Ardy, and Lisa Kennedy, my public relations representative from Championship Group, helped keep me company and pass the time. I had appearance obligations that morning with my primary sponsor, Waste Management, as well as with my associate sponsor, Precision Tune Auto Care.

The light rain persisted and, sure enough, the officials declared a rain delay. A rain delay generally means everybody in the garage area spends time at the track with not much to do. Rain delays are no picnic for the fans, either. They are the ones who spent money on tickets hoping to root for their favorite driver or just be entertained. There are few things worse for a race fan than being at a cold, wet racetrack with no on-track action. It makes for a long day for everyone.

Fortunately, Ardy had made sure I would have a motor home for my debut, so I would have a place of my own and a parking space in the lot reserved for team owners and drivers, conveniently located just behind the garage. It was a little motor home, not a big million-dollar Prevost or Newell like most of the team owners and drivers had. When parked side by side, those premier motor coaches created a mammoth wave of luxury and status. My rented motor home was far more conservative. But I still felt good. I occupied a spot in the driver/owner lot with the big boys and was on the top step of American motorsports.

The rain delay did its best to dampen my enthusiasm. Ardy must've seen the look of trepidation on my face.

"You belong here," Ardy said confidently. "Welcome to the big time."

Those words from Ardy meant a lot to me. Any rookie would feel slightly out of place and intimidated, but the feeling was exaggerated for me. I'd never had anybody that I felt a real bond with in NASCAR, especially not any drivers. Some of them had come to respect me for all that I had accomplished, but I didn't have any true friends. I had acquaintances. My teammates in the Truck Series had helped me up to a point, but their help had a finite end. When we would go to test sessions, I would ask them questions and they would answer. But we were all trying to beat each other and, due to my lack of experience, sometimes I didn't have as much to offer them in return for their help.

"Thanks, Ardy. I can't tell you how much I appreciate hearing that."

He didn't have to say another word, but he continued to raise my spirits.

"Well, you earned it. You couldn't get here without a lot of hard-work and talent."

Ardy always had a way of making me feel more at ease. He knew the importance of an athlete being in the right frame of mind before a competition.

"Much appreciated. But I'm a little worried that today is not going to happen. I'm not liking how that sky is looking," I said, pointing up toward the gloomy-looking atmosphere.

The gray clouds had been circling all afternoon, but they were becoming darker and more ominous as the day dragged on.

"Keep your fingers crossed. But in the meantime, everyone is waiting to see you get out on track and make history."

The stands were chock full of fans eagerly waiting to see if history would be made. Carl Edwards had won two years in a row at Atlanta and was looking for his third straight win. Jimmie Johnson had won three races in a row and was trying to make it four. Everyone was eager to get out there and make it happen.

I was suited up and ready to rock 'n' roll. I looked the part in my impressive white, yellow, and green racing suit and baseball cap that was covered with my sponsors' emblems. There was a sea of reporters down on pit lane, all clamoring to get an interview with me. The press campaign had worked brilliantly. As the cameras began to roll during the opening coverage of the day's event, the announcers mentioned my name within the first thirty seconds and cut straight to an interview with me and Fox Sports reporter Jeanne Zelasko, who had to basically wrestle me away from the rest of the media to secure the coveted first on-air TV interview of the day.

My years of working in corporate America as a project manager had helped me become comfortable speaking in front of people and answering questions on the fly. I was prepared, poised, and ready to address all of her questions.

"It doesn't matter the color of your skin, you are a racer and you made the show. So that is step one. What is step two?" Jeanne asked, turning the microphone over to me.

"To do 500 miles. I need to race the whole race distance. I'm hoping we'll do 500 miles. The weather is going to basically dictate what happens. But really, I just want to finish it. I want to be in a strong position to do battle for maybe a Top 10, at least a Top 20, and basically build my database of information. This is a whole new group of guys that I'm racing against, and it's a different vehicle than I'm used to driving, but I know what to do. I've been here for a while in terms of racing professionally, and this is the top rung of the ladder. I'm happy to be here."

I didn't expect to win my very first Cup Series race. Atlanta Motor Speedway is one of the fastest tracks in all of NASCAR. Cars can get up to 200 mph. I knew it was going to be a challenge getting my bearings at those speeds, in a new environment among a different caliber of racers. There was so much attention being placed on my performance, I wanted to at least have a respectable run.

But Mother Nature had other plans. Despite the fact that the rain had dissipated for a short while, it came back with a vengeance. NASCAR made the official postponement of the race late in the afternoon. The wind had been finally been stripped from my sails. I had worked hard to be able to race at the top level of racing. I had hurdled innumerable obstacles to get to this point, and something as arbitrary as rain was going to be the thing to keep me from realizing my dream that day. It was discouraging knowing that I would need to get psyched up all over again on Monday when the race would be restarted. I was brokenhearted that the delayed start also meant my parents were going to miss seeing me race in person. Their return flight to California was scheduled for Sunday night. But what was troubling me the most was that the track would be "green." A "green" track in a Cup car would be a different situation, one I had no familiarity with.

A green track means the rubber that has been ground into the track during the course of a race weekend has been washed away by the rain. Basically, the extra grip in the track surface produced by the worn tires of the cars during practice and qualifying laps on Friday and the two practice sessions on Saturday would be completely gone. A green track is typically low on grip through the corners until enough rubber has been laid down on the surface by cars continuously running over it.

NASCAR gave the race a Monday mid-morning start of 11:00 A.M. and after a surprisingly sound sleep I was ready to finally make my NASCAR Cup debut. The crowd had significantly decreased in size, and that proved a slight letdown for me. We had dropped to about 40,000 spectators, which may sound like a lot, but this Atlanta track can hold 100,000. Less than half of the fans had returned. I was used to the Truck Series races, which typically hosted the lower spectator number. The other drivers were used to bigger crowds cheering them on, but I wasn't, so I didn't let it faze me too much.

Since all of the prerace pomp and circumstance had occurred the day before, I didn't have to wait long before it would be time to race. I received best wishes from my crew, said a prayer with my nine-months-pregnant wife, and strapped myself into the car. We got the command to start our engines and after a few minutes of warmup, we were cleared to leave pit road.

As my car thrust down pit road, I was rejuvenated by a rush of adrenaline. The gravity of what the day meant was front and center as I propelled my car forward. I knew that the hopes and dreams of many black racing fans and personal supporters of mine would be riding along with me. I had already seen the hue of the fans in the stands begin to change while I had been racing in the Truck Series. But now that I was on the big stage, I was ripe to really make a difference in the fan base. I was proud to serve as a significant catalyst for racial change in the sport.

The race cars slowly followed the pace car for what seemed like an infinite number of laps. Typically, that number would be three, but since the track was green, NASCAR gave us additional laps to warm up our tires, brakes, and lubricants before they deemed the track surface ready for competition. I used this time to check my gauges to ensure my engine was producing proper operating temperatures and pressures and to key the radio with both my crew chief, Ricky Viers, and my spotter to verify that we had clear radio communication. My spotter came over the radio to advise me to pull my seat belts tight one last time and then counted me down to the waving of the green flag. Once it flies, you pay even closer attention to the spotter.

When you get the green, not everybody accelerates at the same time. There's an accordion affect. You make sure you don't hit the guy in front of you and, at the same time, you're looking for a hole or a groove with which to make passes. You start speculating, which guys in front of me can I jump ahead of without hitting?

After accelerating from about 60 mph, I quickly found myself in trouble. A few laps into the race I realized that the fears I'd had about the handling of the car in Friday and Saturday practice were confirmed. My chassis quickly started going loose in the rear and the situation worsened as the laps continued. Soon my car felt completely unstable. I couldn't tell you the exact reasoning why—perhaps the track was the culprit.

My competitors passed me left and right. My car blasted down the straights, but once I got into the turns, I could hardly turn the wheel for fear that the back end of the car would pass the front, and I would go backward into the wall. I had no choice but to slow down when entering the corners. Ricky could immediately tell something was wrong. He saw it on my lap times compared to the pace of the others.

He came over the radio.

"Bill, what's going on? Is the car not handling?" he asked with urgency. His voice sounded panicked.

"It's too loose on entry," I responded.

"On a scale from one to ten, how bad is it?" he asked.

It devastated me to admit it, but it was bad. I knew that my safety and the safety of the other drivers depended on my honest answer, even if it wasn't the answer I wanted to give.

"Probably a ten."

Maximum severity.

I immediately began second-guessing myself. What if I was just being overly dramatic? Maybe I was just agitated by the fact that I was being passed so effortlessly. There had been such fanfare around my entrance into the race, and I couldn't process the fact that I had barely begun and already I was falling desperately behind. Knots were forming in my stomach and anguish in my mind. I had to take a series of deep breaths to steady myself. I had to remind myself that first and foremost, I wanted to finish the race without wrecking the car. Maybe, just maybe, I could push the car harder, but just gaining experience and the respect of my Cup competitors was a win for me. Just don't wreck the car!

During pit stops every forty laps or so, while being serviced with new tires and fuel, the team attempted to discern what the issue was and make the car more compliant. They made chassis changes by adjusting spring rates and tire pressures to improve handling. While the changes helped, we never found the "sweet spot" or the optimum setup. Looking back, it probably had more to do with my inexperience than the inability of the team. On top of my lack of experience in a Cup car, the track itself changed due to it taking on rubber and gaining grip as I raced. We just could not keep up with the dynamics of the situation.

During the race, Ricky called me into the pits for service a lap or two earlier than the rest of the field. Shortly after I rejoined the race, the caution flag came out, which forced me to run at reduced speed behind the pace car while the rest of the field was being serviced. The problem was, the field of cars had run at full speed while I was in the pits. While unfortunate for me, no one could have predicted it would play out that way. The time I lost on the track while pitted could not be made up. I was laps down to the leader at this point anyway. I was nowhere near the front of the pack, so it's not like I was chasing the win, so it was a minor point. Besides, that's just part of racing. A crew chief's split-second decision can often be beneficial or detrimental. They have a saying in racing about such circumstances: "Some days you're the windshield, some days you're the bug."

Late in the race, I got a little too close to the wall in Turn 1 and made light contact. Some slightly visible bodywork damage resulted and a small abrasion appeared on the body where the wall had taken some paint off. It momentarily knocked me out of sorts, but I didn't lose too much momentum. I managed to keep going. Scraping the wall can easily lead to disaster, so I was grateful that I had been able to avoid any significant consequences. Even if a driver makes an error and starts a slide toward trouble, if they can save the car from sustaining serious damage, that's usually considered a testament to a driver's skill.

At least I didn't end up in that graveyard over by the road near the airport!

Despite the fact that I wasn't running at the speed I would've liked, I was still in the race. And I wasn't the only one having a hard time that day. I actually was in good company when it came to drivers and teams figuring out how to race on that day's track surface. Former Cup Series champion Kurt Busch was one position ahead of me and four laps down in a factory Dodge entered by veteran team owner Roger Penske. I was only four positions behind Waste Management's regular driver and two-time Daytona 500 winner Sterling Marlin, who was three laps down to the leader. The full-time driver for Bill Davis Racing Dave Blaney finished thirty-second and two laps down in his Dodge. Only eighteen of forty-three starters finished on the lead lap as eventual race winner, Kasey Kahne.

My team and I may have struggled, but when the checkered flag flew after 500 miles, I was still running on the track. I was relieved that I had accomplished this goal without wrecking the car, but disappointed that I'd finished the race in thirty-eighth position, six laps down to Kahne. I'd known that I was not going to win, but I had not expected to finish so poorly.

I also hadn't expected to feel as good as I did physically. I had run Truck Series races that were so physically demanding that I'd had to go to the infield care center afterward and take an IV in order to recover. This only happened a few times and usually only on extremely hot days. But after 500 miles on the Atlanta track, I felt fine. I had expected the race to be more exhausting, but the air temperature was fairly cool, so I suppose that made all the difference. Since the Cup race was 500 miles, not the roughly 200 miles of a Truck race, I was pleased with my level of fitness. Some drivers never effectively make the step up from the understudy series to the longer races in Cup due to lack of stamina. The fact that I was in my mid-forties and I was able to withstand this level of racing without incident was no small feat. All the years of eating well and all of the hours I'd spent at the gym working to keep myself in top athletic shape had paid off.

However, the race did leave me emotionally spent. It was mentally exhausting racing an ill-handling car for that many laps. It was hard to figure out how to best adjust my driving style and technique to maximize the car's speed while continually racing inches apart from the other competitors on a slippery surface. I preferred driving a line around the track whereby I entered the turn high and dove down to the bottom in the center of the corner, and then drove out to the wall on exit. An extremely loose-handling car is not the fastest way around the track because you are forced to slow down far too much on corner entry to make sure you don't spin out. Since my car was so loose, I'd had to "rim ride," which is driving around the outer circumference of the track without diving down into the center of the corner. Some drivers are accustomed to this style of driving, but I am not a rim-rider, so this technique was uncomfortable and, frankly, intimidating to me on such a fast track.

When you're driving that close to the wall, it's very easy to stripe your car or scrape it along the wall because you are driving literally inches away from it. There is no margin for error. You are relying on a small cushion of air to keep your car from smacking the wall, which, as mentioned, I actually brushed once in Turn 1. Rim-riding was disconcerting for me as a Cup rookie because the cars are careening along at such a high rate of speed. It takes a great level of skill and confidence to pull it off successfully, and when it came to Cup Series, I was as green as the track. But rim-riding allows you to avoid turning the wheel sharply when driving through the corner, and that's what I had to do. Diving down to the bottom of the turn requires much more steering input, and the last thing you want to do is turn the wheel more than necessary with a car that's too loose.

After finishing the race, it was rewarding to receive the congratulations of my team. I think they genuinely felt that I'd done a good job even though I wasn't particularly pleased with the outcome. As is customary with any NASCAR race, the first three finishing drivers were called to the media center to discuss the race and answer questions from the media. I was astounded when Lisa Kennedy told me that I needed to go as well. I couldn't understand why. I had finished thirty-eighth. It was slightly embarrassing to go to the media center after receiving that result.

I arrived to see Kasey Kahne, Mark Martin, and Dale Earnhardt Jr. (the top three finishers) fielding questions. These guys were some of the heavy hitters in the game. All three of them are arguably still considered so even today. I didn't expect anyone to pay much attention to me, but I was wrong. When I entered the back of the interview room, the interview host announced that I was there. Mark Martin took his microphone and welcomed me up to the stage. I didn't feel like I belonged there since it was completely unorthodox for someone who had come in thirty-eighth place to be a part of the interview process.

"Yes! Let's hear from Bill. He's the real story of the race," Mark said graciously.

Of course, I didn't feel that was the case, but I appreciated the way he welcomed me into the Cup Series like he did. He is a legend in the sport, but he took the time to welcome me into the small fraternity of NASCAR Cup Series drivers. He surely didn't have to, but he did. It made a real impact on me that I will never forget.

I was elated to have had the opportunity to make history and race in my first Cup Series race, but I knew that the only reason I was invited into the media center that day was because I was an anomaly: the black guy who made it to the top level of racing. I didn't want that to become my identity and the only thing I was known for. I didn't want my skin color to overshadow my driving abilities or the fact that the reason I had made it to this level was because I had consistently performed well and earned my place in the series, even if I hadn't done as well as I would've liked in my first race.

Once the interviews with the top three drivers ended, the media asked me about my race, how I felt about it, and how many more races I had after this one. I happily answered them all one by one. Then one reporter asked me a question that I felt was kind of odd.

"Bill, who are you representing on the racetrack?" he called out above the others.

I was momentarily taken aback. I thoughtfully formed my response.

"I represented myself. I'm doing this for myself, and for my family. I'm glad so many people, especially from the minority community, have taken note of what it is I'm doing, but I drive for Bill Lester. At the end of the day, if it wasn't for my self-belief, I wouldn't be here." It was a real, honest answer. I added, "I'm looking forward to when it's about racing instead of race."

■ ■ ■

RACING TO THE FRONT

For nearly 500 miles of racing on the high banks of Atlanta, I was out of my *comfort zone* in a big way. It was a matter of believing in my own ability and preparation. Driving under the checkered flag and then getting the acceptance offered by Mark Martin resulted in satisfaction not possible without taking some risk.

Preparation was also a key element. I may have loved playing basketball to stay in shape, but racing professionally meant staying in peak condition. Preventing my fitness from becoming a liability and instead making it an asset required *sacrifice*. The only way to achieve that was by training at a gym, doing the laborious workouts for strength and cardiovascular stamina. I finished the Atlanta race because my conditioning enabled me to stay physically and mentally sharp. I hated going to the gym, but I was rewarded by the effort. Being physically fit meant that I could focus all of my energy on racing and navigating the challenges thrown at me in the race without being exhausted.

Sacrifice is neither fun nor pleasant but often necessary and rewarded in the end.

16

Final Cup Races

After finishing my first Cup race in Atlanta, I felt confident heading into my second. It was held in mid-June at the Michigan International Speedway (MIS), another fast track characterized by a two-mile D-shaped oval with 18° banking and 73-foot-wide turns. I tended to have my best performances on the faster tracks, so I was looking forward to getting out there and seeing what I could do.

MIS is relatively close to my parents' hometown of Chicago, which resulted in a plethora of aunts, uncles, and cousins coming to the race, in addition to my parents, Cheryl, and our two boys. Our newest member of the family had been born at the end of March and coupled with my older three-year-old, our little family was now complete. My sister Allison lived near the Michigan track, so I was thrilled that she would also be able to attend with her husband and two sons, and as many as twenty of Cheryl's relatives drove over from Detroit. My family rallied around me in support, and it meant the world to me. I was ecstatic to be able to share my accomplishments with so many people who loved me and were there to see me racing at the top level. I remember the family turnout more than the race itself. I had hardly any family living in the Southeast, so not as many people were able to see me at the Atlanta race. Beyond my immediate family, I actually can't recall many of the people who were at that race on my behalf. In Michigan, I had the opposite circumstance. The family support became the most memorable thing about the race, more so than the race itself.

On qualifying day, when five of the entered forty-eight drivers failed to make the field, I qualified thirty-fourth. While certainly not setting the track on fire, I was officially in the race, and that's all that mattered. When race day arrived, Waste Management had a huge hospitality area set up at the track to reward special employees and entertain invited guests. It was also a good geographic location for Waste Management because they conducted a great deal of business in the area.

During the prerace activities, Waste Management invited my mother to say a few words to the gathering.

My mother's eyes shined even brighter than her smile as she stepped up onto the podium next to me. She was confident and eloquent as she looked out into the crowd of friendly faces and spoke into the microphone.

"Thank you for having me here to speak," she began, "It's a great honor to be here to support my son as he realizes one of the greatest accomplishments of his life."

Our eyes met as she turned to me with the face of a proud mother.

"You have always, *always* been passionate about racing, long before you were doing it legally on a track."

The crowd laughed in unison.

"That's true," I muttered, nodding.

"He has been obsessed with cars and racing for as long as I can remember. To get where he is today, he has taken risks that lesser men would have shied away from. And I don't just mean behind the wheel. It took great courage and tenacity for him to pursue a field that was so foreign to anything he had ever been exposed to. Even when he faced challenges along the way, and there have been plenty, he persisted. When a door closed, he pushed another one open. He wasn't taking no for an answer. His determination is unparalleled and his resilience is unmatched. I watched him go from having a hobby in the streets to having a successful career on the track. He has come a long way from the boy who liked to stay out all day racing his Stingray bike around the neighborhood."

She grabbed my hand and squeezed it.

"I am so unbelievably proud of you, Bill. You have made it to the biggest stage of your career. You never gave up. You are an inspiration. Your whole family is here today to share this moment with you. Even if you don't win today, you're still a winner in my book."

I pulled her in for a hug, wrapping my arms around her tightly. I was profoundly touched by her words. I never could have gotten as far as I had if it wasn't for the foundation of my family and their unwavering love.

"I love you," she whispered in my ear as we embraced.

"I love you too, Mom. Thank you for everything."

The prerace gathering gave me the chance to catch up with people that I hadn't seen in years. It was surreal to have so many people that I cared about and who cared about me, all in one place. But before long, the race beckoned me to the track.

I wish I could've given them a more compelling show to witness, but I got eaten alive in the race. I couldn't get the car to perform as I would have liked. I fell victim to the effect of what's called the "Hospital Hop," a nuance distinctive to MIS, which is essentially a dip in the track surface in the middle of Turns 3 and 4. I was used to the effect in the Trucks, which didn't reach the same high speeds, but the Hospital Hop was exaggerated for me in the faster Cup car. If you hit the Hospital Hop wrong, the car can get thrown sideways and slide up the track toward the wall, and you risk hitting it. Whenever I hit the Hop I felt like I was on the verge of spinning out in the middle of the corner.

This unsettling feeling made me apprehensive and caused me to not go fast enough through the corners. I over-slowed my speed and didn't carry adequate momentum. As if that wasn't frustrating enough, the clouds overhead had given way to light rain, which created a dangerous situation for the drivers. After the rain became steady, the pace car was dispatched and the field duly followed it onto pit road. With the radar showing no end of rain in sight, the race ended prematurely after 129 of 200 laps were run. Although I hadn't done as well as I would've liked, it was still an amazing experience and a great day overall, in light of having my family and friends present. I also had some pretty good company around me on the track. I finished on the lead lap ahead of Kyle Petty, Jeremy Mayfield, and Clint Bowyer, all Cup veterans with previous race victories. Once again, it confirmed that for all drivers in racing, there are good days and there are bad days.

I had one race remaining with Waste Management sponsorship at the two-mile oval in Fontana, California, over Labor Day Weekend. Prior to the race weekend, we elected to test our Dodge again at the Kentucky Motor Speedway, where I put our team behind the eight ball by backing the car into the wall after a spin, severely damaging it.

BDR did not have sufficient time to fix it nor did it have another new car at its disposal. The team enlisted an older car from its stable, which did not have all the latest performance updates like the one I had wrecked. It showed on the track. Just like in Atlanta, the car and I were not strong in practice. I knew I would need to hustle the car in qualifying, but I believed that when I hit the gas the car would stick, just as it had in Atlanta. But when I hammered the gas exiting Turn 4 to complete the first of two laps of qualifying, the back end stepped out and started coming around, and I couldn't catch it. I did a 180° spin, damaging the tires by flat-spotting them during the slide. The engine also began to overheat because the radiators were taped over for qualifying to produce better aerodynamics and downforce.

I got on the radio to my crew chief, Ricky Viers.

"Should I make another attempt?" I asked.

There was a momentary pause, then I heard, "Yeah. Go for it."

I tried to get up to speed for another lap, but the engine temperature gauge began to spike, and I already knew the tires were ruined because of the slide. Continuing to try to finish the lap risked destroying the engine. I decided that discretion was the better part of valor, slowed down, and then pulled off the track. Not posting an official timed lap prevented us from qualifying for the race.

When I later watched the qualifying session on TV, I saw the speed tracker the producers use to show viewers how a driver's lap is going relative to other qualifiers. Had I not tried to push the car so hard in Turn 4, I would have qualified. I'd made a mistake because I didn't have enough confidence based on the results from practice. I'd tried to get more out of the car than it had in it. If I hadn't made that mistake, we would have made the field and started the race. Instead, we became one of four entries that failed to qualify.

In both Michigan and California, the car was too loose, meaning not enough rear stability. Considering that Southern California was a home race for me and a big market for Waste Management, it was very disappointing. Waste Management already had a season-long contractual commitment to sponsor Sterling Marlin and his racing team. I had looked forward to possibly going back to Waste Management and asking them if we could do more races, but that option fell by the wayside by not qualifying. They had signed up for three races, and I only gave them two, despite my reputation for being a great qualifier.

I have been asked why Championship Group and I decided not to include the Cup Series event on my home road racing circuit at Sears Point and chose three oval races instead. I think it would have been expected of me to perform well on a road course, because of my sports car racing background. But a good result there would not have impressed any potential Cup team owners or sponsors. We were looking for the best way to showcase my skills that would hopefully secure continued sponsorship down the line. While our strategy to focus on ovals produced interest, it did not get any significant follow-up. I had been simultaneously racing in the Truck Series that year, but I ended up losing my BDR Toyota deal at season's end.

I suppose my results had not been good enough in the Truck Series for BDR and Toyota to continue with me on a full-time basis with one of its factory teams. In three seasons and seventy-four starts in a Toyota, I had two Top 5 finishes and four Top 10s, in addition to my two poles. I may not have had the budget, experience, and development opportunities of Mike Skinner and Johnny Benson, but the comparison to those Cup veterans, under any circumstances, was not flattering to me.

Initially, Toyota still remained in my corner. The outgoing Truck Series manager, Lee White, told me I could promise a supply of Toyota racing engines to a truck team owner interested in hiring me. That's a significant factor when considering a truck team's overall budget.

"You can tell a prospective team that you will have a Toyota engine program to bring with you," said Lee.

I was grateful for his promise and looking forward to finding a new way to continue racing at this level, but it was only a short while later that he sat me down and said, "We're not going to provide you with engines."

I can only speculate about what caused Lee to make such an abrupt about-face. He had given a verbal commitment and then had pulled it back. I had not initially asked him to provide this engine program for me. He had offered it, so I couldn't understand why he would do such a thing only to leave me dangling in the wind. By this time, I had already been in discussions with other truck team owners about bringing Toyota engines with me. I was furious, to say the least, not only due to Toyota's breach of commitment but because I would now lose credibility with Toyota team owners since I had to unwind my talks with them.

I can surrender to ill-fated circumstances, unfortunate events that are out of anyone's control, and honest mistakes, but I have a hard time accepting when someone purposely wrongs me in a way that hinders my career and undermines my integrity. There are ample ways that things can so wrong in racing, and taking them all in stride is just part of the business, but I am not okay with someone making me look foolish. It had taken me years to earn respect in the racing community, and in one fell swoop, Lee White could have jeopardized all of my efforts. Luckily, my strong character helped me to persevere.

■ ■ ■

RACING TO THE FRONT

It was difficult to maintain my *enthusiasm* once my three entries in the Cup Series came to an end with not much to show for the effort. Prospects for landing a sponsor or a job driving for a Cup team looked bleak, and so did prospects for my career in the Truck Series. The disappointment ran deep, and at times, I was despondent over not finding a way to continue in the Cup Series. We had created a once-in-a-career opportunity, had given it everything we possibly could, and in what seemed like the blink of an eye, it was over.

My *enthusiasm* came to a low ebb. It took a lot of *discipline* on my part to keep doing the things I needed to do each day to sustain my driving career. The pain and disappointment didn't stop me from continuing to *network* among team owners, and eventually I found a ride in the Truck Series for a partial 2007 season, returning to the Chevy fold. I was *grateful* to continue racing, even if it meant not doing so in the Cup Series.

If all else fails, discipline sustains focus and helps promote enthusiasm.

17

Cup Aftermath (Stars and Bars . . . and Boos)

After we had completed our contract to run three Cup races, my friend and advocate at Waste Management, Carlton Yearwood, gave me a 4-inch-thick binder. In it were the reports about media coverage related to our three-race program. Put together by Stevens/FKM, a public relations agency working on behalf of Waste Management, the report included all the TV, print media, and online stories we had generated as well as information and photos from prerace personal appearances on behalf of Waste Management. This book made for some interesting reading.

Many media outlets across the country found our "Driving into History" program a reason to cover NASCAR. The stories often summed up its historical import and had quotes from me as well as statistics on my career. There were other markers of my influence on NASCAR. The City of Atlanta honored me with "Bill Lester Day" confirming that new fans could be engaged by my attempt to race at NASCAR's top level. I doubt many Atlantans knew who I was, knew about my career in NASCAR, or even that I lived in Atlanta prior to having a day named in my honor.

The media found the story of my quest to join the Cup Series newsworthy and was eager to provide substantial editorial coverage. The binder contained a report that concluded that we had produced $25 million in sponsor value for the Atlanta race, a figure generated by Joyce Julius & Associates, the accepted industry method of calculating the ad value of the TV time and print media space dedicated to stories.

The investment made by Waste Management for the Atlanta race comprised roughly $325,000. Considering the value we generated for our sponsor, you didn't have to be a business genius to figure out we had created an excellent return on their investment. In light of the tremendous interest and exposure we garnered across the motor sports landscape, I would have thought we'd receive a fair number of sponsorship proposals from corporate America. I was frankly astounded when we didn't.

At the time, I didn't understand. Why weren't any of our efforts to land a sponsor being converted? I had accepted that there were no more races or opportunities with Waste Management. They already had a contract with the MB2 racing team and Sterling Marlin. But why couldn't a new sponsor come in from outside the sport of NASCAR and back this car of mine and Bill Davis Racing? Or why couldn't a sponsor work with me to go to another team if they so desired? The press opportunities alone would make it worth their while. Granted, I hadn't qualified in that one race, but I was still a solid driver with a lot of potential. There were eight American drivers with stats lower than mine that year, three of whom acquired sponsorship and continued on the following year. So why was I hearing crickets?

The situation did not result from Championship Group being unprepared or not doing their homework. The company had previously helped generate millions in sponsorships across a wide variety of sports, including the Olympic Games. They had an established history of success. They knew what they were doing. In NASCAR, Championship Group brought Mars, Inc., into the sport, which was a company that later backed Cup Series champion Kyle Busch for many years with its M&M's brand.

Championship Group sent out proposals to all the Fortune 1000 companies, including a unique pitch to 200 of those companies where African Americans were represented in the upper levels of management. No serious inquiries to Ardy Arani and Championship Group resulted. Ardy concluded that any calls from potential sponsors were going to NASCAR and that the sanctioning body was derailing our chances. NASCAR typically acted as a gatekeeper when it came to sponsors entering the privately owned sport. If we generated a sponsor prospect, inevitably that potential sponsor would call NASCAR, not Championship Group. All we expected from NASCAR was a confirmation that I was welcome in the Cup Series and would be competitive if a potential sponsor talked with their officials. All we asked from NASCAR was a fair shake. We didn't get it.

I thought NASCAR was ready for a black driver at the Cup level. If anything, my presence in the Cup Series would provide more of a global focus on NASCAR. If the sanctioning body had been receiving any pressure from political activists, such as Jesse Jackson or other equal-rights organizations, it may have helped me to gain more traction. Instead, I became a man alone on an island, watching the ships sail by.

If NASCAR as an organization had made a valiant effort to expand its diversity efforts and support me as a valued driver, I truly believe that it would have greatly increased the opportunities for Championship Group to secure sponsorship. It would have made all of the difference for mainstream corporate America or for a successful black-owned business to take an interest in becoming my sponsor. I had done as much as I could to bring attention to myself and the sport. I had put in the work on the track, and reaped decent enough results that should have translated to sponsorship and a continued career at the Cup level. Though I ride solo in the car, racing is very much a team effort. I could not get to where I needed to be without other people to work with me, believe in me, and support me, including financially. If the powers that be didn't want me to succeed, I wouldn't.

And I didn't. Unfortunately, no help emerged. This response by NASCAR to my Cup Series bid came as a shock and was in direct contrast to what had happened in the Truck Series, where concerted diversity efforts in NASCAR had first taken hold, starting with the program by Dodge.

I realized then how political a sport racing truly was. It didn't matter how hard you worked, how well you raced, or how much publicity you generated: at the end of the day, if NASCAR didn't stand behind you and support you (or worse, hindered you), you were doomed to fail. It had been a struggle to get to the top as a black man, but I'd never expected that once I got there, it would impossible for me to stay. I had been given one shot at the big leagues, and because I hadn't blown their socks off, I was dismissed.

I appreciated the support I'd received from NASCAR while driving a truck for Toyota. Without the support NASCAR helped deliver, my Toyota program might have ended quickly, along with my career. But when it came to our independent effort at Championship Group to move up to the Cup Series level, the major league of NASCAR, we discovered the door was closed. I suspect that from the beginning the goal to become more diverse had to do with American manufacturers, like Dodge, pushing the sanctioning body as opposed to NASCAR's internal channels being the driving force. American automakers employ men and women from a wide variety of backgrounds and sell their vehicles to a vast array of ethnicities. Those factories sold a lot of cars to these same constituencies and played a major role in NASCAR. The same went for large corporations like General Mills and Coca-Cola that, at the time, were some of the biggest sponsors in the sport. It was in all of their best interests to appeal to a more diverse audience, and with the amount of money they poured into the sport, they had a definite say in how the sport was run. I think NASCAR had gone along with the diversity incentive to appease them, and dropped off when they felt they had successfully done so.

There had been recent examples of other African Americans breaking into what had always been white sports bastions. Serena Williams, Venus Williams, and Tiger Woods had all come onto the scene in the mid- to late nineties, which spawned increased viewership among African Americans in both tennis and golf. Once Tiger Woods won his first Masters title at age twenty-one, professional golf benefited mightily with increased support and interest from fans of all colors. I might not have been a threat to win a Cup Series race at Bill Davis Racing, and I was long past my twenty-first birthday, but I could help the entire NASCAR diversity effort by competing on their biggest stage. A credible candidate, I had led laps and won pole positions. I would venture to say that I had demonstrated more talent than at least a dozen of the drivers in the Cup Series at the time, including those who failed to qualify regularly.

Given its private ownership by the France family, NASCAR is City Hall and all the participants know that you can't succeed if the sanctioning body is not supportive of what you are doing. I supported NASCAR and represented the sport, my sponsor, and team professionally. I always conducted myself with professionalism and believed in the mission to move diversity forward.

Over the years, I have regularly received numerous questions about racism in the sport. Despite all of my negative experiences, I have repeatedly come to NASCAR's defense, trying to downplay the friction that had become commonplace. But it was extremely difficult to look past a Confederate flag being waved in the stands. Yet I did. Not only have I taken the high road time and time again, but I have looked for ways to not be affected and insulted by the actions of strangers.

One time, when I was interviewed, I was asked if the presence of the Confederate flag made me uncomfortable. The obvious and unavoidable answer is "Yes!" Not just as a black man but as a human being who understands the symbolism of what the flag represents and the horrors that took place during slavery in particular. Anyone who truly understands what it means should be disgusted by the Confederate flag. And I am no exception.

But that's not the politically correct answer. That's not the response that would keep me in NASCAR's good graces, if ever I was. I didn't want to alienate the NASCAR audience that was already hesitant about me. Instead, I chose to be diplomatic and carefully crafted my words.

"Yeah, the Stars and Bars make me uncomfortable. But I don't hold that against the fan per se, or NASCAR. I hold it against the culture. This is part of Southern culture and how they were raised. They were brought up believing in it. So, I typically consider that to be ignorance about how others may see the flag differently."

It is a slippery slope when talking about racism. It did me no good to make snap judgments, bold accusations, or blanket assumptions. It would be impossible to actually know what every person was thinking. I tried my best to avoid directly answering if NASCAR or its fans were racist. It's a loaded question with many layers and a variety of answers that needs to be addressed on a case-by-case basis.

If a fan put a Confederate flag in front of my face, did it mean that fan was a racist? Not necessarily. Perhaps not all of them fully grasped the weight of what the Confederate flag means and the message they were silently conveying, perhaps some of them only viewed it as a Southern symbol and did not equate the flag with being racist against black people. It may simply have meant that this was the culture they had been reared with. But some of them, and it may very well have been a great number of them, knew *exactly* what they were doing and did it anyway. Some of them were overtly racist and absolutely proud of it. Whatever their reason, knowingly waving a Confederate flag in front of a black man showed a serious level of insensitivity, ignorance, and disrespect. It was an image I was not comfortable with.

An interviewer once asked, "Do you feel there's racism in the sport?"

Images of a lawn jockey that had been dressed in my likeness, being burned, formed in my mind. Memories of NASCAR fans using the n-word floated through my brain. Visions of a red flag adorned with a blue cross being proudly waved in the stands flashed back to me. In the wake of all that had transpired over my years in racing, it was hard not to speculate that, on some level, racism existed in NASCAR.

But again, I did not want to make controversial waves, so I formed an answer that was both honest and discrete.

"I find things that I'm uncomfortable with, but I don't know if its racism. I have heard some racial slurs. So, yes, there are some racists out there. But would I call NASCAR fans racists? No. There are some. Yes. As a whole I'm not going to sit here and categorize them all as racists. That would be ignorant, as ignorant as them thinking I'm going to be comfortable with them waving the Stars and Bars in front of my face."

There were times when it was difficult for me to race in NASCAR. One memorable event took place when I was at Martinsville, Virginia, back in 2004, and was racing in the Truck Series. Martinsville is a short half-mile track, which means that the top speeds are much lower than on the long tracks. As a driver, you can't hit much more than 110 mph before it's time to slow down and turn. Because of this, there's less of a chance that a car is going to get collected by another and go flying off into the stands, and so the fans are much closer in proximity to the actual track.

Before every race, a makeshift stage is driven out by an eighteen-wheel flatbed. Atop the stage are both NASCAR officials and local dignitaries—usually the mayor of the city is in attendance. All of the drivers are behind the backdrop. When our names are called, we each individually come out from behind the banner and wave and smile to the crowd. With the fans so close, I was able to not only see spectators holding up Confederate flags and wearing Confederate hats, but I could also hear their contempt for me.

When my name was called, I walked out to the sounds of some people clapping and cheering, but a louder, more obtrusive noise permeated my ears, one that I still cannot fully fathom.

"Driving the twenty-two Toyota is Bill Lester for Bill Davis Racing."

"Boo!"

"Booo!!"

"Boooooooooo!!!"

Never in my life had I ever been received so poorly. I was being booed by a huge crowd of people, for some unknown reason. It was shocking. While I didn't expect everyone to love me, I couldn't understand what I had done to deserve such hostility. I had never spoken ill of NASCAR, other drivers, or its fans, and had never made any disparaging remarks. I had always been polite and professional. I didn't engage in any of the antics to antagonize fans that some NASCAR drivers did. I was a clean driver who didn't push people off the track or drive dirty, yet the animosity coming from the stands was unequivocal.

I tried not to let it bother me. I ascribe to the theory that those that anger you control you, so I held my head high, smiled, and continued to wave.

Jeff Gordon, a white driver who is also from California, was booed consistently in the first few years of his career, so it's entirely possible that I was merely being booed because I was not a Southerner. I'll never really know for sure. But as one of the only black men in the history of the sport, it's hard not to consider that the motive was racially charged.

It was also extremely uncomfortable and intimidating to be the only black man in a sea of thousands of white men who were loudly and obviously hating my presence. The track was so small that the truck haulers could not park inside of the track, so I would have to walk—often unaccompanied—back and forth through the thick crowd, to and from my trailer. I always walked swiftly and kept my head down, hoping not to be noticed. It may sound paranoid, but when you are the only black man in the South and you've had thousands of white people boo you, you tend to quicken your pace.

Suffice it to say, Martinsville was my least favorite track.

■ ■ ■

RACING TO THE FRONT

They say that bravery is acting in the face of fear. Remaining calm, staying positive, and proceeding forward in the face of an extremely uncomfortable position is not an easy thing to do. When I was faced with thousands of people who were adamantly rooting against me, it rattled me, but I did not let it deter me. I faced opposition internally from the NASCAR executives and externally from the fans who didn't want me infringing on their territory. Finding the courage to hold my head high despite so many people trying to bring me down was challenging but necessary. Martinsville was the ultimate experience of getting out of my *comfort zone*, but I stayed the path.

In life there are often obstacles that will test our merit and our desire to succeed. It's easier to give in to overwhelming forces that push against us, but you will never reach your true potential by giving up. I refused to allow others to dictate my mindset or affect my outcome. Rising above the hostility and being better than the ones who dared to drag me down was the key to enduring the injustice I experienced. Harnessing my inner strength helped me withstand the many levels of discrimination I faced over the course of my career.

Sometimes circumstances warrant finding the additional courage necessary to stay out of your comfort zone, as opposed to only having to get out of it.

18

Diversity Adversity

As time went on, it became evident that the idea of a black driver in the Cup Series may have actually agitated those at the top of the NASCAR hierarchy. When it came to drivers competing at the top, the diversity program may have been more about laying some groundwork to welcome established racing stars like Juan Pablo Montoya, a famous Formula 1 driver from Colombia, and Indy car sensation Danica Patrick to the Cup Series. Forecasting to the NASCAR community that changes in the makeup of the faces crossing the stage during driver introductions might change one day soon appeared to be the new goal.

Surprisingly, NASCAR proved uninterested in a face like mine competing at the Cup level on a regular basis. While trying to satisfy the needs of manufacturers interested in diversity and various corporate sponsors, NASCAR had another important constituency—track promoters.

Bruton Smith is the chairman and CEO of Speedway Motorsports, Inc., and has been inducted into the NASCAR Hall of Fame. In 2005, he was ranked number 207 on the Forbes 400 list, coming in with an estimated net worth of $1.5 billion dollars. His tracks hosted twelve of the thirty-six Cup races in 2006.

During my "Drive into History" campaign, he was interviewed by the *Tampa Bay Times* regarding his thoughts on me. His remarks raised a few eyebrows, including my own. When broached about the subject of diversity at the tracks, he stated that he didn't expect black fans to flock to the track to watch me.

"I don't see it happening," Smith said. "Look at your other sports, the NBA, NFL. Black people are playing, but they don't rush in and buy the tickets."

Not only was his comment inaccurate—both of the sports he mentioned have HUGE African American fan bases—but they were downright offensive, not just to me but to the entire black community. He had insinuated that black men liked to play sports, but we were too cheap to actually pay money to watch them. I can't think of a less inviting thing to say to a group of people you supposedly want as a new target audience.

As soon as Smith made those remarks, my phone began ringing off the hook. Everyone wanted me to comment. If I had allowed myself to say what I really wanted to say, it may have been the end of my career. I swallowed the fire that was burning in my throat.

"I have no inclination to respond to that," I said curtly.

Smith tried to backpedal from his defaming words. He remarked that he was happy to have me in the Cup Series.

"It's a great news story, and Bill deserves a shot because he's a good driver."

That statement spoke volumes. I was a "news story," something that people could talk about briefly and then forget shortly after, a gimmick to generate publicity, and a scratch to satisfy a pesky itch. News stories don't have staying power. He didn't expect me to do well or have a lucrative, successful career. In hindsight, it was a red flag that I never anticipated.

Bruton Smith was a titan in NASCAR. His words reflected what so many of the fans were likely thinking. His commentary inadvertently pulled the curtain back. If black people started showing up in the stands, it had the potential to hurt attendance by white fans. "White flight" is a very real phenomenon where large clusters of white people migrate from minority and urban areas to less diverse areas. And the power brokers behind the sport were not about to stand idly by and watch their cash cows migrate to another field.

Bruton Smith was not alone in wanting to thwart my NASCAR career. I learned years later that NASCAR's own marketing director, George Pyne, had campaigned against my efforts to come into the Cup Series. He took active measures to deter me from making it to the top level. Pyne was NASCAR's ranking member of the Steering Committee for its diversity effort. With members like that, it's no wonder that more black drivers had not penetrated the Cup Series barrier. The Steering Committee's sole goal was to expand diversity within NASCAR, and included representatives from corporations active in NASCAR, such as the Coca-Cola Company and Nextel Communications, as well as prominent black businessmen like Earvin "Magic" Johnson, who briefly joined the group.

In 2005, before I ever attempted to qualify for a Cup Series race, Pyne told Ardy Arani that I should stay in the Truck Series, and that his sports marketing team should abandon any efforts to put together a program for me in Cup. This statement effectively meant the NASCAR marketing department would offer no help when it came to finding more sponsorship to continue in the Cup Series with Bill Davis Racing once the three-race deal with Waste Management concluded.

After I had qualified for the Atlanta race, an executive with Toyota's racing effort, Pat Wall, was asked about my Cup ambitions by a journalist. He echoed Pyne's attitude.

"Bill Lester," he said, "should stay in the Truck Series until he retires."

I was excited when basketball icon Magic Johnson joined the NASCAR Executive Steering Committee to help move forward minority business opportunities and participation in the sport. I hoped that as a successful former black athlete and high-profile businessman, he would have the presence and acumen to actually bring about the type of significant change to the sport that would increase minority involvement across the board. He had talked publicly about going to racing events with his father, detailing how much he loved them and how racing was effectively in his blood. He indicated that NASCAR offered no direct compensation for his involvement. I was optimistic and eager to work together toward a mutual goal.

I reached out to him through his assistant to have a face-to-face meeting with him so that we could talk more fluidly. She arranged for us get together at the Four Seasons Hotel in downtown Atlanta during one of his business trips.

At this point in my career, I had met more than a few celebrities, but having been an avid basketball fan my whole life, I was thrilled to meet Magic Johnson. He was a legend on and off the court.

As if that wasn't daunting enough, the lobby of the Four Seasons was just as overwhelming. The ceiling was three stories high and was adorned with a chandelier that may have cost more than my house! There was a grand staircase straight ahead that looked as though Scarlett O'Hara was due to amble down it at any moment. Instead, it was Johnson who made this entrance as he descended the stairs to meet me. I wasn't sure if he knew what I looked like, but I certainly knew what he looked like.

I promptly made my way over to him and extended my hand.

"I'm Bill Lester. It's great to meet you. Do you prefer to be called Earvin or Magic?"

"My friends call me Earvin," he replied.

I took that as a good sign. He invited me back up the stairs where we retreated to a secluded sitting area where he took the couch and I sat in the adjoining chair.

"I don't know how much you know about me," I began. I proceeded to tell him about myself and my racing career.

"I love racing and I have been following your career. You've achieved quite a lot in the sport so far," he acknowledged.

I was energized that he actually knew who I was and understood the efforts I had been making up until then.

"Thanks, man. I can't tell you how much that means to me. It's been a real struggle, though. I have had an extremely hard time getting funding and securing sponsorship. Corporate America has not exactly been forthcoming. I could really use your assistance opening doors."

Earvin nodded his head in agreement. He seemed very receptive to my plight.

"No doubt. Anything I can do to help," he said graciously.

"That's fantastic. Thank you so much."

I was relieved and elated. We chatted for a while longer and then parted ways. He seemed sincere and definitely gave me the impression that we were on the same page. I left with optimism and an extra spring in my step.

I followed up a few days later with a call to his assistant, who acted as his gatekeeper. She took a message for me, but I didn't receive a call back. Not thinking anything of it, I tried again a few days later. Maybe she hadn't given him the message or maybe he had gotten busy and had forgotten to reply. When I didn't receive a reply yet again, I decided to wait a while. I figured that he may have been traveling, and I didn't want to be annoying. A few weeks passed, and I tried a few more times, to no avail.

I could not understand what had gone wrong. Had I somehow been ostracized? Why was he not responding after such a great first meeting? Had I read the situation incorrectly? Was my ask too big?

His assistant became just as elusive. Needless to say, nothing ever materialized. Saying that I was disappointed would be an understatement. I had attached high hopes to the idea that Magic Johnson was going to be the catalyst that NASCAR needed to propel the sport forward and help me become better received by NASCAR fans, sponsors, teams, and officials. Maybe his efforts did pay dividends for the minority business community and vendors associated with NASCAR. Who knows? I do know Earvin ended up leaving the Executive Steering Committee on Diversity rather inconspicuously, as opposed to the massive fanfare he'd generated when he arrived.

Indications are that Magic Johnson must have gotten word from NASCAR officials like George Pyne, who didn't think I was Cup Series material, and had been warned against aiding my cause. It's unfortunate that the higher-ups would apparently taint his vision of me and sabotage my career's trajectory. I suppose that he was so new to the inner workings of NASCAR that he didn't anticipate being manipulated through political influence. It took me a long time to come to terms with the NASCAR undercurrent myself. I don't begrudge Earvin for his decisions, but I do wish that he had communicated with me so that I might have enlightened him on exactly why my head was being held under water.

NASCAR had certainly benefited from the presence of Juan Montoya and Danica Patrick, and I think it would have also benefited from having me regularly behind the wheel in the Cup Series. Montoya ended up winning just two Cup races and Patrick did not come close to winning a race, yet they still had a very impactful influence on the NASCAR fan base and drew a lot of attention. I was glad that other minority groups were getting some sort of recognition on the track, but in the end, neither of them was African American, so my demographic was still severely unrepresented.

It was easy for some NASCAR executives to say that I hadn't paid my dues to race in Cup because so few people knew just how many dues I had paid. It was convenient to feed the rumor mill that I didn't belong, and that I just wanted to turn a quick buck along with my representation by Championship Group. My record in the Truck Series suggested otherwise, and Championship Group had an impeccable track record of success as a sports marketing agency.

Not getting any additional opportunities to race in the Cup Series became the most heartbreaking setback among the many I had already experienced in my racing career. It felt like my potential had been extinguished before being given a chance to thrive.

Over the 2006 season, and even the following year, the lack of opportunity in the Cup Series gnawed at me. I had spent years fighting to get to the top of American racing and once there, life looked pretty good. The competition was fiercer, the crowds were more robust, and the purses were heftier. Driving such powerful cars was extremely exhilarating. Despite a rocky start, I felt strongly that my lap times would improve once the learning curve wore off. The next hurdle would have been improving my race craft, such as honing exactly when or how to pass in a Cup car and learning the on-track tendencies and nuances of the other Cup drivers. With my proven driving abilities, I knew I would get better. I had established the advantage of my endurance capabilities. I had already improved in all these areas over the course of my career. I believed I could produce Top 10 results—possibly even Top 5—as well as some laps led and maybe a victory, if the right circumstances allowed. But none of that could happen without seat time in a good car. And that couldn't happen without the sanctioning body's approval and support, since I hadn't been born with a silver spoon in my mouth and would have to rely on outside funding.

Being overlooked by Dodge early on was disappointing, but being dismissed so soon in the Cup Series was painful. I don't let anger live inside me or take over my state of being, but I would be lying if I said that I wasn't, on some level, mad that this was how the chips were falling. At the very least, I was disheartened and disenchanted. My overall love for racing had been skewed by these experiences, which negatively affected my enjoyment for racing for longer than I like to admit.

Racing is a sport where losing is the predominant experience, so I had to compartmentalize what had happened and keep going, as if I had spun out of contention late in a race and needed to straighten myself out and continue on toward the finish line, even though winning was no longer an option. I had to accept the situation and keep the big picture in mind; I had gained enough recognition to open other doors, so all wasn't completely lost. I reminded myself that other drivers got to the top rung in racing before they moved to successful careers elsewhere in professional auto racing. I forced myself to keep my focus on the goal of making a living as a race car driver. I just needed to reinvent my career, once again.

Having built up a rather formidable network of contacts, I had developed the relationships necessary to find opportunities. I made the conscious decision to accept that some things were out of my control, and that I wasn't going to allow myself to be defeated by it. I had to recognize that the only good response was to keep striving to compete in a sport I had always loved, provide income for my family, prove the naysayers wrong, not let them destroy my passion for racing, and help create a path for others to follow. It wasn't only about me.

I had always known that my journey was not for the faint of heart. Despite the impediments, I was going to continue to find a way through the obstacle course.

I had been chosen to walk this path for a reason.

■ ■ ■

RACING TO THE FRONT

I couldn't allow myself to get discouraged after realizing my dreams of competing regularly at the top of NASCAR would likely not happen. By maintaining my *enthusiasm* and love for racing, I spent another four years driving sports cars professionally on world class road courses—including Laguna Seca, where my *passion* for racing had started.

I always tried to make friends, not enemies, and to never burn a bridge. My constant *networking* set me up to talk with every available manufacturer in NASCAR about continuing to race. As it turned out, I decided to compete in the Grand-Am Series owned by NASCAR, thanks to the support of the sanctioning body's then vice chairman Jim France and the relationship I continuously nurtured with him.

Too often, the demands of motor racing kept my focus on the sport—not unlike my father putting in the hours to get ahead in his profession. But it is important to have *gratitude* about what you have accomplished, even if it becomes just a fleeting moment at the top, like my NASCAR Cup Series career.

Networking with others can be reenergizing and one of the best ways to keep moving forward, especially if your journey seems stagnant or the future looks bleak.

19

The Bare Minimum

During my tenure in NASCAR, formalized efforts to create diversity councils, programs, departments, and summits were put in place by the organization. When the pressures from the sponsors, manufacturers, and black activists kept coming, the organization obliged by creating the NASCAR Diversity Council, which was equipped with several high-profile African Americans. The NASCAR Diversity Council was created in 2000 by Brain France, the chairman and CEO of NASCAR.

When I was asked to join the council, I was happy to serve as a member and help bring change to the sport that had changed my life. We had regular meetings to discuss the state of the sport and how we could implement changes that would increase diversity in the grandstands, in the pits, and behind the wheel. I was involved with the council for four years, but because my racing schedule began to demand so much of my time, my ability to contribute diminished.

One of the other members was Brad Daugherty, a black man who stood seven feet tall and had symbolized diversity in NASCAR long before I arrived. Brad had been an All-American basketball player at the University of North Carolina before moving into a pro career with the Cleveland Cavaliers. A North Carolina native, he had been an avid NASCAR fan growing up. He wore the number forty-three in recognition of his favorite driver, Richard Petty. Even before retiring from his pro basketball career and becoming a NASCAR team owner, Brad had spent a lot of time at NASCAR events and became friends with the NASCAR hierarchy, including Brian France. Over the years, Brad became a TV commentator for ESPN at NASCAR races in addition to a Cup Series team owner. Recently, Brad jumped back into the fray of sports commentating as a NASCAR analyst for NBC Sports Network.

Brad told me that he would sometimes take Brian aside and try to counsel him on how to expand NASCAR to include people of color.

"This is what you need to do if you want to really achieve diversity," he would say.

Brad would rattle off a list of ideas that would generate a more inclusive sport. Brian would respond to Brad by shooting down his advice every time.

"We're not going to do that," Brian would assert.

It seemed as though there was a limit on how much NASCAR really wanted to do to make progress on diversity.

Reverend Jesse Jackson established the Rainbow PUSH/Rainbow Sports program in an attempt to increase diversity across all motorsports, including NASCAR. When NASCAR received an invitation to participate in the Rainbow Push Sports Conference in 2004, Brian France requested that I accompany him. He was concerned that he might face some backlash.

Essentially, I was there to deflect from the lack of diversity in NASCAR and serve as a symbol (or prop) to show that NASCAR was changing in the right direction. France was fearful that the crowd would point out NASCAR's long history of failing to include people of color, and if I was by his side, he could negate that argument. He could insist that I was proof that the sport was becoming more progressive.

I was apprehensive about sending this message since I believed that NASCAR was not diverse enough, and still had miles to go before they accomplished the goal of truly being diverse. I hadn't made it to this level because of NASCAR's inherent efforts to invoke change. I had come up through the ranks primarily due to my own efforts. The Drive for Diversity program had not yet been established. I'd had to fight to get to where I was, and I didn't want anyone to think it had come easily or that NASCAR was kicking down doors for me. It was quite the opposite actually. I'd had to kick the doors down.

I agreed to go to the summit in order to shed light on the facts. I wanted to serve as the face for change, not as the poster boy for the bare minimum. One African American NASCAR driver among hundreds of white drivers was not enough to constitute the word "diverse." We were leaps and bounds away from where NASCAR needed to be in order to accurately and comfortably use that word. My presence in the sport was only just the beginning.

During a panel discussion at the conference, I straddled the line of being diplomatic and being honest. I was not willing to compromise my integrity and say something that was clearly false.

"NASCAR doesn't have to do anything for diversity as a privately owned company. But they are trying to put checkmarks in the boxes that would make the sport more inclusive. Not just on the track, such as with pit crews, but with opportunities outside the track, like internships and jobs at major corporations that participate in NASCAR. So, they are doing some things to broaden the net."

I thought that NASCAR was making efforts toward progress, but I remained unconvinced that NASCAR fundamentally wanted to change.

A friend who worked in NASCAR's diversity department told me that the top officials at NASCAR were often worried about comments I made to the media.

"The brass," she told me, "is concerned about what you might say."

Was I not falling into line the way they would've liked? Did they want me to follow a prescribed script that would make them look good? Did they think that I should just be glad that a black man had made it this far? Did they want me to be grateful for a career that they had little to do with? Perhaps it was a blend of all of the above.

I was not doing anything detrimental to NASCAR, but on the other hand, I didn't roll over and sing endless praise for their handling of the situation. The simple truth is that they could have done more. My position was that NASCAR needed to do more than provide lip service and check the right boxes if it really wanted change. This was not the era of the civil rights movement; this was the early 2000s. The country was only a few years away from having a black president, and yet the second largest sport in the country had only eight African Americans in a Cup-level driver's seat in its entire seventy-plus-year history. When you think about it that way, it's shocking!

During the years I competed, there were lots of interviews and photo sessions set up by the sanctioning body that really tried to exemplify NASCAR being about diversity. I remember one photo shoot in particular at the short oval in Mansfield, Ohio. Besides myself, there were two female drivers, Kelly Sutton and Deborah Renshaw, and a Japanese driver, Shigeaki Hattori. None of us particularly wanted to be in the photo. We were all well aware that our images were being used by NASCAR to send a message. At least the women smiled, unlike Shige and me. I would have preferred for us to be recognized for our racing, not our gender, race, or ethnicity. And I would wager a bet that Kelly, Deborah, and Shige felt the same way.

I remember doing what felt like far too many diversity stories with the media, answering the same leading questions over and over:

"Why aren't there more black drivers in the sport?" and "How soon will we see more black fans in the stands?"

Reporters weren't getting a whole lot of new information out of me, especially since they often didn't ask, or appear to care, about my racing performances or stats. Most of the reports reflected much more interest in the color of my skin than in my racing career. I often felt like the token spokesman filling in the blanks for their diversity story.

NASCAR's marketing department also exemplified a real lack of effort. NASCAR president Mike Helton was always a great advocate for me, and I have a lot of respect for him. But he had to work within the marching orders of Brian France, since he ultimately steered the ship. Mike recommended that I speak with the head of marketing at NASCAR, Steve Phelps. I could tell by the reception I got from conversations with Steve, and the subsequent lack of action, that the marketing department held little interest in me or in helping me pursue sponsorship. This made for a huge disconnect between Mike's vision of transformation for the sport and what some of the other executives were actually willing to do. Steve was cordial and willing to listen. There wasn't a negative response or an outward rejection of my ideas, but there was also no follow-through or measures taken. After numerous attempts to make progress, I concluded no significant effort would be expended by him. He said all the right things, but there was no movement forthcoming. Nothing ever came of our meetings. It was very frustrating after being recommended by Mike in the first place.

So which NASCAR was I dealing with? The one built on conservative values that held to the way things had always been done and favored white faces in the stands and behind the wheel? Or the NASCAR that pledged to make the sport more diverse and was willing to take active measures to support participants of color?

It's difficult to say you are one way when a culmination of behaviors suggests otherwise. And, as we all know, actions speak louder than words.

Despite popular belief, I wasn't a member of the formal Drive for Diversity program. Most people assumed that I had come into NASCAR by this route, but I didn't. Drive for Diversity, also known as D4D, was created after I had landed my job driving for Dodge. The support I later received from NASCAR while driving a Toyota in the Truck Series for BDR was also not part of the D4D program.

NASCAR launched D4D in 2004 to increase participation by minorities and women. This included not just drivers but all aspects of the sport including team ownership, team membership, and staffing at all levels within NASCAR and its corporate partners. When it came to drivers, NASCAR began with a grass roots effort to identify young minority and female talent competing on local short tracks in entry level stock cars. Their objective was to help these drivers move up to one of its national touring series. Drivers selected for the program would compete in cars fielded by D4D. Additional assistance from D4D came in the form of financial support beyond what a driver may have already had in place, which usually meant some form of family backing.

In 2008, Cheryl and I received an invitation to meet with NASCAR executives in Daytona Beach about the future of the D4D program. We flew down to Florida and were greeted at the Daytona office by NASCAR president Mike Helton and Marcus Jadotte, an African American who managed public affairs and the diversity department at NASCAR.

After some small talk and catching up, Mike got right to the point.

"You know that we have the Drive for Diversity program. It's been run by an outside vendor for the last four years, and although we still believe in the mission of the program, we're not overly satisfied with the way it's being managed. The results have not been satisfactory."

I think I knew what he meant, but I wanted some clarification.

"In what way?" I asked.

Marcus took the lead in response.

"Drivers participating in the Drive for Diversity program have moved up from the entry-level, local tracks to the regional touring series, but no driver has advanced to one of our three national touring series."

I knew this to be true, but I was also aware that NASCAR was only helping fund drivers up to the regional level—therein lay the problem.

"I have noticed that," I commented tersely.

I wanted to let them steer the conversation because I wasn't quite sure what point they were getting at.

"We'd like you to run the Drive for Diversity program," Mike explained. "You know the ins and outs of NASCAR, you have a vested interest, and you have the leadership experience from your years as a project manager."

"We think you would be great at directing this program for us," Marcus added enthusiastically.

Mike knew how much I had struggled to make it in professional racing and likely thought that I would jump at the opportunity to help up-and-coming drivers find a better way. I certainly wanted there to be a more efficient path for drivers of other genders and ethnicities, but I wasn't sure that this particular venture was the right fit for me. As soon as I started asking questions about what this would entail, a plethora of red flags started waving. I was informed that we would have to secure our own operating budget. After spending a lifetime fighting to barely find funding for myself, I was less than enthused by the idea of having to do it all over again, but on a much broader scale. It seemed like an almost impossible task, filled with catch-22s, that would drain all of the joy out of racing for me.

"Gentlemen, I appreciate that you have that much faith in me, but I am not convinced that I'll be able to find sponsorship for a bunch of kids racing on short tracks with no TV coverage. I honestly don't know if I have the ability to successfully carry out an undertaking of that caliber at this point in my life."

"It won't be easy, but we think that if anyone can do it, it's you, Bill," Mike said confidently.

I turned to Cheryl to try to read the expression on her face. She had always been my sounding board for big decisions and this was not something that I would feel comfortable agreeing to without getting her input and opinion.

"It's a big commitment, and I wouldn't want to rush to any decisions. I think it's something that I'd like to marinate on and talk over with my wife. I want to make sure that anything I devote myself to also works for my family."

"Of course. We completely understand. But I believe that with your management skills and racing knowledge, coupled with Cheryl's business acumen, you can run this program. I have complete faith that you'd be the best person to move this program in the right direction," Mike declared.

We left the meeting telling Mike that we'd be in touch soon. Based on my years in racing, Cheryl knew the upward battles that we would face and shared my hesitation. It was a daunting task that I just wasn't ready to embrace. We quickly decided this offer was far too risky and simply not in our best interest to pursue further.

NASCAR later ended up moving forward with Max Siegel, a black executive from the music and entertainment industry, who had far more corporate connections than we did.

Despite not being a part of the D4D program, either as a participant or a leader, I was still a catalyst for change. The hue in the stands began to change when I raced in the Truck Series. Unfortunately, I wasn't on a grand enough stage to make a significant or lasting impact to the overall sport. But I feel a sense of fulfillment knowing that any nonwhite driver who came after me (or has yet to come) has benefited from the bricks I laid and the accomplishments I was able to achieve.

■ ■ ■

RACING TO THE FRONT

I had a lot of appreciation and *gratitude* for the fact that there were efforts being expended to diversify a sport that had always been copiously white. Though NASCAR had—and still has—a long way to go to achieve a more diverse work force and audience, the Diversity Council and the Drive for Diversity program are steps in the right direction. NASCAR created a diversity department, brought in people from all walks of life to lend their voices to a diversity council, and created the Drive for Diversity program. If those efforts had been realized twenty or thirty years sooner, I may not have had to fight as hard as I did. I am *grateful* that I was able to be a part of the transformation that will help the next generation, so that their path forward will not be as rigorous and cumbersome as mine was.

I was humbled and honored that the president of NASCAR thought that Cheryl and I would be a good fit to take on a huge project like the D4D program. I am *grateful* that I was able to earn enough respect from high-level executives to warrant an opportunity of that magnitude. Unfortunately, it was not the right fit for me and my family, but the fact that I was considered meant a great deal. However, one should never underestimate the importance of having the wisdom to know when to say "no."

Not every situation pans out the way we hope it should, but having gratitude for the experiences and opportunities that life offers is an essential part of the journey.

20

Returning to First Love—Sports Cars

While racing in NASCAR, I made a conscious effort to network within the sport, which proved helpful when the 2007 season came along and I no longer had a team to call my own. As I had suspected, Bill Davis Racing did not move forward with me, so I was on the hunt for my next opportunity.

The 2007 season began with my return to the famed Rolex 24 at Daytona in January for the first time since the ill-fated finish of the 2001 race, when Joe Varde had crashed on pit exit and the coveted Rolex eluded my grasp. I was thrilled to have another chance at bringing home the wristband trophy. I raced with Roger Schramm, Jack Baldwin, Justin Bell, and John

Heinricy, and we drove a Pontiac Riley in the Daytona Prototype class of the Grand-Am sports car series. This was in the Rock Valley Oil (RVO) car Roger owned, which unfortunately did not do very well in the race. We only finished 458 laps out of 668 due to a mechanical failure with the car. At that point, I didn't know if or when I would be racing again and in what capacity. I was trying to do whatever I could to extend my career and find a port in the storm. Not yielding good results in the Rolex 24 weighed on me heavily, especially since I loved the rush of endurance road racing and desperately wanted to make my mark after my return from NASCAR.

The most well-known twenty-four-hour endurance race is the 24 Hours of Le Mans that takes place in France. It is the most prestigious race in the world and the best sports car drivers from around the globe compete for the win. If we had performed better in the Rolex 24 in Daytona, I may have been able to position myself better to have a shot at securing sponsorship to try my hand at Le Mans, but I was never very successful in this race. To this day, not having the opportunity to compete in the 24 Hours of Le Mans is my one biggest professional racing regrets. Being able to say that you ran that race is like saying you got to play in the Super Bowl. But the elusive Rolex 24 was still evading me; ergo, Le Mans was not in my sightline, either. With Daytona behind me, I was unsure what my next move would be. Luckily, I had established some connections over the years that I was able to tap back into.

During my time in the Truck Series, I had begun to build a relationship with Jim France, a son of NASCAR founder Bill France Sr. and the uncle of NASCAR CEO and chairman Brian France. Once my efforts to join the Cup Series full-time were derailed, Jim helped me move back into sports car racing in the Grand-Am Series and assisted me in finding the budget to do so.

NASCAR had created Grand-Am, one of America's top road racing series, largely through the work of Jim France, who directed it on a day-to-day basis after its launch in 2000. Jim, as a diehard sports car enthusiast, controlled his own capital in this series. As the director of Grand-Am, Jim needed to keep as many teams competing as possible. The series competed for fans, sponsorship, and manufacturer recognition against the rival American Le Mans Series and needed to keep a full field of entries on the track. If not for Jim's love of sports car racing, there wouldn't have been a Grand-Am. He kept it afloat. When it came to sustaining the number of teams and cars entered in the premier Daytona Prototype (DP) class, Jim worked in various ways, including the direct funding of some teams. In my case, Jim helped fund a team and I was paid out of the team's budget to drive for it.

I had the impression that Jim thought a lot of me for showing up in NASCAR through my own efforts and proving that I could be competitive. He knew all of the challenges I faced as a man in my mid-forties trying to make it in a professional sport that I had considerably less experience in than even the majority of the young guns in the field. He was also keenly aware of the political struggles I had to endure. NASCAR had more bureaucracy because they were a much larger organization with a bigger financial footprint than the Grand-Am series. Essentially, NASCAR had too many cooks in the kitchen and they were all fighting over the money to buy ingredients and the ability to make their own recipes. In Grand-Am, decisions belonged to Jim alone. A virtual czar, he had complete authority to run things the way he saw fit without outside influences or pushback.

Jim was a visible presence within Grand-Am: He could often be seen going to and from his relatively old Newell motor home. Sometimes he cruised around the track incognito on his motorcycle while hidden beneath a helmet (most people didn't realize it was him). Many times, he was front and center, engaging participants on the track. That was how I got to know him. I went out of my way to speak to him and sometimes when I was in the area visited him in his personal office, which was located in a completely separate location from the corporate NASCAR/Grand-Am offices in Daytona.

I liked Jim a lot. He wasn't an extrovert, but once you got to know him, he was quite personable. He could also be very quiet, making it difficult to know exactly what he was thinking. He enjoyed listening. Frankly, I wouldn't want to play poker with him. I made it a point to show my appreciation for everything he had done for me. I always went out of my way to chat with him and even sent him an annual Christmas card during the holidays. Having a guy like Jim think enough of me to invest in me and look out for my interests made a huge difference in my career and meant the absolute world to me.

Jim connected me with the RVO Grand-Am team based in Rockford, Illinois, for the Rolex 24. Roger Schramm was a nice gentleman who was excited to have me drive on his team with him. The team manager, Dave Watson, was an easygoing veteran racer who had started his career driving stock cars and competing on Wisconsin short tracks. Dave and the crew would often share stories between our practice sessions about their wild adventures in snowmobile racing, something I had little appreciation for. The team did not operate at quite the same level as the top teams in the series, but the other RVO drivers and I were dedicated to doing the best we could with our car against the better-financed entrants. Our team was primarily made up of weekend warriors who were passionate about racing, but were simply not as skilled as members of the other teams. But it didn't really matter to me because they were great guys who worked hard and shared my love of the sport.

Going back to sports cars was like returning home, especially since I immediately stepped into a DP, which competed at the top race class, as opposed to the slower GT class car. Sports cars, in general, were much more responsive than a Cup car or a NASCAR truck. They were typically lighter, with wider tires, and had additional downforce, better braking, and nimbleness in the corners that made them outperform their NASCAR rivals. Due to the car's light weight and high grip, a DP was easier to drive to its limits. While extremely fast through the corners, it felt relatively slow in a straight line since a DP only had about 550 horsepower, much less than the 750-or-so horsepower I had become accustomed to in a NASCAR truck or the roughly 900 horsepower of a Cup car.

I was much more comfortable in the sports car parking area known as the paddock. (Sports car racing doesn't have the same financial backing as NASCAR and the tracks tend to be in more rural areas, so instead of garages there is a "paddock," which is the open area where drivers park their trailers side by side while leaving enough room between them to work on their cars.) In sports car racing, I didn't have to worry as much about being different or fitting in. Those involved in sports car racing were generally more accepting of racial and cultural differences because there was increased international diversity in the makeup of its teams and fans. The Rolex 24 was comprised of teams from all over the world. Germany, Italy, France, and England, for example, all had a strong presence in endurance racing. I was no longer an outcast among a sea of close-knit teams who shared the same pale complexion and Southern drawl. There were accents from all over the world. No one race or nationality was more dominant than the other. There wasn't a need for a formal diversity program within the Grand-Am series.

Sports car racing was not nearly as well-known or viewed as widely as NASCAR. At this point in my career, when people asked what I did for a living and I responded, "I'm a sports car racer," the usual reply was, "What's that?"

When I was racing with NASCAR, everyone knew what it meant when I told them that I was a NASCAR driver. I would often make the distinction by saying, "I race sports cars and also raced in NASCAR."

After the Rolex 24, I returned to Daytona in February 2007 to start what turned out to be my final season in the Truck Series with Billy Ballew

Motorsports. A truck team owner since 1996, Billy had been watching me and told me he had respect for my efforts with Dodge and Toyota. Just as importantly, he also knew I had some financial support from NASCAR. Coupled with his assets and technical assistance from Chevy, that took us through the first fifteen races, a little past halfway into the season. Billy did what he could do to keep me in the saddle, usually selling sponsorships to small, local businesses he had relationships with. We once had backing from a company called Christian Debt Consolidation. I had never heard of them before their logo graphics appeared on my truck.

I wondered how he remained financially solvent but, somehow, he always found a way. Billy just loved racing and had strong connections of his own. He stayed completely engaged with everything happening on his team. As a used car dealer from Georgia, he knew how to hustle and how to sell. His race trucks were pristinely prepared, which was no easy feat considering the financially limited platform he had to work with, including a very modest shop. But his trucks were always immaculate and the black paint was silky smooth and shiny. He left the preparation to crew chief Richie Wauters, but Billy was always at the track, either watching intently or working to strengthen business relationships with those he came across. This was in stark contrast to Bill Davis, who often enjoyed the races from the comfort of his top-of-the-line motor home with his wife, Gail. Billy may not have been turning the actual wrenches, but he was involved in some aspect of his team every step of the way.

Over the course of seventeen years in the Truck Series, Billy Ballew Motorsports won twenty races, a majority of them with NASCAR star Kyle Busch. In my case, I managed to finish eight races on the lead lap in fifteen starts with a best finish of eighth in Kentucky. These lackluster results weighed on me and finally began to dim my enthusiasm for NASCAR.

I had become accustomed to the high-performance trucks fielded by the Bill Davis Toyota team. It was a frustrating adjustment to revert backward with the limited sponsorship dollars currently at our disposal. We were so underfunded that we couldn't afford all the bells and whistles that undeniably helped win races. With Billy's team, we used what were referred to as "customer" engines that provided good horsepower, but were not the robust factory-built motors supplied by Toyota that I had grown used to. Consequently, while my entries were well prepared, I didn't run at the front like I had with Bill Davis. I couldn't get the results I was after and be a contender to lead laps, which meant that I also couldn't win races.

In retrospect, even though I had some success in the Truck Series over the course of my career, I had come to the party too late and was not fully able to master continuously running on the edge in a NASCAR truck without sometimes overstepping it. I could not make up for all of the time I should have been racing as a kid and as a young adult. It was hard to play catch-up as a relatively inexperienced driver in his forties against guys who had been racing these types of vehicles since they were teenagers.

NASCAR Cup Series Champion Kyle Busch is an example of extraordinary talent developed from a young age. Like his older brother Kurt, also a Cup Series Champion, Kyle had benefited from being on a team run by their father in Las Vegas, and believe me, experience is every bit as important as money.

Similar to Kyle Busch, Aric Almirola is another driver who won for Billy who had substantially more experience than I did. After having raced early in his career, Aric ran the full season with Billy in 2010 at age twenty-six with full commercial sponsorship. He won two races and finished second in the championship. I would've loved to have started my professional career in my mid-twenties, but such was not my luck.

It didn't take away from how much I loved the sport. I may not have started out as young as I would've liked, I may not have gotten the financial support I had hoped for, and I may not have won the biggest races, but I was doing something that only a small handful of people in the entire world have ever had the pleasure of experiencing. I didn't need trophies, Rolexes or a lap around Victory Lane to feel blessed and successful, because I was living my dream. I was no longer stuck behind a desk watching the clock, watching for the little hand to strike five, and that was monumental. I was able to keep a roof over my family's head and food in their mouths all the while having the time of my life. In NASCAR, I was making a living driving up to 200 mph in top-tier race cars in a sport with an almost rabid following. There were so many fans who followed my career and cheered me on. Having complete strangers care about my achievements and seek my autograph was a humbling feeling that I will appreciate until my dying day. There are so many things to be grateful for.

The dynamic of racing sports cars in the Grand-Am series was much more welcoming and much less stressful than at the top level of NASCAR. I went on to happily race in Grand-Am for five years. In 2008, I drove thirteen Grand-Am races for Steve and Martha Southard's team in a Lexus-Riley DP co-driven by Shane Lewis. Steve had raced at the amateur level and went on to own a car parts business with his wife, Martha. Owning a professional racing team was a natural progression for them. Being a part of their organization felt like being a part of their family. In sports car racing, I finally began to forge real friendships with my teammates, who offered me sound advice on the track.

In 2009, I raced with the Orbit Racing team owned by Roger Hawley in a BMW-powered Riley DP chassis. Englishman Darren Manning, one of my co-drivers there, really opened my eyes about how to most effectively drive a DP. Darren drove a DP like an Indy car, not a sports car. There is a distinct difference between Indy cars and stock cars and an even greater difference in the way Indy car drivers take to the track. Indy car drivers are solely fueled by speed as opposed to stamina. Since Indy car races are usually shorter in duration, there is no room for error. Longer endurance races offer more leeway for slower pit stops and the opportunity to recover from costly mistakes such as spinning a car out. Indy car races do not lend the driver that luxury. It's a sprint format, not endurance, and many drivers have tried unsuccessfully to master the art of playing both fields.

Darren had spent several seasons driving Indy cars prior to our first co-drive in the Rolex 24. His style of driving was much more aggressive than my own, but I wanted to learn his tricks. He taught me how to maximize the car's stopping potential through threshold braking, which meant braking hard for as little time as necessary and then immediately switching back to the gas. The throttle was either full on or off. You were either on the brake or on the throttle. I had never learned to drive that way in a sports car. Upon corner entry, I would brake, and then coast briefly in the middle of the corner before accelerating out of it. In other words, I would let the car free roll for a moment and stabilize before I went back to power.

Initially, I looked at the computer telemetry traces of Darren's throttle and braking application and could not fathom how he was able to manage driving all the way around the track without nearly any pedal modulation. In sports car racing the cars were equipped with real-time telemetry, which is a computer system that captures the data of each lap in a graphical presentation, which includes throttle, steering, and brake inputs. It's an invaluable tool for drivers because we can analyze our performance as compared to our co-drivers to see where time was gained or lost over the course of the lap. I was able to precisely assess how Darren was best optimizing the capabilities of the car.

I would never have attempted his approach if the data had not convinced me that it was the secret to his success. It was an entirely different style than my own and commanded a new level of bravery that I needed to conjure from within. In my practice laps, I listened to his instructions and attempted to emulate his method. I couldn't do exactly what he was doing because of the instability it produced in the balance of the car, but I tried and it improved my speed through the corners. Fortunately for me, Darren proved to be an excellent mentor.

Ironically, after learning some new techniques from Darren, my best finish in the Prototypes came in partnership with Ryan Dalziel, a Scotsman who had experience in Indy cars as well. At a July sprint race in the blistering heat at Daytona, we finished on the podium in third place. (A sprint race is any race under the normal two-hour-and-forty-five minute mark. Anything over that is considered an endurance race.) Finishing third was an extremely satisfying result of my producing a good opening stint and then handing the car over to Ryan during the pit stop, who then drove even more impressively to the finish. Much like Darren, Ryan was able to stay hard on the throttle until it was time to threshold brake and then transition immediately back to the gas with no coasting in between.

Daytona is the official headquarters of NASCAR and is known as the World Center of Racing. It is a track that I have had the joy of competing on many times in a wide variety of racing cars. To stand on the podium in Victory Lane at Daytona was one of the highlights of my life and a moment I will always remember fondly.

When I switched to Starworks Motorsports in 2010, I raced against Ryan in the Rolex 24. He co-drove on a rival team, Action Express Racing, which ended up winning the coveted endurance race. It wasn't long after that he came over to Starworks and became my teammate. Once at Starworks, Ryan was regularly paired with another young driver, a Canadian named Mike Forest, in the team's No. 8 DP. Together they scored a number of Top 10 results, landing them on the podium three times. Due to budget constraints, I co-drove with myriad other drivers that year in the sister No. 7 DP to marginal success. I began to recognize that there were clearly better drivers than me competing in DPs.

Indy car team owners like Roger Penske, who competed with a Porsche-powered DP, and Chip Ganassi, who was backed by a variety of manufacturers including Lexus, were the benchmark in Grand-Am. That's what I was up against: Indy car team owners, Indy car drivers, and Indy car technology, all of which was unfamiliar to me. Meanwhile, I had been lumbering around in big ol' NASCAR vehicles for six seasons, which wasn't doing me any favors now.

I had fun racing in Grand-Am DPs, but I wasn't setting the world on fire. My initial infatuation for racing had started with seeing Prototypes in the Can-Am Series race at Laguna Seca as a boy, and I relished the opportunity to earn a living driving the latter-day Prototypes. But, once again, I found myself racing in reverse. The chance to drive sports car Prototypes had finally arrived, but the timing was late.

Some things just weren't meant to be.

■ ■ ■

RACING TO THE FRONT

Given the setbacks and disappointments I had experienced in NASCAR, it would have been easy to stay bitter about that situation and give up on racing. But I knew my overall *enthusiasm* for competing behind the wheel had not diminished, which helped me stay focused on moving forward and finding another way to achieve my goal of continuing to race professionally.

By employing the power of *networking*, I sustained my relationship with Jim France, which enabled me to move into Prototype sports cars for the first time and enjoy new challenges. It was a classic case of recognizing a glass being half full instead of half empty. That's another way of stating that my *gratitude* for having future opportunities stayed in focus instead of being diminished by the hopes that didn't get fulfilled.

Instead of focusing on shortcomings
or what might be missing,
being thankful and grateful for opportunities
helps keep attention on priorities.

21

A Historic Season

The 2011 season began, and although the DPs afforded higher speeds, better braking, and faster cornering, without ample funding it was not possible to continue driving them. NASCAR kept me afloat by providing a budget of a half million dollars. Although that sounds lofty, in the expensive world of professional auto racing, it's not nearly enough to even partially support a DP team. Sedan-based racing programs, on the other hand, didn't have the same costly financial requirements, so I shifted my focus to them. I began to look at who had the best options available.

There is one constant in racing that doesn't change no matter what top professional category you may be competing in: If you want to win races and championships, it's incumbent to get on a team that has factory support. After reviewing all the possibilities, I returned to the Chevrolet fold by joining Autohaus Motorsports. Team owner Bob Kirland had decided to run a full season in 2011, following several partial seasons, and I was ready to be a part of it.

Each year, my agreement with NASCAR worked differently. In this case, the Autohaus team received a half-a-million dollars from NASCAR, and I was paid under a separate consulting agreement with NASCAR. I had moved to Orlando a few years earlier and since Autohaus had its shop in Delray Beach, the commute was relatively short. I could easily head over for shop visits and to test at the nearby road course at Palm Beach International Raceway.

With Autohaus, I would be driving a Chevy Camaro, originally engineered and built by Pratt & Miller, a highly successful race car builder. It paled in comparison to the stiff chassis platform offered by the Riley DP, and I had a hard time adjusting to the differences. The Camaro had a comparatively soft chassis and suspension setup, so, far more than I liked, the car tended to pitch and roll (which meant the front of the car raised up upon acceleration, dove down under braking, and leaned over when cornering due to the lateral g-forces). I was often concerned that the tires would unexpectantly abandon their grip and break loose, since the car felt numb and did not provide me with the feedback I had come to expect from the stiffly sprung DP. For my style of driving, the only advantage from a soft chassis came in the rain; the suspension was more compliant in slippery conditions and less inclined to suddenly let the tires break loose.

My move to Autohaus highlighted what many professional drivers constantly face throughout our careers: needing to adapt to a variety of cars, often with dramatically different driving characteristics. I'm not entirely sure that even veteran fans recognize all of the challenges and nuances of moving from one type of race car to another.

In NASCAR, the suspensions were also relatively soft, which is what a driver needs on short ovals or a road course. But it had been a long time since I had driven on a short track or a road course, so I didn't have a recent frame of reference for driving a soft chassis. Immediately following my days in NASCAR, I had moved into DPs that rode lower to the ground on stiff chassis platforms. After moving away from sleek Prototypes, I found myself in an unfamiliar GT coupe, struggling to come to grips with its high pitch and roll handling characteristics. I even wrecked our Camaro in a mid-season test at Watkins Glen, New York, trying to find the limit of grip. The car was able to be rebuilt, but it further shook my confidence in my ability to master its tendencies. It also meant lunch was on me for the crew that day to show my appreciation for the extra effort they had to expend loading up a damaged race car for the long trip back home to the shop.

I was paired at Autohaus with a bright young talent named Jordan Taylor who was a nineteen-year-old college student at the University of Central Florida. The son of two-time road racing champion Wayne Taylor and the younger brother of DP driver Ricky Taylor, Jordan had established himself as a driver on the rise while racing a privately entered Mazda RX-8 in the GT category the year before. The move to the factory-assisted Autohaus team was the next step in his budding career, which was being closely guided and monitored by his father.

At this point, I was a veteran in Grand-Am, and I didn't need to establish myself. Many years of experience behind the wheel in top divisions had solidified my reputation as a professional driver. But Jordan and I needed to learn to work together, setting up the car for races and meshing as teammates. The team was also unfamiliar with me and wanted to evaluate my capabilities as a driver. Jordan was recommended to Autohaus with support from Chevy, which had long been supporting his father's DP team, Wayne Taylor Racing.

In the age of computers, our general manager, Marcus Haselgrove, together with team engineer Cody Ragone, was able to generate a wealth of key data about braking, acceleration, and maximizing speed from the car. After Jordan ran a particularly good lap time, I looked at his data and asked myself, "How the heck did he do that?" Jordan's driving style wasn't like that of the Indy drivers whom I had tried to emulate. His prowess came from his experience driving GT sedans. He was much more comfortable feeling the grip limit of the tire under a car equipped with soft suspension. In short, a GT car was not numb to him.

Jordan was still relatively new to racing and had not bounced around as much as I had, so he had a much easier time conforming the car to his will. He did not have preconceived notions or old habits to break. It was at the season-opening Rolex 24 at Daytona when I first saw the emerging talent of my young teammate on display. Jordan qualified second in the GT class, right on the heels of a veteran factory Porsche driver. Car manufacturers often installed their highly successful factory drivers on Grand-Am teams, racing their brand to boost results in qualifying and fortunes in the race.

When you run in the same car with factory drivers, it's another barometer of how you stack up. I was in the twilight of my career, whereas Jordan was only beginning and was already at a comparable level to the Chevrolet factory drivers. Johnny O'Connell, a factory driver for Corvette Racing in the rival American Le Mans Series, joined our Autohaus driving team for the Rolex 24, and Jordan discovered he could post similar lap times.

At age forty-nine, maybe my driving skills had peaked, I don't know, but Jordan could feel the car's behavior in a way I couldn't. He had been racing only production-based GT cars throughout his young career. I did a decent job maneuvering the DPs after leaving NASCAR, but the GT cars proved to be more challenging.

Jordan and I had a unique relationship. I mentored him off the track and he often mentored me on it. Jordan did not need any guidance on the track; he was outperforming me at almost every turn, but the breadth of my career gave me invaluable experience that enabled me to mentor him on the ins and outs of racing and the politics that ensued. We spent time together since we both lived in the Orlando area. When we had to go to Delray Beach and visit the Autohaus shop, we rode down together. It was during these rides that I encouraged him to pursue NASCAR opportunities.

"Jordan, you really need to consider making a move into NASCAR. Your footprint will be so much bigger. It's such a larger stage. Sports car racing is a great platform for now, but with the way you drive, you should broaden your horizons for the long term. You can make it in the biggest league, which is NASCAR, and I think you should go after it."

Being thirty years older than him, I almost felt like a father figure. I wanted him to realize his full potential professionally, so I felt it was imperative that he have belief in his abilities reinforced by someone outside of his family.

"I would love to. I just wouldn't know where to begin," he admitted.

"You can try to find a ride in the road course events. The NASCAR Xfinity Series is a great place to show teams and sponsors what you can do."

I wanted to pay it forward and help him out the way Willy T. Ribbs had influenced my career all those years ago. I shared countless NASCAR stories with Jordan on our rides back and forth to Delray Beach.

Jordan got to actually see firsthand the level of intensity that NASCAR fans bring. During autograph sessions in the Grand-Am paddock that accompanied the race weekend, NASCAR fans often brought paraphernalia for me to sign, such as die-cast Waste Management Cup cars and hero cards (the large trading cards used in professional motorsports) from the Truck teams I'd raced for. I had been out of NASCAR for years, but people still recognized me, were following me on my sports car journey, and brought NASCAR items to Grand-Am tracks they wanted me to autograph.

"This is what I'm talking about. These are the kind of rabid fans that NASCAR has," I told Jordan as we walked back to our team hauler.

Jordan nodded in agreement.

"I see. You're practically a celebrity," he said jokingly.

"If you're in NASCAR, people know who you are. It's a whole different deal than sports cars. Sometimes when I'm out to dinner with Cheryl and the kids, fans come up and ask for an autograph. It's wild! If I had only stayed in sports car racing, I never would've received that kind of recognition. Being able to race in NASCAR is when you can really start making money and a name for yourself."

"That sounds amazing. Just tell me what you think I need to do, and I'm game."

I don't know if Jordan would have ever considered NASCAR racing before our talks. I'm glad that what I said resonated with him. Although he has yet to compete in NASCAR, it's not for lack of trying. Not only have I tried to open doors for him, but so has NASCAR Cup Series champion Jeff Gordon, whom Jordan also befriended. It's a great shame that the opportunity for him to compete has not presented itself yet, because I believe he will turn heads. But his struggles are a testimony to how difficult it is to break into NASCAR. While I was much older than Jordan, we forged a friendship that I truly enjoyed and still do. There was one race in particular that cemented our bond.

Virginia International Raceway (VIR) is a beautiful, fast, and perilous track consisting of seventeen turns through the foothills of the Blue Ridge Mountains. We arrived there after finishing fourteenth in our class in the season-opening Rolex 24 Hours of Daytona endurance race, sixth at Homestead-Miami Speedway, and seventh at Barber Motorsports Park.

In Grand-Am, the rule book stipulated that the qualifying driver had to start the race, so I drove in qualifying. With the race at VIR lasting only two hours and forty-five minutes; there wasn't much time for both Jordan and me to drive. The strategy at Autohaus called for me to start the race and switch drivers at an early pit stop after I had satisfied the minimum time of thirty minutes to earn points. That allowed Jordan to drive the bulk of the race and finish it. All teams that had one driver who was faster than the other ran their strategy this way.

The race started under what seemed like monsoon conditions. The rain was relentless. I had qualified sixth, just behind the Brumos Porsche driven by Andrew Davis. After the green flag dropped, I stayed close to the Brumos car's rear bumper and made sure to never lose sight of its tail lights. The challenge to do so was heightened by the horrendous visibility and inevitable fogging of the windshield that results from competing with race cars in the rain.

The Porsche had an advantage in these conditions due to its engine being in the rear. The engine's weight over the rear wheels provided superior traction in the wet. But we had an advantage as well due to our characteristically soft suspension. In the rain, the last thing a driver wants is a rigid chassis, which makes cars more skittish on a wet surface. Some pitch and roll under slippery conditions helps in keeping the car more compliant, and thus easier to drive.

Even on rain tires, I struggled to keep the car on the track. The first four qualifiers slid off-course or spun. That quickly put me and Andrew into first and second place. To his credit, he didn't make any errors or put a wheel wrong. I stayed hot on his trail. Having the Brumos Porsche out front offered a clear path to follow. Had I lost him I might not have been able to maximize my speed through each corner due to such poor visibility.

The downpour remained steady for my entire thirty-minute run behind the wheel. I decided not to take any unnecessary risks in trying to pass Andrew since he maintained a strong pace and nobody closed from behind. I also firmly believed that giving Jordan a car anywhere near the front could produce a winning result. In the end, I brought the car into the pits in second place. Given the conditions, I had completed a flawless stint.

Once Jordan took to the track, the rain mercifully began to let up and then ceased altogether. Although he started out on grooved rain tires, he called in over the radio for slick tires to be bolted to the car on his next scheduled pit stop, since the track was drying. Pit stops momentarily shuffled the running order, but by the time all the pit stops were completed, Jordan had worked himself into the GT class lead. A nod must go to the Autohaus crew as well. Led by Marcus Hasselgrove and car chief Bill Welsh, the crew really rose to the occasion. At the shop, our team worked hard during its pit stop practices and those efforts paid off. Excellent pit crew execution is as crucial to success as driving performances.

I started to realize that we had a real shot at winning. As the laps wound down, Jordan continued to lead the race. I anxiously watched the cars come roaring past on the main straight and then, once they had gone by, looked over at the race scoring monitor on a screen mounted on the back of our pit wagon, to compare lap times. We were getting closer and closer to a possible victory.

When a late-race caution flew, I heard Jordan come over the radio to our crew chief, Charlie Ping.

"I like the way the car's handling."

A sense of relief washed over me. As long as the car continued to handle well, I knew Jordan was capable of bringing it home.

Once the race went green again, with only a handful of laps left, I stationed myself at the front of our pit area with my feet pressed against the pit wall, anxiously waiting to see Jordan come onto the main straight again.

My heart pumped furiously, but I tried not to get too excited. I knew anything could happen in the closing laps of a race. As I knew from the closing laps at the Truck race in Nashville, the claws come out the closer drivers get to the finish line. Drivers become more emboldened and take chances in the last few moments that can change everything. You never knew who was going to strike a risky or dangerous move, causing you to spin out trying to avoid hitting them, or who was going to clip you on a pass and send you both flying into the wall. You never knew who was going to steal the inside line and push you further out, or if another driver under you would take the turn too wide, allowing more drivers to overtake you both. The last few laps of a race were often the most tumultuous.

I had been here before and didn't want to suffer the same level of disappointment because I allowed myself to get prematurely enthusiastic. The excitement, however, kept building despite my better judgment. All around me smiles began to appear and started widening on the faces of my teammates, along with a heightened pitch in their voices. They were clearly thinking the win was coming. I tried to stay grounded. I had come too far and had experienced too many upsets in racing to let my guard down until I saw the checkered flag.

On the last lap, we saw Jordan come through the final turn and onto the main straight in the lead. By now, we were all standing up on the pit wall in nervous anticipation. Our car came barreling up the track at the front of the GT class! The last of my worries dissolved.

"He's still out front!" I announced with bated breath. "We're going to win!"

When the checkered flag fell over the number 88 Autohaus Camaro, we all erupted into cheers of pure elation. My own screams of happiness were echoed in my teammates. We had just won the Bosch Engineering 250 at Virginia International Raceway! Sheer pandemonium broke out as we took turns hugging, high-fiving, and congratulating each other.

Jordan completed his cool-down lap and momentarily entered our pit box. Since this was our first win, he didn't realize he needed to head directly to Victory Lane. Once informed, he stuck the Camaro back into gear and headed to the end of pit lane, made a right, and parked the car under instruction of the officials.

The crew and I raced over on foot. I rushed right up to Jordan, threw my arms around him, and pulled him into a huge hug.

"Way to go, man! You drove a great race!"

He had a big grin on his face, but was surprisingly tranquil. He barely said a word. Jordan was either overwhelmed by his first career victory at a top professional level or completely spent from his driving efforts, and was almost in a state of shock.

At the podium, it was tremendously satisfying to step up to the top. It had been such a long drought between victories for me. Flanked by the second and third place finishers, we received our victory trophies. Once we popped the champagne corks, I doused Jordan and our Autohaus crew assembled below the podium. In Jordan's case, that turned out to be unfair. He actually didn't know how to uncork a champagne bottle! He had won many races in his youth, but none of his victory celebrations had included champagne. He was only a teenager, so he wasn't of legal drinking age yet. After watching him struggle with the bottle, I took pity on him being drenched with spray by the other drivers on the podium. I quickly uncorked his bottle for him so he could join in on the fun.

After we emptied the champagne bottles and all of the Victory Lane photos were taken, Jordan and I went to the media center to talk with the assembled reporters about our race.

"Everything came together for us. We knew at the beginning of the season that this team had a lot of potential." I turned and pointed to Jordan. "Watch out for this guy right here. Jordan Taylor is going to be a household name. He's one of the most talented drivers I've ever seen, and I can't wait to see what he does next," I proudly told reporters.

Jordan was gracious and similarly complimentary toward me.

"Bill handed me over a perfect race car, giving me the chance to contend for the win."

I'm proud to say that I did a solid job behind the wheel during my short stint in extremely difficult conditions, but not too proud to declare that Jordan's performance superseded mine.

"Jordan is the real hero of the day. It was his stellar performance that brought us home a win."

Once the interviews ended, we headed back to our pit box where the team had nearly finished breaking down the equipment and was loading it on the transporter. It had been a long time since my last victory, and I literally pinched myself a time or two just to make sure it was real. I had run ten full seasons and thousands of laps without getting the ultimate prize, a victory, so I was definitely savoring this one.

Since Grand-Am was owned and operated by NASCAR, my victory marked the first time an African American driver had won a nationally sanctioned NASCAR race since Wendell Scott won a Cup race in Jacksonville, Florida, in 1963. Serendipitously, VIR is the hometown of Wendell Scott. Experiencing my first victory so close to Scott's home in nearby Danville brought a unique and surreal feeling of accomplishment. I was proud to help sustain the legacy he had established as a successful black racing driver. Wendell Oliver Scott passed away in 1990, so I never got the chance to meet him, but I had the pleasure of meeting his family on two previous occasions.

In 2003, I helped induct Wendell posthumously into the National Black Sports and Entertainment Hall of Fame during ceremonies held in New York City. It was an occasion I will never forget. I got to spend time with Wendell's widow, Mary; his sons, Wendell Jr. and Frank; and daughters, Sybil and Debra. They extended an open invitation to visit whenever I came for one of my NASCAR Truck races in Martinsville, Virginia, which was about thirty miles from Danville. After learning so much about Wendell early in my Truck Series career, the chance to gain a better understanding and appreciation for the man who paved the way for me was an opportunity I relished. I promptly responded to the Scott family's invitation.

Not long after meeting the Scott family, I flew from Atlanta into the Greensboro, North Carolina, airport, headed for my Truck Series race in Martinsville. But first, I drove my rental car into the city of Danville. My drive through the city with its narrow streets and older, very modest homes gave me a glimpse of the small-town South, a much more conservative way of life than I had grown accustomed to.

Wendell Jr. and Frank greeted me at the front door of the Scotts' home. Inside, Mary and Sybil welcomed me into the living room. After exchanging pleasantries, I quickly noticed the room was rich with family photos and mementos of Wendell's legacy in racing. I sat down and marveled in the history and the stories that the Scott family shared. I truly felt blessed to be given a very personal tour of their lives.

Before long, I started asking questions about some of the cars in the photographs. They ranged from Wendell's earliest days of driving at the local dirt track to the cars he had driven in NASCAR during the 1960s and 1970s. Wendell Jr. and Frank provided most of the answers, but Sybil offered great insights as well. Being so much younger, her memories were often different. Mary occasionally offered some perspective, but she mostly watched in contentment as her children led the dialogue. I was intrigued that each of the Scotts had their own unique thoughts and recollections, but the stories fit together well and gave me a sense of who Wendell had been and the challenges he'd faced.

Talking to the Scotts was a humbling experience. They offered startling accounts of the racism and poverty they had endured. I could only try to envision what it had been like to race in NASCAR during the era when Wendell had raced. My racing experiences and hardships seemed trivial by comparison and it helped to put my journey into perspective. I had heard the n-word at the track, and I knew what it was like for conversations to stop and fingers to be pointed when I walked by. All this paled in comparison to what Wendell and his family had experienced when they went racing. Even if the NASCAR environment made me uncomfortable on occasion, at least I felt my family was safe when at the track. The same could not be said for Wendell and his family.

My continual questions about Wendell's race cars prompted Frank to ask if I would be interested in going across the street to the garage and seeing one of them. I couldn't believe they had one of his cars there, much less that they were offering me a chance to see it!

To my surprise, the garage—as they called it—turned out to be a large barn. When I think of a race car garage, my mind envisions a huge 20,000-square-foot building capable of housing at least a dozen race vehicles and equipment. The old wooden barn that I saw looked like it could accommodate little more than two cars.

We entered the garage and there in the corner sat the silhouette of a car under a cover. The garage was filled with tools and mechanical equipment, but my eyes focused squarely on the shape under the tarp.

"Do you want to see what's under it?" Frank asked.

"Absolutely!" I replied.

A chill ran up my spine and through my fingers as I carefully helped the guys roll back the tarp, revealing a race car in impeccable condition with the number thirty-four painted on the side. Crude and primitive by modern standards, this car represented a historic, national treasure.

I closely inspected the car as I circled around it. I was in awe of its majesty.

"Do you want to sit in it?" Frank offered.

I couldn't believe it! Sit in Wendell Scott's car?!

I did my best to keep my cool before blurting out, "Sure!"

I gingerly climbed in, making sure I didn't hit, scratch, or damage anything. Once inside, I immediately realized how dangerous it must have been to race this car. Sanctioning bodies and drivers alike considered safety in the 1960s and 1970s almost an afterthought. This car had a bench seat with thin safety belts, nothing like the custom-made racing seats and thick, six-point racing harnesses in our modern race vehicles. The interior had almost no padding to protect the driver, unlike the deeply padded head surrounds, leg supports, and roll bar padding required in race cars today.

I put my hands on the steering wheel and tried to envision what it must have been like to wrestle with such an ungainly beast on the high banks of Daytona or on a bullring like the South Boston Speedway in the heat and humidity of summer. After coming back to reality, I noticed Frank and Wendell Jr. watching me proudly, satisfied to see the impression this experience had left on me.

The Scotts welcomed me into their home and into their lives like I was one of their own. They made it clear they were proud of me and my racing accomplishments.

"Daddy would have been proud of you," Sybil said sincerely.

Wendell Scott was a true pioneer. Accordingly, NASCAR inducted him into the NASCAR Hall of Fame in January of 2015. To accomplish all he did under the circumstances he faced, he deserved it! The time I spent with the Scott family was priceless. It truly gave me a greater appreciation for the sport of NASCAR and my presence as an African American in it. It reminded me I had a legacy to uphold.

■ ■ ■

RACING TO THE FRONT

I always believed that one day I would win a professional race. Without knowing when or how long it might take, I relied on *persistence*—doing my best every day to reach that goal, no matter how slim the prospects for success at any point in time. In and out of the car, I strived to do my best and learn from mistakes. I don't believe Wendell Scott could have scored his lone career victory without this kind of *persistence*. It's part of the DNA of any champion.

I can't imagine any American professional athlete making more sacrifices to pursue their dream than Wendell Scott did during his racing days in NASCAR. I may have felt isolated at times during my career, but I rarely faced any serious challenge to my dignity like he faced on a daily basis while racing in the 1960s. Getting to know more about Wendell reminded me of the importance of being willing to *sacrifice* in order to reach an important goal. If I hadn't been willing to *sacrifice* with a move to the South from Northern California, I could not have advanced my career in racing. At times, I felt isolated and was occasionally insulted by boos during my time in NASCAR, but without these sacrifices, my victory at VIR never would have taken place.

It's rare to achieve challenging goals without some form of sacrifice due to adverse circumstances.

22

GT Championship Pursuit

The last eight races of the 2011 season turned out to be quite a ride. After our victory at VIR, the fifth race of the season took place at Lime Rock Park in Connecticut, where we backed up our rainy victory with a second-place finish. Stevenson Motorsports won the race while driving a Camaro. One of the early favorites to win the championship title, the Stevenson team had two veteran drivers in Scotsman Robin Liddell and Ronnie Bremer of Denmark. Although they were victorious at Lime Rock, they had experienced some mechanical issues and driving miscues earlier in the season that hurt them badly in the points and would ultimately leave them out of contention for the season-ending championship.

Although drivers are racing to win each race—earning a trophy and a victory at each track if successful—they are also cumulatively accruing points throughout the season. In both sports car racing and NASCAR there are three championships awarded at the end of the season: the Driver Championship, which is given to the driver with the most points for the season (sometimes drivers switch teams during the season, so this is for the individual driver); the Team Championship, which is given to the team with the best results (if a driver stays on the same team all season and wins the Driver Championship, they are likely to also help their group win the Team Championship); and the Manufacturer Championship, which is given to the car manufacturer whose race cars amass the most points over the season.

Since Jordan and I had contrasting driving styles, my team strived to set up more of a compromise car, one that suited both Jordan and me, for the first few races of the season. But once I saw Jordan's talent, I set my ego aside. If I had to drive less or if I had to drive a car more to his liking, I was willing to do that to improve the chances of the team's success.

By the middle of the season, our Autohaus team began focusing on making the car's chassis setup to Jordan's liking, and I adjusted my driving style to live with it. I would do my best in my opening stint, then turn the car over to Jordan, so he could work his magic.

Corvette Racing factory driver Tommy Milner, a regular in the rival American Le Mans Series, joined us at the Watkins Glen International six-hour race in June, and again we finished second behind the Brumos Porsche. Prior to the start of this classic endurance event, Jordan had boosted our confidence by winning the pole position. That was when the idea of a championship season truly began to look feasible.

When we returned to the Glen for the late summer event and the season's tenth race, we finished second again and took the lead in points. We then finished ninth at the famed Formula 1 circuit in Montreal, Canada. When we arrived at Mid-Ohio Sports Car Course for the season finale, we were leading Brumos drivers Andrew Davis and Leh Keen by just three points. But despite being in a strong position, I was conflicted about our chances.

Jordan and I had begun to flow like a well-oiled machine, but I knew that having to finish our season at the Mid-Ohio track could be problematic. Mid-Ohio had always been a difficult track for me, from the time I had run the Trans-Am race with Tom Gloy and his Gloy Sports racing team in 1990. I'd learned back then that the tight, twisty layout didn't suit my driving style. I needed to be on top of my game more than ever because there were Driver, Team, and Manufacturer Championships hanging in the balance, but trepidation was brewing under the surface for me.

During the qualifying session the day before, I couldn't adjust to the way the car handled and ended up qualifying back in ninth position. With eight other drivers in front of me, I would have to make up time right out of the gate, which is certainly possible, but not ideal.

Race day came and I was prepared for the showdown. Out of the ninety-six laps run during the two hours and forty-five minutes, thirty-two of them were under the yellow flag, making it very hard to make up lost time and pass other drivers. I was already behind the curve in ninth place, and as my stint wore on, I began losing more positions, which triggered me to respond aggressively. I started pushing the car harder and harder to stay on pace, but that is a classic mistake in the racing world. You can't continuously overdrive the car to gain back positions. It rarely works, and in this case, it derailed our chances further. I spun out and stalled the engine in the Carousel, a tricky portion of the track. I had nosed into the tire barrier, the engine died, and now would not fire back up, no matter how many times I hit the push button starter and slammed down the gas pedal.

Thirty seconds feels like a lifetime when you are sitting still, at zero speed, watching all your competitors fly past you, along with your chances of victory.

"I can't start this thing!" I yelled desperately into my radio.

Panic had completely taken hold of me as I frantically tried to get the car to start. I was a sitting duck on the side of the track and soon enough, the other cars would circle back around. If I couldn't get it started immediately, I would have to be towed from the track and brought back into the pits, which would cost me even more time and positions. I couldn't afford for that to happen. I cycled battery power and manipulated both the ignition switch and the starter button. The car finally came back to life.

I rejoined the track and radioed in to let them know, but it wasn't soon enough. My heart sunk when the yellow caution flag waved for me.

"Damn it!" I screamed, punching the steering wheel in frustration.

I am usually composed in high-pressure situations, but with so much at stake, I couldn't keep the anxiety and frustration from pumping at full throttle. The gravity of the moment was gnawing at me. This was the last race of the season and after years of competing, I finally had a championship within my sights. I was nearly fifty years old, and I was well aware that my professional racing days were nearing an end. I wasn't even certain that there would be a next season for me.

"It's not over yet. Anything can happen," my pit crew chief, Charlie Ping, replied.

Charlie was a sharp guy who knew how to strategize and adjust for unforeseen complications. He came back on the radio and walked me through the revised strategy.

"Bill, do what most of the cars in front of you do when pit lane opens," Charlie said. "If most cars pit, then come in; if most of the other cars stay out, then stay out."

I parroted back what he'd said, but I didn't internalize it after being so flustered about our dwindling track position that resulted from my driving blunder.

When pit road opened, most of the GT cars came into the pits, but I still was in my own head. I was completely focused on advancing our position forward and clearly wasn't thinking straight. Adding insult to injury, I stayed out. I didn't follow the strategy that Charlie had suggested. My car was positioned toward the back of the field and, due to the configuration of the track, my view of the leaders was partially obscured, but the fact remains, I made another mistake. I simply blew it!

I was forced to make a slow lap around the track behind the pace car before finally entering the pits to switch drivers. After coming to a stop in our pit box and hopping out, Jordan jumped into the driver's seat, ready to fight our way to the front. In a race with six more yellow flags flown, Jordan had trouble improving our track position. We kept fluctuating between being a lap down or at the tail end of the lead lap.

By that point, I was behind our pit area, almost in tears. My despair had morphed into sheer torment. I was distraught. The championship was ours to lose, and I'd lost it. Even Jordan couldn't rescue our title hopes after my snafu. The added pressure I'd placed on him resulted in a rare spin of his own that he quickly recovered from. We ended up finishing eighth and the Brumos guys, who'd started nineteenth, came home fourth, beating us to the championship by just two points!

We lost both the Driver and Team Championships. Being so close to a title and watching it slip away was agony. The loss lingered with me for a long while and remained heavy on my mind as I tried to stay focused on what my career might look like moving forward. Being a champion would have certainly cemented longevity in racing, but losing left my fate uncertain. For Jordan, there would be other chances at titles and championships. For me, this was my best opportunity, and I had just squandered it. Had we won the race, I was set to be interviewed by Lester Holt of NBC. That would have undoubtedly raised my national profile and probably opened up future opportunities.

My father had flown in from California to attend, and I was grateful to have him there with me. He met me on the back side of our pit area after the completion of my stint. His eyes were sympathetic as he reached out for a much-needed hug.

"It's okay. You did the best you could. It's not your fault that the car stalled and you lost time," he said soothingly.

"Maybe, but I didn't start us off in a good position, and I couldn't even hold onto that," I said, shaking my head. "It's like a kick in the gut. We were so close!"

"Bill, you can't beat yourself up over this. Look at all that you have accomplished. Nobody expected you and Jordan to even get as far as you did. Sure, it would've been nice to win, but it doesn't change the fact that you guys fought hard and made it further than most other drivers."

His calming presence helped console me. I knew he was right. I drew in a long, slow breath.

"It's just so disappointing to lose, again, and to be the reason why we lost . . . especially with so much on the line."

My father reached over and put his hand on my shoulder.

"Nobody said life is fair or that it will ever go your way. More often than not, it doesn't. You weren't able to capitalize on an opportunity, and that's unfortunate, but it happens. Life goes on. All you can do is learn from your mistakes and keep moving forward."

My father had been with me on my journey the whole way through, unconditionally offering me sound advice and support. He was exactly what I needed in that moment.

The heartbreak of the loss took a long time to get over. I'm not completely sure I ever have. Not winning the Grand-Am championship with Autohaus and Jordan far outweighed the disappointment over my Cup racing career not going forward.

I purged the emotions as best I could and allowed myself to grieve the loss, but then I had to pick myself back up and get on with it. A race car driver has to compartmentalize. If you want to go forward, you can't dwell on the past. It's not healthy and won't get you anywhere. To keep things in perspective, I would give myself little pep talks in the form of daily affirmations:

Racing a car is what I do;
it's not who I am. It does not define me.

I always try my hardest and give my all, and that's all I can do. Nothing is ever promised in life. Sometimes I'll win, and sometimes I'll lose. At the end of the day, I'm proud of the way I've continually handled myself and the effort I put forth. I've been fortunate enough to have a ten-year professional career in the sport I love. I would rather lose in racing and still have an incredible, life-changing experience than win at project management and be stuck at Hewlett-Packard. It has been a bumpy road riddled with ups and downs. I've rejoiced in the highs and lamented the lows that come from taking chances, all of which were absolutely worth it.

Even though I was disconcerted by the loss of the Driver Championship, not *all* was lost. We did win a title! We helped Chevrolet capture the Manufacturer's Championship. Out of twelve races, our Camaro GT.R was the top-finishing entry from Chevy in four of those races, giving Chevy the edge over Mazda by two points. It was rewarding knowing that mine and Jordan's efforts had led to a prosperous result after all, even if it wasn't the one we'd had our hearts set on.

The 2011 season turned out to be my final full year of racing. In 2012, I needed to take a more traditional approach to shopping myself around to team owners because NASCAR decided to no longer provide a sponsorship budget for me. It was nothing personal. The sanctioning body had begun making plans to merge Grand-Am with the separately operated American Le Mans Series to unify professional sports car racing in the United States. That meant budget reallocation. I could hardly argue since I had received just enough backing from them over a period of many years to remain in the sport. I also felt like I had done the best job I could with the platforms I had available to diversify and expand the fan base away from the traditional mold of being white and Southern. I held up my end of the bargain.

A Grand-Am championship might have enabled me to sign on with another team looking to improve its prospects. But the absence of a budget and a title, plus my advancing age, all worked against me. To their credit, NASCAR supported my strong desire to participate in the 50th Anniversary Rolex 24 at Daytona. With all of the attention afforded to the milestone race, I wanted to end my professional driving career with one last shot at the special edition Rolex Daytona chronograph given to the race winners.

I drove in the Rolex 24 one final time in 2012 for the Muehlner Motorsports team from Germany, which had some help from the Porsche factory. My teammates included Davy Jones, who had been a phenomenal IMSA sports car driver for Jaguar in the late '80s and early '90s and had scored a win in the 24 Hour of Le Mans and a runner-up finish in the Indy 500. He was trying to spark a comeback after a devastating neck injury he sustained back in 1997 while driving an Indy car. Davy and I shared the car with two other drivers, Mark Thomas and John McCutcheon, who were enthusiastic about racing but were not career professionals.

During practice, I didn't feel as though the car was handling well and performing at its best. I complained to the team owner, who went to Porsche and borrowed one of the German marque's fastest factory drivers to run a lap and see what his thoughts were. Nick Tandy jumped in our Porsche GT3 Cup car and knocked a couple of seconds off our best lap time, which I had set. The issue wasn't the car, it was me. That was a final day of reckoning.

Clearly the time to consider retirement had truly arrived.

While our Porsche finished the race thirty-ninth overall in the standings and twenty-sixth in the GT class, that clearly did not warrant a Rolex Daytona. Apparently, I was not destined to wear the coveted watch after all.

I competed in one more Grand-Am race for Autohaus Motorsports at the Indianapolis Motor Speedway, which had been added to the Grand-Am schedule for the first time. The Racing Capitol of the World (as it is commonly called) again reminded me of how far I had come in my career. I had never anticipated competing at Indy. To race there was a blessing.

For my last run as a professional race car driver, I again co-drove with Jordan Taylor, who would move on to Corvette Racing in the American Le Mans Series as a factory Chevy driver the following season. When Jordan and I had won at VIR the year before, during his stint, he'd held off Corvette Racing factory driver Oliver Gavin. I'm quite sure that had made Corvette Racing sit up and pay attention. I was happy to see his success and proud to have been his teammate.

My last two seasons of racing presented more challenges, provided more upsets, and introduced a convoluted mix of emotions that I never would have anticipated. I had to work harder than ever to keep life in perspective and remain positive in the face of adversity. I had to go back to my roots and remind myself that the car has always been a symbol of freedom, independence, and self-expression for me. No matter what result a race brought—a trophy, a title, or a tear-stained cheek—winning was in the overall experience. The thrill I got every time I slid in the driver's side window and strapped myself in before a race is something that I wish every person on Earth could experience. When the blood rushes through your body with such vitality, you feel truly alive. Having all of your senses heightened is almost like an out-of-body experience. There's nothing that compares to it. While I got paid to do it, I loved it so much I would have almost done it for free.

As I look back on all of the losses I've suffered over the course of my career, I am grateful to have had the chance to suffer them. I also consider myself fortunate that after all my hard work and exhausted efforts, I was able to win a professional race before retiring. It is a feather in my cap that I wear proudly.

■ ■ ■

RACING TO THE FRONT

There's an old cliché that says, "You win as a team and you lose as a team," and that holds true to sports car racing. Over the course of one season, Autohaus and I had meshed well enough as a team to learn how to exploit our strengths and put ourselves into position to win a championship. The same skills I had used to *network* with individuals to help advance my career also worked when it came time to integrate myself into a new team. Ultimately, racing is about human systems more so than mechanical ones. Encouraging others to invest in my dreams as well as their own through teamwork proved to be a winning formula. It helped us to win a race that began a pursuit of the championship.

We lost the title at Mid-Ohio when I became the weak link in our system. At times like that, the *network* of relationships you've built and maintained gives you support when you need it the most. Thankfully, once the pain of losing wore off, everybody recognized and appreciated how far we had come together. Our bond and our camaraderie pulled us all through a hard moment.

Networking is very similar to teamwork and can build beneficial relationships over time.

23

Is There A Future for Black Race Car Drivers?

African Americans drive cars and more than a few like to speed. So why aren't there more of us participating in major league motor racing? It's a fairly simple answer that hasn't changed much over the years.

It's about exposure and opportunity. For the black community, both are lacking.

Many African American children don't have the chance to experience motor sports growing up. They are not exposed by a family member who watches the sport at home on TV or takes them to the track so that they can immerse themselves in racing the way they do with other sports. Sports form a multigenerational bond that is passed down. How many times do you hear someone say they love the same team as their parents or their older sibling, because that's what they grew up watching at home? It happens all the time. But motor sports are not an African American tradition the way they are for many white people. Few black kids grow up watching the Daytona 500 in their homes.

Children can typically walk out their front doors and throw a football in their yard, they can go to the park and shoot hoops with their friends, and they can join the baseball team at school. Kids can't partake in the sport of racing with the same ease. The closest thing is karting, but racing a go-kart is not something you can find everywhere, and it can be very expensive. Most serious kart racers are the children and grandchildren of professional race car drivers who have been brought up in the sport, most of whom are white. There are no motorsport racing teams in grade school for young kids to join. There are no college scholarships given to up-and-coming race car drivers. The only way a child is going to become interested in racing is if someone introduces them to it.

Kids want to grow up and be like their sports heroes, but not having black race car drivers to look up to sends a clear message to the children of the black community. The African American community is not afforded the same opportunity to excel in motorsports. It is unlikely that an African American child is going to watch a sport in which he is not reflected by either the athletes or the fans and has no real chance of partaking in should they develop an affinity for it. And with most other sports being significantly more diverse, little black boys and girls know that they can grow up to be successful basketball, baseball, football, and soccer players.

So why would they take an interest in NASCAR?

It takes a committed effort to be a true fan, and the black community is justified in feeling unwelcome in a sport that condoned the flying of Confederate flags for decades, but times are changing.

Darrell "Bubba" Wallace Jr. is the only black driver to race in the Cup Series since me. While he enjoyed solid financial support from his family,

Bubba has not had an easy road either, but he has already galvanized mammoth changes within NASCAR. When tragedy struck, Bubba stood up and used his platform to speak out against social injustice and set forth a series of events that I never dreamed possible.

After the murder of George Floyd in Minneapolis on May 25, 2020, at the hands of four police officers who knelt on his neck until the breath was depleted from his lifeless body, a movement was ignited. Protestors took to the streets day and night, refusing the turn a blind eye to any more police brutality against black men. Demonstrations took place in big cities and small towns all across America, demanding justice and change. Celebrities, athletes, and politicians of all races came out in droves to support the Black Lives Matter movement. Companies, organizations, and corporations worldwide began issuing statements rebuking racism. A global shift in collective consciousness took hold centralizing on the importance of obtaining racial equality and ending systemic racism.

Twelve days later, at the Atlanta Motor Speedway, Bubba Wallace wore a black t-shirt that read, I Can't Breathe, Black Lives Matter under his fire suit in a show of solidarity for all of the black men that have been lost at the hands of police officers. He aimed to inspire listening, learning, and awareness in the hopes that people would pay attention to the message that black lives also matter.

But he didn't stand alone.

NASCAR honored George Floyd with a thirty-second moment of silence before the race began, accompanied by an announcement by Steve Phelps, who had been recently promoted to the president of NASCAR.

"Our country is in pain and people are justifiably angry, demanding to be heard. The black community and all people of color have suffered in our country and it has taken far too long for us to hear their demands for a change. Our sport must do better. Our country must do better. The time is now to listen, to understand, and to stand against racism and racial injustice. We ask our drivers, our competitors, and all our fans to join us in this mission to take a moment of reflection."

Moments later, a video aired with a dozen or so NASCAR drivers delivering a sympathetic and humbled address which had been prepared by the sanctioning body. The video cut back and forth between drivers so that the sentences blended together as one uniform speech. Bubba Wallace was the first to speak.

"The events of recent weeks highlighted the work we still need to do as a nation to condemn racial inequality and racism. . . . The process begins with us listening and learning because understanding the problem is the first step in fixing it. We are committed to listening with empathy and an open heart to better educate ourselves. We will use this education to advocate for change in our nation, or communities and most importantly in our own homes. . . . It is all of our responsibility to no longer be silent. We just can't stay silent. We have a long road ahead of us, but let's commit to make that journey together. Our differences should not divide us. It is our love for all mankind that will unite us as we work together to make real change."

Only a few miles away, I sat at home in my living room, watching it on television. Chills ran up my arms and a lump formed in my throat. There are no words to fully and accurately describe the tsunami of emotions that washed over me in that moment: *pride* for the sport that I love for finally recognizing its limitations and need for education and understanding; *happiness* that changes were actively being discussed; *sadness* that it took such a catastrophic incident to finally get NASCAR's attention on the subject of racism and racial equality; *shock* that after years of my words falling on deaf ears, finally NASCAR was listening; *respect* for the executives who made the decision to acknowledge this moment in time and pay tribute to the fallen; *delight* with Bubba's courage, knowing that the white fan base could turn against him the way many had with Colin Kaepernick; *trepidation,* worrying that perhaps this was merely an instance of NASCAR offering the public what they wanted to hear in order to be politically correct and on trend with the times; and *optimism*, genuinely hoping that this was the beginning of a new era for NASCAR.

This was a markedly different stance than any NASCAR had ever taken, so various news and sports outlets took notice and reported on it. Suddenly, Bubba Wallace was a household name being interviewed left and right as the only current black driver in the top level of NASCAR. The whole country was realizing the lack of diversity within the sport.

Although, at this point, I had been retired from racing for quite a few years, I had met with Bubba several times and considered him a friend. When I watch the races on Sundays, it's Bubba I am primarily cheering on and rooting for. I immediately reached out to him to share my support and let him know how proud I was of him and the legacy he is creating for the next generation of black drivers to come.

I also wrote a heartfelt email to Steve Phelps expressing how much I appreciated what he had done. I offered to assist in any way I could to lead diversity discussions and move initiatives in the right direction. Steve responded promptly welcoming the overture.

The next day, Bubba appeared on CNN to discuss with Don Lemon what had transpired at the race and what it meant to him.

"I am proud of NASCAR for stepping up to the plate and delivering in a huge way," Bubba stated.

"What are you going to do when someone raises a Confederate flag? What's the next action, Bubba?" Don asked pensively.

Bubba's answer would forever change NASCAR.

"That's a good question. . . . My next step would be to get rid of all Confederate flags. There should be no individual that is uncomfortable showing up to our events to have a good time. . . . It starts with Confederate flags. Get them out of here. . . . It's time for change."

NASCAR stayed true to their word that they were listening this time.

Bubba is a part of the Richard Petty Motorsports team, which is practically a dynasty within NASCAR racing. The team created a bold design for the number 43 car that Bubba drives. For the Martinsville race two days later, Bubba's car was painted black with #BlackLivesMatter emblazoned in white along the side. And the words Compassion, Love, Understanding were displayed on the hood below the powerful image of a white fist and a black fist, tightly gripping hands that drove home the message of unity. Considering how uncomfortable I always felt as a black man at that track, it was both profoundly karmic and fitting.

Richard Petty stood with Bubba and supported his beliefs, knowing that it would be met with friction by some of the Confederate flag–waving fans. But that wouldn't be for long.

Shortly after the race began that day, NASCAR issued an unexpected—and controversial—statement that floored me: "The presence of the Confederate flag at NASCAR events runs contrary to our commitment to providing a welcoming and inclusive environment for all fans, our competitors and our industry.... The display of the Confederate flag will be prohibited from all NASCAR events and properties."

I honestly never envisioned a day when NASCAR would actually ban the Confederate flag, but here it was happening before my very eyes. I could hardly believe it.

Any doubts I had were alleviated right then and there. Steve Phelps and the executives at NASCAR were indeed serious about progressing the sport and making it more inclusive.

Overjoyed, I retweeted the post with the caption, "The movement is real!"

No black driver, official, or crew member would ever again have to be subjected to the Stars and Bars as they prepare for their day's work. No African American spectator would ever have to be reminded of their ancestor's enslavement while watching this sporting event.

I wish I could say that the decision was unanimously accepted by all the fans, but such was not the case. Plenty of outraged fans took to social media saying that they would be boycotting the sport indefinitely. It seems as though their affection for a flag that serves as the face of white supremacy and a symbol of racism, segregation, and discrimination means more to those "fans" than the sport they claimed to love.

The following week, the race was at Talladega. The rain was relentless, so the event was delayed until the following day, but not before what was thought to be a noose was found in garage number four, Bubba's garage. NASCAR quickly launched an investigation and the FBI was immediately called in. The incident was viewed as a possible hate crime and was taken very seriously.

Between the nation's civil unrest, the escalating divisiveness of our country, and the outspoken hostility of those NASCAR "fans" that refused to accept change, NASCAR became the unlikely epicenter for controversial politics. A plane flew over the raceway trailed by an enormous Confederate flag. Vendors across the street from the track continued to sell hats and shirts with the Confederate symbol and told reporters that sales had gone way up since the ban went into effect. Although the sanctioning body was ready to move into the 21st century, not everyone was so willing.

My phone began to ring off the hook. Everyone wanted the last black NASCAR driver before Bubba Wallace to weigh in, and I was happy to use my voice and my platform to do just that. I appeared on CNN the next day, hours before the postponed Talladega race was set to begin.

"So is this the moment of change?" asked CNN reporter Poppy Harlow.

"Well, I hope it is. It's definitely a step in the right direction; the fact is that the public is aware that change is in the air. NASCAR has made some very strong statements and put some processes in place such as the banning of the flags, which lets folks know that we are serious; NASCAR is serious and that it is time for change. . . . The banning of the flag is the first step in a number of many."

My interview concluded, and I anxiously waited for three o'clock to roll around for the start of the race broadcast. Curious spectators from all around the globe also tuned in as an incredible sight began to unfold on my television screen.

The commercial broke away, replaced by the coverage of every NASCAR driver and their crew walking down the track, pushing the number 43 car with Bubba Wallace sitting inside of it. The world was in the throes of COVID-19, so Bubba sported an American flag mask which was a poignant message: NASCAR is not a white sport. It's America's sport.

The car came to a stop at the end of pit lane. Bubba lifted the removable wheel up and out of the way and pulled himself out of the driver's window. He sat there with his legs still inside the car and rested his elbows on top of the roof. Bubba solemnly lowered his head as if he was overwhelmed by the weight of the monumental, historic moment.

Nothing like this had ever occurred on a NASCAR track, or in the history of any other sport. Every single white driver and all crew members rallied together and stood with the lone black driver to show the world that they were one team that would not be divided by hate. Race car drivers are competitive by nature, and that day they refused to allow racism to win. Their silent statement spoke volumes.

This was what I had been waiting a long time for. This was the change I tried to actualize, but was unable to. This was the shift I wanted to see come from all facets of NASCAR, from the officials to the drivers to the crew members, but never thought would come. The world wasn't ready when I voiced my concerns and stated my resolute opinions in the late '90s and early 2000s, but NASCAR was finally ready and listening.

Richard Petty walked over to Bubba and put his hand on Bubba's back. He patted Bubba's head and rubbed his back, almost the way a father would console a child.

That image was impactful. It was an accurate portrayal of how racism feels. Bubba's body language depicted the heartbreak of having someone trying to bring you down and make you feel inferior, but Richard's simple, yet meaningful actions displayed the beauty of those who lift you back up.

Few people have experienced what Bubba and I dealt with and endured as black drivers in NASCAR. Between the Confederate flags in the stands and the n-word jokes back in the race shops, I had walked his path and shared his pain.

The FBI's investigation showed that even though the rope in the Talladega garage stall had all of the characteristics of a noose, it was not a deliberate act of racism specifically directed at Bubba. It was used as a pulley for closing the garage door and had been there since the year before. It was the only one fashioned that way, but it was a relief to know that it wasn't a vicious message to black drivers. They certainly don't need any more reasons not to want to pursue racing. It is, however, unfortunate the track staff allowed that symbol to remain in place that long.

In light of NASCAR's new welcoming culture, I hope that more African Americans will be encouraged to step out of the shadows and consider participation in the sport. But it's not just the black community that has been underrepresented in NASCAR, though the other minority groups have had slightly more success, NASCAR has had drivers from Spanish-speaking countries in its Cup Series such as Daniel Suarez of Mexico, Cuban American Aric Almirola, and Juan Pablo Montoya of Colombia. Danica Patrick, who spent seven seasons in the Cup Series, moved the gender line the furthest when she arrived in 2012.

The Drive for Diversity program still exists, but it has so many glaring holes that continue to make it cumbersome for minority drivers to gain traction. Many drivers of color are still not able to come up through the NASCAR ranks without securing their own sponsorship or having family-funded financial backing, which defeats the purpose of the program. NASCAR is one of the most, if not the most expensive sport to partake in. Unfortunately, talent, hard work, and determination are not enough. Drivers need more corporations to be willing to invest in drivers that are not Caucasian.

Banning the Confederate flag was a major step in the right direction, but the next step has to be NASCAR investing more in the D4D program to broaden participation in the sport, as opposed to the current trend of D4D fielding less cars and drivers each year. If the sanctioning body at NASCAR wants to seriously diversify their sport, they need to be more aggressive with helping drivers gain support and secure sponsorship from corporate America.

Exposure and opportunity.

My wish is that the next generation of black drivers won't have to fight and claw their way into NASCAR like I did. If a driver is putting in the work, establishing themself as a worthy contender on the track, and wins races, sponsorship should follow, no matter their gender, age, or race.

Plain and simple.

I hope that by the time my children are grown and they have children of their own that we will be able to sit around the television, watching as drivers from all walks of life, all ethnicities, and all races stand together on NASCAR's pit road, listening to the National Anthem and feeling as though it represents each and every one of them.

■ ■ ■

RACING TO THE FRONT

It's universal that overcoming adversity is necessary for success in most endeavors. If in the course of history not many blacks have pursued motor racing, then only participation by those of us eager and willing to get out of our *comfort zone* can bring about change. No matter whom you are or what your background, any individual seeking to advance needs to learn what it takes to get out of their *comfort zone* and expand opportunities.

Making it as a professional race car driver—from whatever background—is a laborious and arduous journey that isn't guaranteed. One has to be willing to suffer the pain and discomfort of setbacks but then be able to pause long enough to revel in the joys of success. The best way to improve long odds typically requires *sacrifice*, which means working harder and employing a *disciplined* approach that keeps the focus on reaching goals. No matter how daunting the road ahead may seem or how disheartening the disappointments have been, never give up on a dream that you are passionate about pursuing.

Sacrifice and discipline are twin pillars of long-term advancement and success.

EPILOGUE

Final Reflections

FROM AN EARLY AGE, I knew that cars were not just an interest, and racing them would be more than a pastime for me. I was blessed with an innate propensity for driving fast: I had above average hand-eye coordination, quick reflexes, and the ability to assess a situation and make advantageous decisions in a split second. My natural abilities validated a talent that I chose not to waste. The bold choices I made shaped the man I became and changed the professional course of my life late into my existence.

My journey through racing spanned over three decades, beginning at the SCCA amateur level and progressing all the way to the top level in NASCAR. Leaving a steady six-figure career to pursue my one true passion was a huge risk, but it was well worth it. There were innumerable struggles and setbacks along the way, but I was resilient and determined, refusing to accept defeat. I'm proud of all my efforts because it took a strong constitution to face down extreme odds and the internal fortitude to prevail.

Navigating the politics behind racing and obtaining the finances needed to sustain a career in it ended up being the most difficult and frustrating part of the process. I persevered through the pushbacks from some executives at the sanctioning body of NASCAR as well as corporate America, and rose above the backlash from fans who weren't willing to accept a black driver from California. Years ago, Willy T. Ribbs told me the actual driving itself would be the easy part of being a race car driver, and though I didn't understand it at the time, I came to realize that he was absolutely right.

There was plenty of heartache for me to encounter in professional race car driving, but there was also an abundance of happiness.

My experience afforded me the opportunity to travel the country, meet people from all walks of life, and build friendships that would last a lifetime. I got to drive some of the fastest cars in the world, on the hardest courses, and was paid to do so. I won't ever have to look back and wonder "what if" I had done something differently because I lived my life with no regrets. I started professional racing at an age when many athletes are retiring, but I proved that I could still be as competitive as the younger generation. Having my career play out in reverse presented unique challenges, but it also taught me invaluable lessons that I may never have learned otherwise.

In the grand scheme of things, my racing life has been a thrill-ride that many could argue I should not have even been allowed to partake in, but it became an adventure that I would not trade for any trophy or championship. While perfecting my craft and living my dream, I was even able to carve out a place for myself in history. Along the way, I created memories that will become my legacy and enjoyed success while doing it. I have always hoped I will inspire others to do the same, whether it's in cars on a track or in some other endeavor. It's never too late to pursue your passion, convey gratitude to those who have supported you, and knuckle down and persevere toward your dream. Now go out there and get out of your comfort zone!

ACKNOWLEDGMENTS

Many thanks to Jonathan Ingram, whose insightful perspective I highly admire on more subjects than just racing. You have forgotten more about the history of motorsports than I ever knew, and your help getting my thoughts and memories on paper has proved invaluable. I deeply enjoyed our collaboration.

I would also like to thank my literary agents, Regina Brooks, for convincing me to see this memoir to the end and Kelly Thomas, for bringing my story to life. You were both great to work with. And thanks to Tracey Moore for connecting me with Serendipity Literary Agency.

To those employees I had the privilege of managing at Hewlett-Packard, thanks for your understanding when I left early on Friday afternoons to prepare my race car. Please know you were the best part of my job and were the only thing I really missed when I left.

Thanks to my racing fans, especially those in NASCAR. It was always humbling to sign autographs for you while I was competing, and I still find it amazing to continue doing so over a decade after leaving the sport.

Lastly, a huge debt of gratitude to all those black racers who came before me, broke barriers, and paved the way for me. It is you whose shoulders I stand upon and who made my journey possible. God bless you.

ABOUT THE AUTHOR

Bill Lester was born in Washington, D.C. attended University of California Berkeley. Before becoming a professional race car driver, he worked at Hewlett-Packard. Lester competed in NASCAR and IMSA, two of America's most prestigious racing series and earned six podium finishes and one victory during his 10 full seasons. Bill has received various awards including "Trailblazer in Motor Sports" and the "Jackie Robinson Award" from the Rainbow/PUSH organization and the "Sam Lacy Pioneer Award" from the National Association of Black Journalists in 2013. He was a broadcast analyst for Fox Sports South show "Around the Track" and the NBC Sports show "NASCAR America." Follow him @Bill_Lester and billlester.com.

Recognized for his definitive books and articles on motor racing, Atlanta author **Jonathan Ingram** has written eight books, including *CRASH!*, part of the library collection at the National Museum of American History, and is the winner of awards from the National Motorsports Press Association and the Georgia Racing Hall of Fame.